MULTIPLE-CHOICE AND FREE-RESPONSE QUESTIONS IN PREPARATION FOR THE AP UNITED STATES GOVERNMENT AND POLITICS EXAMINATION

(SIXTH EDITION)

By

Bonnie Herzog
Joe E. Newsome High School
Lithia, FL

Ethel Wood
Princeton High School
Princeton, NJ
(retired)

D&S MARKETING SYSTEMS INC.
1205 38th Street Brooklyn, NY 11218

w w w . d s m a r k e t i n g . c o m

ISBN # 978-1-934780-04-6

Printed in the U.S.A.

PREFACE

Understanding United States government and politics continues to be an elusive, often complicated challenge. The founding fathers purposefully established a complex governmental structure based on separated powers and federalism, designed to guard against the tyranny of both the powerful ruler and the masses. Changes brought by important historical events, as well as the intrigue of informal politics, add to the complex mix that often puzzles even the most astute experts. For students enrolled in a high school Advanced Placement Government and Politics course, the challenges are to understand the basic concepts of government and politics as well as the sizable body of *information* necessary for mastery of the subject.

MULTIPLE CHOICE AND FREE RESPONSE QUESTIONS IN PREPARATION FOR THE AP UNITED STATES GOVERNMENT AND POLITICS EXAMINATION assists students in assessing their level of understanding of both basic concepts and factual information in United States government and politics. The questions simulate as closely as possible the AP United States Government and Politics Examination administered each year in May by the College Board. Part I consists of an overview of the United States Government Course and Examination. Part II of the book presents a 16 chapter narrative review and questions grouped by topics, and Part III presents four practice exams of 60 multiple-choice questions and 4 free-response questions each that include concepts and facts in the following proportions as recommended by the College Board:

    I. Constitutional underpinnings of democracy in the United States............................5-15%
    II. Political beliefs and behaviors of individuals 10-20%
    III. Political parties, interest groups, and mass media 10-20%
    IV. Institutions of national government: the Congress, the Presidency, and the
           Federal Courts 35-45%
    V. Public policy..5-15%
    VI. Civil rights and civil liberties...5-15%

The book prepares the students for both the multiple-choice and free-response portions of the AP Examination. The narrative review will help students understand the concepts that multiple-choice questions and essays cover.

All communications concerning this book should be addressed to the publisher and distributor:

D&S Marketing Systems, Inc.
1205 38th street
Brooklyn, New York 11218

TABLE OF CONTENTS

PART I

THE UNITED STATES GOVERNMENT COURSE AND EXAMINATION

The United States Government Course and Examination

The study of government and politics in the United States is an important and intriguing sojourn. After all, democracy will not work if a citizenry does not understand political issues and processes. With that goal in mind, the College Board's Advanced Placement Program established a curriculum and examination for United States Government in the late 1980s. Today the course is one of the largest and fastest growing of all AP programs, reflecting our nation's resurging interest in government and politics. Young people in particular seem to have a special enthusiasm for political participation not readily apparent in the recent past. In the election campaign of 2004, young voters, along with all others, supported new types of interest groups and came out to vote in much larger numbers than in previous elections. The political involvement of young people continued to increase through the 2008 campaign. You, as a high school student almost old enough to vote, have a unique opportunity to learn about your political system because you are studying the AP Government and Politics curriculum. No matter what your political views, it is important to understand concepts and facts that form the basis of government and politics in the United States. It is in this spirit that this book is written.

In the pages that follow are a description of the course, the major topics of the curriculum, an overview of the examination and the skills you will need to do well, and a section on how the exam is scored. Read through this part very carefully because it will provide you with a general outline of the course that will help keep you from getting lost in the complexities and challenges that the study of United States government always presents.

A DESCRIPTION OF THE COURSE

The most important thing to keep in mind as you study the U.S. Government and Politics curriculum is that it is not all about facts. Yes, information about specific government policies, laws, court cases, political tactics, and demographical features of voters can help you to better understand the concepts. However, the course is really all about analyzing concepts that will help you to keep up with government and politics throughout your lifetime no matter how much the particular landscapes may change over the years. This analysis may be broken down into six major content areas that you will be responsible for. These content areas are outlined below in the proportion that they will be tested on the examination.

CONTENT AREA I: CONSTITUTIONAL UNDERPINNINGS OF UNITED STATES GOVERNMENT (5-15%)

This content area is more history based than any of the other areas because it examines the kind of government established by the U.S. Constitution, paying particular attention to the concept of federalism and the separation of powers. However, don't assume that you know this material already because you have studied it in history class. You do have to know something about the historical situation surrounding the Constitutional Convention, but you also have to understand the ideological and philosophical traditions that shaped the framers' work. For example, theoretical perspectives you will need to know are democratic theory, theories of republican government, pluralism, and elitism.

CONTENT AREA II: POLITICAL BELIEFS AND BEHAVIORS (10-20%)

This section starts with a study of U.S. political culture – the complex mix of beliefs, values, and expectations that shape our political system. Here you will examine how these political beliefs and values were formed over time, as well as the modern day results. Topics include political socialization, political ideologies, and factors that shape political opinions. You should comprehend and appreciate how political beliefs and behaviors differ, as well as the political consequences of these differences. A second focus of this content area is on political participation, including voting behavior. You should understand why individuals engage in various forms of political participation and how that participation affects the political system.

CONTENT AREA III: POLITICAL PARTIES, INTEREST GROUPS, AND MASS MEDIA (10-20%)

This content area focuses on "linkage institutions," or organizations that link citizens to the government, such as political parties, interest groups, and mass media. You should be able to answer these important questions once you study this section: How did our party system evolve historically? What are the functions and structures of political parties, and what effects do they have on the political system? What are the processes and consequences of political campaigns for office, and what reforms have been attempted in recent years? What election systems are used on the state and national levels, and what are their consequences? What roles do interest groups and PACs play in the political process and in shaping public policy? Which people are better represented to government by interest groups, and why? What role does the media play in the political system, and what impact does media have on public opinion, voter perceptions, campaign strategies, electoral outcomes, agenda development, and the images of officials and candidates?

CONTENT AREA IV: INSTITUTIONS OF NATIONAL GOVERNMENT (35-45%)

This section is by far the longest, and you should study it in proportion to the percentage that it will be represented on the exam. It includes the "branches" of the national government, including the legislature, the executive, the bureaucracy, and the judiciary. You should be familiar with the organization and powers, both formal and informal, of these major political institutions in the United States. However, it is not enough to understand the institutions individually, but you must know basically how they interact to make public policy. Powers are separated, but they also are shared, checked, and balanced. You should also have a general idea about how powers and relationships have evolved over time. Additionally, you should understand how these institutions are tied to linkage institutions (Content Area III), such as interest groups, political parties, and the media.

CONTENT AREA V: PUBLIC POLICY (5-15%)

Politicians and institutions interact with one another to bring about public policy. How are agendas set for policy? In other words, why and how are some issues addressed and not others? The very nature of our political system determines that policies are made by numerous players and institutions. Congress interacts with the president who interacts with members of the bureaucracy who in turn communicate their wishes back to Congress. Political parties set agendas and run candidates who will give voice to their opinions. Interest groups pressure members of Congress and executive branch bureaucrats to pay attention to their needs. State governments interact with national and local levels to represent their citizens. You should investigate policy networks, iron triangles, and other forms of policy subgovernments in both the domestic and foreign policy areas.

CONTENT AREA VI: CIVIL RIGHTS AND CIVIL LIBERTIES (5-15%)

You probably will find this content area particularly interesting to explore. It focuses on the development of individual rights and liberties and their impact on citizens. Since the courts have been prime shapers of policy in this area, you can put to work your knowledge of Supreme Court procedures (learned in Content Area IV) through examining significant decisions that have defined the civil rights and liberties of American citizens. You will need to be able to analyze judicial interpretations of freedom of speech, assembly, and expression (civil liberties); the rights of the accused, and the rights of minority groups and women. At the end of this unit, you should be able to assess the strengths and weaknesses of Supreme Court decisions as tools for social change.

THE EXAMINATION

The AP United States Government and Politics Examination is 2 hours and 25 minutes long. It consists of a 45-minute multiple-choice section and a free-response section that consists of four questions. The time allotted for the free-response questions is 100 minutes, with the expectation that you will spend approximately 25 minutes on each one. You must answer ALL questions; you will have no choices. The multiple choice section is worth 50% of your grade on the exam, and the four free-response questions collectively count for the other 50%. In other words, each free-response question is equally weighted against the others and counts 12.5% of your total grade.

Time	Type of questions	Number of questions	Percent of grade
45 minutes	Multiple choice	60	50%
100 minutes	Free response	4	50%

SKILLS AND ABILITIES

What do the questions require you to know, and what skills do you need?

- First, you need to know your facts, concepts, and theories. Content knowledge is very important!

- Next, you need to understand patterns, principles, and consequences of political processes and organizations. Constantly ask yourself *why* particular behaviors and organizations are important. For example, what consequences do voter patterns have on who gets elected to office? The fact that people with higher levels of education are likely to vote does make a difference on who gets to make policy in this country. Why is it important that each state is represented equally in the Senate and in proportion to population in the House of Representatives? You can memorize those facts, but you also need to be able to consider what effect that organization has on policy decisions.

- You must be able to analyze and interpret data on charts, graphs, and tables, and to occasionally interpret political cartoons.

- Pay close attention to the structure and wording of the free-response questions and allow the structure and wording guide your answer. Never begin to answer a question until you are absolutely sure what the question is asking. For example, don't read through a question and say to yourself, "This question is about campaign finance reform," and just begin writing. Be sure that you answer *precisely* and *completely* what the question is asking. Answer the whole question and nothing but the question!

THE MULTIPLE CHOICE QUESTIONS

This book is full of sample multiple-choice questions modeled after the ones that you will have on the exam. Practice is important, as is a careful reading of the question stem and all choices available. Since you will be penalized (see the next section) for questions you miss, it is usually best to skip questions that you have no idea how to answer. However, if you can eliminate one or more choices, it will usually benefit you to select the best answer from the remaining choices. Most of the questions are straight-forward, and all of them have five answer choices. A few questions will be based on charts, graphs, tables, and/or cartoons.

FREE-RESPONSE QUESTIONS

For free-response questions, follow this mantra carefully: Answer the whole question, and nothing but the question! Spend a minute of your allotted time to literally tear the question apart and take note of *everything* that it asks you to do. If you don't get around to answering part of the question, you will be punished in the score, sometimes severely. A special caution: when a question asks you to explain something, be sure that you do that as thoroughly as possible. Many rubrics give two points for an explanation, and if you cut yours short, you may end up with only one point credit, a frustrating situation, especially if you know the answer.

Each free-response question will test different content areas. In other words, you will not get two questions only about political parties, or two questions only about Congress. Of course, you probably will not be questioned in all six content areas, although most questions require you to bring together knowledge from two different areas.

In all likelihood, you will be more confident of some questions than others. Most students remember some content areas better than others. Be prepared to expect that, and most importantly, don't panic. Answer each question the best that you can, and don't miss some parts of the question that you know just because you are concerned about a part that you are unsure of.

Writing style matters only in the sense that you need to express your answers clearly, accurately, and completely. You will not be evaluated on the quality of a thesis statement, although including one will often insure that you get some of the points of the question. The most important thing is that you answer everything that the question asks as clearly and completely as you have time for. Be sure to keep up with the time and allocate approximately 25 minutes for each question. If you finish before the time limit, be suspicious that your answers might not be as complete as they should be, and go back to enhance any explanations that you need.

HOW YOUR EXAM WILL BE SCORED

You will receive 0 to 60 points in Section I (Multiple-Choice), and 0 to 60 points in Section II (Free-Response). You will not see your raw scores in these sections. Instead, your scores will be converted to grades on an AP 5-point scale, with a "5" being the highest.

- **Multiple-choice section** – To adjust for guessing, 1/4 of the number of wrong answers is subtracted from the number of right answers. This fraction is based on the five-choices that each question has, so that the expected score from random guessing will be zero.

- **Free-response section** – Each of the free-response questions are assigned a certain number of points when they are designed, generally ranging from 5 to 8 points. No matter what the point scale, each question is equally weighted against the others, so that each is worth 12.5% of your total grade (or 25% of the 50% that the free-response section is worth.)

The multiple-choice section is graded by a machine, but the free-response questions are graded by real people – faculty members from high schools and colleges from around the country that gather in one place to grade questions in a marathon 7-day effort that takes place in early June after you take the exam in May. The grader will not know your name or school and each of your four questions will be graded by a different person, so don't worry that the grader will be influenced by one weak answer when evaluating another question. He or she will only see and grade one free-response question. After the grading of free-response questions is completed, your exam will be sent back to the College Board and Educational Testing Service to calculate a composite score. The maximum composite score is 120. Finally, you will receive your grade in the mail sometime in July.

OVERVIEW OF THE REVIEW BOOK

Part II of this book takes each of the six content areas of the AP United States Government and Politics curriculum and addresses the major points that each area requires you to know. Each content area is broken into chapters focused on a review in narrative and review terms. At the end of each unit are practice multiple-choice questions in proportion to the weight of the section. For example, Units One and Six have 25 questions each to reflect the 5-15% weight of each section, but Units Two and Three have 30 questions to reflect the 10-20% weight. Each unit also includes one free-response question based on the material reviewed.

Part III consists of four Sample Examinations, each with 60 multiple-choice and 4 free-response questions. Each sample exam is modeled after the AP test, and you should allot 45 minutes to take the multiple-choice section and 100 minutes to take the free-response section.

The purpose of this book is to help students make their way through the myriad of information presented by college textbooks on the subject of United States government and politics. Additionally, you will have the opportunity to test and improve your test-taking skills that will help you to understand the content. The book is as concise as possible, and it provides help in making connections among all the various content areas that make up the study of the all-important world of government and politics in the United States.

UNIT ONE

THE FOUNDATIONS
OF GOVERNMENT

CHAPTER ONE
CONSTITUTIONAL UNDERPINNINGS

The Founders created the Constitution during the late 18th century – an era when European philosophers were strongly criticizing governments dominated by imperialism and monarchy. The design of the Constitution reflected the influence of the European Enlightenment and the newly emerging beliefs in democracy, liberty for more individuals in society, and the importance of checking the self-interest inherent in ordinary human interactions. At the same time, the founders were far from unanimous in their admiration for direct democracy, and the Constitution they created reflects restraints on democracy. While they believed that monarchies were repressive, they knew that complete freedom would lead to disorder. Their main challenge was to fashion a government that struck a balance between liberty and order.

THE INFLUENCE OF THE EUROPEAN ENLIGHTENMENT

The **European Enlightenment** grew out of the Scientific Revolution of the 16th and 17th centuries, a time of amazing discoveries that form the basis of modern science. Scientific success created confidence in the power of reason, which Enlightenment thinkers believed could be applied to human nature in the form of natural laws. Every social, political, and economic problem could be solved through the use of reason.

THE SOCIAL CONTRACT

A seventeenth century English thinker of the 1600s – **John Locke** – believed that in the **"state of nature"** people are naturally free and equal, but that freedom led inevitably to inequality, and eventually to chaos. Locke agreed with other philosophers of the day (such as Thomas Hobbes) that the state of nature changes because humans are basically self-centered. However, he believed that they could be rational and even moral. Even though people serve self-interests first, they fear violence, particularly violent death. He argued that people have **natural rights** from the state of nature that include the right to "life, liberty, and property." In his *Second Treatise of Government*, Locke stated that people form governments to protect these natural rights, giving up their freedom to govern themselves through a social contract between government and the governed. The only valid government is one based on the **consent of the governed**. This consent creates a **social contract** – an agreement between rulers and citizens – that both sides are obligated to honor. If for any reason the government breaks the contract through neglect of natural rights, the people have the right to dissolve the government.

3

LOCKE IN THE DECLARATION OF INDEPENDENCE

The founders generally were educated men who had read Locke and Hobbes, as well as French philosophers, such as Montesquieu, Voltaire, and Rousseau, who were concerned with freedom, equality, and justice. John Locke, in particular, directly influenced the thinking of the founders, as reflected in the Declaration of Independence. Compare the words of Jefferson with those of John Locke:

LOCKE IN SECOND TREATISE OF CIVIL GOVERNMENT	JEFFERSON IN THE DECLARATION OF INDEPENDENCE
"When any one, or more, shall take upon them to make laws whom the people have not appointed so to do, they make laws without authority, which the people are not therefore bound to obey; by which means they come again to be out of subjection, and may constitute to themselves a new legislature."	"When in the course of human events, it becomes necessary for one people to dissolve the political bands that have connected them with another, and to assume, among the powers of the earth, the separate and equal station to which the laws of nature and of nature's God entitle them..."
"Whosoever uses force without right...puts himself into a state of war with those against whom he so uses it, and in that state all former ties are canceled, all other rights cease, and every one has a right to defend himself, and to resist the aggressor..."	"But when a long train of abuses and usurpations, pursuing invariably the same object, evinces a design to reduce them under absolute despotism, it is their right, it is their duty, to throw off such government..."
"A state also of equality, wherein all the power and jurisdiction is reciprocal, no one having more than another..."	"We hold these truths to be self-evident: That all men are created equal;"
"[men] have a mind to unite for the mutual preservation of their lives, liberties, and....property."	"that they are endowed by their Creator with certain unalienable rights, that among these are life, liberty, and the pursuit of happiness."
"To great and chief end, therefore, of men uniting into commonwealths, and putting themselves under government, is the preservation of their property...."	"that to secure these rights, governments are instituted among men, deriving their just powers from the consent of the governed."

THEORETICAL PERSPECTIVES

John Locke and other Enlightenment thinkers, such as Voltaire, Montesquieu, and Jean Jacques Rousseau, created theories of democracy, republican government, pluralism, and elitism that guided the founders as they shaped the new government of the United States in the late 18th century.

DEMOCRATIC THEORY

At the time of the founding of the United States almost all other political systems in the world were **authoritarian regimes** in which rulers fully controlled the government, and often held sway over economic and social institutions as well. Ironically, the European country with the most controls on the power of its monarchs was England, the very political system that the Americans so protested for its oppressiveness. In fact, democratic theory has very strong roots in British history, although it may be traced back to much earlier civilizations, such as Ancient Greece. **Democracy** is a form of government that places ultimate political authority in the hands of the people. Democratic theory has two basic models:

- **Direct Democracy** – In this form of democracy, citizens debate and vote directly on all laws. In Ancient Athens, the legislature was composed of all of the citizens, although women, slaves, and foreigners were excluded because they were not citizens. Direct democracy requires a high level of participation, and is based on a high degree of confidence in the judgment of ordinary people. Many of the founders of the United States were skeptical about the ability of the masses to govern themselves, being too prone to the influence of demagogues (charismatic leaders who manipulate popular beliefs) and too likely to overlook the rights of those with minority opinion. The latter leads to **majoritarianism**, or the tendency for government to do what the majority of people want.

- **Representative Democracy** – The founders chose to establish a **republic**, or an indirect democracy in which people elect representatives to govern them and to make laws and set policies. This form is also referred to as an **indirect democracy**. In the United States, the people came to hold the ultimate power through the election process, but all policy decisions were to be made by elected officials or those that they appoint. A representative democracy, then, is a compromise between a direct democracy and an authoritarian rule, and has become the most accepted form of democracy in the world today.

ELITE THEORY

How can a republic claim to be a democracy if only a few people actually make political decisions, even if they are elected by the people? **Elite theory** holds that a "representative democracy" is not really based on the will of the people, but that there is a relatively small, cohesive elite class that makes almost all the important decisions for the nation. Another version of elite theory argues that voters choose from among competing elites. New members of the elite are recruited through a merit-based education system, so that the best and brightest young people join the ranks of the elite. Elite theorists argue that the founders believed that a privileged majority should rule in the name of the people with a controlled amount of input from citizens.

PLURALIST THEORY

Another theoretical perspective is **pluralism**, the argument that representative democracies are based on group interests that protect the individual's interests by representing him or her to the government. The theory is grounded in the notion that in a diverse society such as the United States, too many interests exist to allow any one cohesive group of elites to rule. Government decisions are made in an arena of competing interests, all vying for influence and struggling to speak for the people that they represent. Some pluralists have argued that the founding fathers represented different interests (such as rural vs. urban, or north vs. south), and that many points of view were actually represented. The model still works today, as pluralists argue, creating strong links between government officials and their popular base.

THE CONSTITUTION

The Constitution reflects the founders' attempt to balance order with freedom. They generally did not believe that people were fully capable of ruling themselves, but they also wanted to check any tendency toward monarchy. The Constitution is based on five great principles designed to achieve this balance:

- **Popular Sovereignty** – the basic principle that the power to govern belongs to the people and that government must be based on the consent of the governed.

- **Separation of Powers** – the division of government's powers into three separate branches: executive, legislative, and judicial.

- **Checks and Balances** – a political system in which branches of government have some authority over the actions of the others.

- **Limited Government** – the basic principle that government is not all-powerful, and that it does only those things that citizens allow it to do.

- **Federalism** – the division of governmental powers between a central government and the states.

These principles resulted from the agreements and compromises made at the Constitutional Convention in 1787.

BACKGROUND TO THE CONVENTION

During the Revolutionary War, the Continental Congress wrote the **Articles of Confederation** to provide unity for the separate states that loosely formed the new country. The Articles allowed state governments to retain their powers, and the newly formed central government had severe limitations:

- The central government consisted only of a Congress in which each state was represented equally.
- No executive or judiciary branches were created.
- The central government could not levy taxes. It could only request money from the states.
- The central government could not regulate commerce between states. The states taxed each other's goods and negotiated trade agreements with other countries.
- No law enforcing powers were granted to Congress.
- No process for amending the Articles was provided.
- States retained all powers not specifically granted to Congress.

When the war was over, the immediate need for unity was past, and chaos threatened to undo the new nation. States quarreled over borders and tariffs, the country was badly in debt, and foreign countries saw the lack of a strong central government as weakness that could easily be exploited. Many leaders began to push for a government strong enough to settle disputes, to regulate commerce, and levy limited taxes. An important turning point occurred when farmers in western Massachusetts, in debt and unable to pay their taxes, rebelled against foreclosures, forcing judges out of court and freeing debtors from jails. **Shay's Rebellion** was eventually controlled, but it encouraged leaders to seek a stronger central government.

THE CONSTITUTIONAL CONVENTION

Fifty-five delegates arrived from the thirteen states in May 1787. Most were important men in their states: planters, bankers, businessmen, and lawyers. Many were governors and/or Congressional representatives, and most had read works by Hobbes, Locke, and French philosophers, such as Voltaire and Montesquieu. Several famous delegates were:

- **Alexander Hamilton**, the leading proponent of a strong, centralized government.
- **George Washington**, the chairman of the Convention, and the most prestigious member, who also was a strong supporter of a centralized government.
- **James Madison**, a young, well-read delegate from Virginia, who is usually credited with writing large parts of the Constitution.
- **Benjamin Franklin**, the 81-year-old delegate from Pennsylvania, who had also attended the Continental Congress in 1776.

Absent were **Thomas Jefferson**, serving as ambassador to France, and **John Adams**, ambassador to England. Other absent leaders were **Patrick Henry**, who refused to come because he "smelt a rat," and **Samuel Adams**, who was not selected by Massachusetts to attend. The absence of Patrick Henry and Samuel Adams almost certainly tilted the balance of the convention toward order and freed the delegates from criticism as they created a stronger central government.

Agreements and Compromises

The founders' common belief in a balanced government led them to construct a government in which no single interest dominated. They were concerned with the "excesses of democracy" (Elbridge Gerry, delegate from Massachusetts), demonstrated by Shay's Rebellion, and they agreed with Locke that government should protect property.

Benjamin Franklin – a strong proponent of liberty and equality – proposed that all white males have the right to vote, but most delegates believed that only property owners should have the franchise. In their view, ordinary people would either scheme to deprive property owners of their rights or become the "tools of demagogues." In the end the founders did not include specific voting requirements in the Constitution, leaving each state to decide voter qualifications for its citizens.

A major issue at the convention was the balance of power between the large states and the small. The large states favored a strong national government that they believed they could dominate, and the small states wanted stronger state governments that could avert domination by the central government. These different interests are apparent in the first discussions of representation in Congress. Most favored a bicameral, or two-house, legislature, similar to the organization of most state legislatures since colonial times.

The Great Compromise (The Connecticut Compromise)

The delegates from Virginia opened the Convention with their **Virginia Plan** that called for a strong central government. Although proposed by Edmund Randolph, the plan was almost certainly the work of James Madison, who, along with Alexander Hamilton, reasoned that a suggestion as boldly different from the current government would not be accepted, but might at least inspire major revisions. Their plan succeeded beyond their hopes. The delegates took the plan seriously, and began the debate with the assumption that the central government would be strengthened greatly. The plan called for a bicameral legislature: the larger house with members elected by popular vote and the smaller, more aristocratic house selected by the larger house from nominees from state legislatures. Representation in both houses was to be based on wealth or numbers, giving the large states a majority in the legislature. The Virginia Plan also called for a national executive and a national judiciary.

Delegates from the small states countered with the **New Jersey Plan**, presented by William Paterson. Just as Madison and Hamilton had hoped, the counter plan did not argue with the need for a stronger central government, giving Congress the right to tax, regulate, and coerce states. The legislature would be unicameral, and each state would have the same vote. The delegates from small states were determined that the new legislature would not be dominated by the large states, and the debate between large and small states deadlocked the Convention. Finally, a committee was elected to devise a compromise, which they presented on July 5.

The Great Compromise (also called the Connecticut Compromise) called for one house in which each state would have an equal vote (the Senate) and a second house (the House of Representatives) in which representation would be based on population. Unlike the Virginia Plan, the Senate would not be chosen by the House of Representatives, but would be chosen by the state legislatures. The House of Representatives would be directly elected by all voters, whose eligibility to vote would be determined by the states. The Compromise was accepted by a very slim margin, and the Convention was able to successfully agree on other controversial issues.

Other Compromises

Another disagreement at the Convention was based on North/South differences, particularly regarding the counting of slaves for purposes of apportioning seats in the House. The South wanted to count slaves in order to increase its number of representatives, and the North resisted. The delegates finally agreed on the **Three-fifths Compromise**, which allowed southern states to count a slave as three-fifths of a person, allowing a balance of power between North and South.

Another debate concerned the selection of the president. The initial decision was for the president to be selected by Congress, but the delegates were concerned about too much concentration of power in the legislature. On the other hand, they feared direct election by the people, especially since the House of Representatives were to be popularly elected.

The Compromise was to leave the selection of the president to an **electoral college** – people selected by each state legislature to formally cast their ballots for the presidency.

All but three of the delegates signed the document on September 17, 1787, with others who opposed it leaving before that. The drafting of the Constitution took about three months, but the document has lasted for more than two hundred years, making it the longest lasting Constitution in world history.

AMENDING THE CONSTITUTION

The Founders designed the amendment process to be difficult enough that Congress could not add so many amendments that the original document would end up with little meaning. The process requires action by BOTH the national government and the states before an amendment may be passed.

Formal Amendments

The Constitution may be formally amended in four ways:

- Amendments may be proposed by a 2/3 vote of each house of Congress and ratified by at least 3/4 of the state legislatures. All but one of the amendments have been added through this process.

- Amendments may be proposed by a 2/3 vote of each house of Congress and ratified by specially called conventions in at least 3/4 of the states. This method was used once – for the 21st Amendment that repealed Prohibition – because Congress believed that many state legislatures would not vote for it.

- Amendments may be proposed by a national constitutional convention requested by at least 2/3 of state legislatures and ratified by at least 3/4 of the state legislatures.

- Amendments may be proposed by a national constitutional convention and ratified by specially called conventions in at least 3/4 of the states.

The last two methods have never been used to amend the Constitution.

Informal Amendments

The Constitution is written broadly enough that change can occur within our political system through interpreting the words to fit changing needs and events. All three branches have contributed to informal amendment of the Constitution.

- **Legislature** – Congress has passed laws that reinterpret and expand Constitutional provisions. For example, the Commerce Clause allows Congress to regulate and promote interstate and international commerce. Over time, Congress has passed many laws that define the Commerce Clause, including regulations on forms of commerce that didn't exist in 1789, such as railroad lines, air routes, and internet traffic.

- **Executive Branch** – Presidents may negotiate executive agreements with other countries, an authority not mentioned in the Constitution. The Constitution requires that foreign treaties be ratified by the Senate, but executive agreements do not. These agreements are used to circumvent the formal process, especially for routine matters that might simply slow the work of the Senate down.

- **Judicial Branch** – Of all the branches, the judiciary has been the most influential in interpreting the Constitution. Article III defines the power of the judiciary very broadly, but does not specifically mention **judicial review** – the power of the courts to declare statutes unconstitutional and interpret the Constitution when disputes arise. That power was first established in *Madison v. Marbury* in 1803, when Chief Justice John Marshall claimed judicial review as a prerogative of the court in his famous majority opinion issued in the case.

BEARD'S CRITICISM OF THE FOUNDERS

The founders' interest in protection of property has led some scholars to question their personal interests as motives in writing the Constitution. Charles Beard argued in *An Economic Interpretation of the Constitution*, written in 1913, that the founders created a constitution that benefited their economic interests. According to Beard, the major conflicts and compromises resulted from the clash of owners of land as property, and owners of business or commercial interests. Many scholars today disagree with Beard because voting at the Convention did not follow these divisions closely. For example, Elbridge Gerry, a wealthy Massachusetts merchant and politician, refused to sign the Constitution. James Madison and James Wilson, men of modest means, were two of its biggest proponents. However, the founders did tend to base their votes on the economic interests of their states, as reflected in the famous compromises at the convention.

FEDERALISTS VERSUS ANTI-FEDERALISTS

The delegates agreed that the Constitution would go into effect as soon as popularly elected conventions in nine states approved it. The debate over **ratification** – the formal approval of the Constitution by the states – raged throughout the country, with supporters of the new government calling themselves **Federalists**, and their opponents, the **Anti-Federalists**. Federalists supported the greatly increased powers of the central government and believed that the Constitution adequately protected individual liberties. The Anti-Federalists believed that the proposed government would be oppressive and that more individual freedoms and rights should be explicitly guaranteed. Pamphlets, newspapers, and speeches supported one view or the other.

THE FEDERALIST PAPERS

Ratification of the Constitution was defended by the **Federalist Papers**, written by Alexander Hamilton, James Madison, and John Jay. These documents contain some of the most basic and brilliantly argued philosophical underpinnings of American government. Two famous papers are *Federalist #10* and *Federalist #51*.

The *Federalist #10* argued that separation of powers and federalism check the growth of tyranny: If "factious leaders...kindle a flame within their particular states..." leaders can check the spread of the "conflagration through the other states." Likewise, each branch of the government keeps the other two from gaining a concentration of power. *Federalist #10* also argued that Constitutional principles guard against the dangers of a direct democracy, or the "common passion or interest…felt by a majority of the whole…such [direct] democracies have ever been spectacles of turbulence and contention." Madison argued that a long-lived democracy must manage its interest groups, even though these "factions" can never be eliminated.

The *Federalist #51* explained why strong government is necessary: "If men were angels, no government would be necessary. If angels were to govern men, neither external nor internal controls on government would be necessary."

THE BILL OF RIGHTS

A compromise between Federalists and Anti-Federalists was reached with the agreement to add ten amendments that guaranteed individual freedoms and rights. With this agreement, the Constitution was finally ratified by all the states in 1789, and the **Bill of Rights** was added in 1791. Without these crucial additions, the Constitution would not have been ratified in several key states. Many of the recommendations from state ratifying conventions were considered by James Madison as he wrote the Bill, and he and a specially appointed committee submitted seventeen amendments to Congress. Congress eliminated five of them, and two were not immediately ratified by the states. These two did not become part of the original Bill of Rights, with one (dealing with apportionment of representatives) later clarified by Supreme Court decisions, and one (addressing salaries of members of Congress), added as an amendment 203 years later in 1992.

IMPORTANT DEFINITIONS AND IDENTIFICATIONS:

- Anti-Federalists
- Articles of Confederation
- authoritarian regimes
- Bill of Rights
- consent of the governed
- democracy
- direct democracy
- *An Economic Interpretation of the Constitution*
- elite theory
- electoral college
- European Enlightenment
- *Federalist Papers*
- *Federalist #10*
- Federalists
- formal amendment process
- The Great Compromise
- informal amendment process
- judicial review
- John Locke
- majoritarianism
- natural rights
- New Jersey Plan
- pluralism
- ratification
- representative democracy
- republic
- *Second Treatise of Government*
- Shay's Rebellion
- social contract
- "state of nature"
- Three-fifths Compromise
- Virginia Plan

CHAPTER TWO
FEDERALISM

Federalism, a central feature of the American political system, is the division and sharing of power between the national government and the states. The balance of power between the two levels of government has spawned some of the most intense controversies in American history. Historically, national interests have clashed with states' rights, and even today, when most Americans think of the government in Washington as vastly more powerful than the state governments, federalism is still one of the most important founding principles of the United States.

UNITARY, FEDERAL, AND CONFEDERAL POLITICAL SYSTEMS

All political systems may be evaluated according to their geographic distribution of power. A unitary system is one that concentrates all policymaking powers in one central geographic place; a **confederal system** spreads the power among many sub-units (such as states), and has a weak central government. A **federal system** divides the power between the central government and the sub-units. All political systems fall on a continuum from the most concentrated amount of power to the least. **Unitary governments** may be placed on the left side, according to the degree of concentration; confederal governments are placed to the right; and federal governments fall in between.

UNITARY SYSTEM (China, Britain, France)	FEDERAL SYSTEM (U.S. Canada)	CONFEDERAL SYSTEM (U.S. under the Articles of Confederation; Confederate States of America during the civil war)

THE HISTORICAL DEVELOPMENT OF FEDERALISM

Federalism was carefully defined in the Constitution as a founding principle of the U.S. political system. Even so, the nature of federalism is dynamic and has been shaped through the years by laws, Supreme Court decisions, and debates among prominent elected officials and statesmen.

14

FEDERALISM AS PROVIDED IN THE CONSTITUTION

When the colonies declared their independence from Britain in 1776, they reacted against the British unitary system in which all political and economic power was concentrated in London. Although the British did not impose this power consistently until after the French and Indian War ended in 1763, new controls on the colonial governments during the 1760s became a major source of friction that eventually led to war. During the American Revolution, the states reacted to Britain's unitary system by creating the Articles of Confederation that gave virtually all powers to the states. The framers at the Constitutional Convention tried to balance the perceived tyranny of the unitary system with the chaos created by the confederal system by outlining a hybrid federal system in the Constitution. Federalism, then, became a major building block for preserving freedoms while still maintaining order in the new nation.

Delegated Powers

The Constitution grants the national government certain **delegated powers**, chief of which are the war power, the power to regulate interstate and foreign commerce, and the power to tax and spend. Delegated powers (also called expressed or enumerated powers) are those that are specifically granted to the federal government by the Constitution.

- **The War Power** – The national government is responsible for protecting the nation from external attacks and for declaring war when necessary. Today, defense includes not only maintaining a standing army, navy, and air force, but also the ability to mobilize industry and scientific knowledge to back the efforts of the military.

- **The Power to Regulate Interstate and Foreign Commerce** – The national government has the responsibility to regulate commerce between the U.S. and foreign nations, as well as trade between states (interstate commerce.) The commerce clause (Article One, Section 8, Clause 3) gives Congress the power "to regulate Commerce with foreign Nations, and among the several states, and with the Indian Tribes." The government regulates a wide range of human activity, including agriculture, transportation, finance, product safety, labor relations, and the workplace. Few aspects of today's economy affect commerce in only one state, so most activities are subject to the national government's constitutional authority.

- **The Power to Tax and Spend** – Even when Congress lacks the constitutional power to legislate (for example, education and agriculture), its power to appropriate money provides Congress with a great deal of control. When Congress finances an undertaking, it determines how the money will be spent. Congress may threaten to withhold funds if a project does not meet federal guidelines. In recent years Congress has refused to finance any program in which benefits are denied because of race, color, or national origin, and more recently, gender and physical handicap.

Other powers specifically delegated to the national government include coining money, establishing a postal system, and the right of the government to borrow against its credit.

Concurrent Powers

All powers not granted in the Constitution to the national government are reserved for the states. States, however, may hold some of the same powers that the national government has, unless they have been given exclusively to the national government, either by provision of the Constitution or by judicial interpretation. **Concurrent powers** are those that both national and state governments hold. Examples are the concurrent powers of levying taxes and establishing and maintaining separate court systems. Even so, federalism limits state powers in that states cannot "unduly burden" their citizens with taxes. Neither can they interfere with a function of the national government, nor abridge the terms of a treaty of the United States government.

Reserved Powers

Reserved powers are those held by the states alone. They are not listed (as delegated powers are), but they are guaranteed by the 10th Amendment as "reserved to the states respectively, or to the people." Reserved powers include establishing local governments and regulating trade within a state. States also have police power – the authority to legislate for the protection of the health, morals, safety, and welfare of the people. However, because these powers are not listed in the Constitution, there is sometimes a question about whether certain powers are delegated to the national government or reserved for the states.

Prohibited Powers

Prohibited powers are denied to either the national government, state governments, or both. For example, the federal government can't tax exports, and state governments cannot tax either imports or exports. States can't make treaties with or declare war on foreign governments.

The "Necessary and Proper Debate"

From the beginning, the meaning of federalism has been open to debate. In the late 18th century, Alexander Hamilton – the first Secretary of the Treasury – championed **loose construction**, the view that the Constitution should be broadly interpreted. The national government created by the Constitution represented "the supreme law of the land" (Article Six), and its powers should be broadly defined and liberally construed. The opposite view of strict construction, articulated by Thomas Jefferson, was that the federal government was the product of an agreement among the states and that the main threat to personal liberty was likely to come from the national government. Jefferson's **strict construction** required that the powers of the national government should be narrowly construed and sharply limited. This famous clash in interpretations of the Constitution shaped the political culture of the United States for many years, well into the mid-twentieth century.

Realizing that they could not make a comprehensive list of powers for the national or the state governments, the founders added to Article I the **"necessary and proper clause."**

This clause states that Congress shall have the power "to make all laws which shall be necessary and proper for carrying into execution the foregoing powers." Hamilton's arguments for national supremacy relied heavily on the "necessary and proper" (or "elastic") clause. Jefferson's states rights point of view rested partially on the 10th Amendment that reserves powers to the states.

McCULLOCH V. MARYLAND

During the early 19th century, the Supreme Court tipped the balance of the debate to **national supremacy**, the point of view that the national government should have relatively more power than the states. Chief Justice John Marshall advocated this view in a series of decisions, including the influential 1819 case known as *McCulloch v. Maryland*.

The case arose when James McCulloch, the cashier of the Bank of the United States in Baltimore, refused to pay a tax levied on the bank by the state of Maryland. When state officials arrested him, McCulloch appealed to the Supreme Court. The Court's opinion set an important precedent that established national supremacy over states rights. The case questioned the right of the federal government to establish a bank, since no such right is enumerated in Article I.

Marshall ruled the Maryland law that established the tax unconstitutional with his famous statement: "The power to tax is the power to destroy." The power to destroy a federal agency would give the state supremacy over the federal government, so the states may not tax a federal agency.

THE NULLIFICATION CONTROVERSY

The issue continued to rage during the early 19th century. Eventually James Madison and Thomas Jefferson defined the states rights point of view as **nullification**, the right of a state to declare null and void a federal law that in the state's opinion, violated the Constitution. Before the Civil War, John C. Calhoun led the charge for southern states that claimed the right to declare "null and void" any attempts by the national government to ban slavery. The issue was settled with the northern victory in the Civil War that determined once and for all that the federal union is indissoluble and that states cannot declare acts of Congress unconstitutional.

THE "COMMERCE CLAUSE"

The meaning of the commerce clause was at issue in the 1824 ***Gibbons vs. Ogden*** case. Aaron Ogden had been given exclusive license by the state of New York to operate steam-powered ferryboats between New York and New Jersey. Thomas Gibbons obtained a license from the U.S. government to operate boats in the same area, and when he decided to compete with Ogden, Ogden sued, and the case went to the Supreme Court. Several issues were at stake in defining federalism:

- The definition of commerce – When New York's highest court ruled against Gibbons, defined commerce narrowly as only the shipment of goods, not navigation or the transport of people.

- National government's powers over intrastate commerce – Does the national government have the right to control any commerce within a state's boundaries?

- State government's powers over interstate commerce – Is interstate commerce a concurrent power that states may share with the national government?

John Marshall wrote the majority opinion in the case, an expansive interpretation of the commerce clause that increased the national government's authority over all areas of economic affairs. Marshall defined commerce as all business dealings, not just the transfer of goods, and he ruled that the national government could regulate within states' jurisdiction. On the other hand, interstate commerce is solely the right of the national government, and so the New York court had no right to prohibit Gibbons' trade.

Expansion of the Commerce Clause

With the booming Industrial Revolution of the late 1800s, the debate over the balance of power between state and national government focused on the interpretation of the commerce clause, which gives Congress the power "to regulate Commerce with foreign Nations, and among the several States, and with the Indian Tribes." At first, the Court tried to distinguish between interstate commerce, which Congress could regulate, and intrastate commerce, which only the states could control. Because most companies participate in both types of commerce, the Court had a great deal of trouble distinguishing between the two. If a company is canning vegetables, some of which will be shipped within the state, and some outside the state, should different regulations apply to canning the same product? Is a shipment destined for another state under state control as long as it travels to the border? At what point does it become interstate commerce?

In the late 19th century the use of the commerce clause was questioned when it came to the federal regulation of child labor, dangerous working conditions or even tainted consumer goods. The Supreme Court declared this use unconstitutional because the federal government would be regulating the workplace or the manufacturing of goods rather than regulating interstate trade. The use of the commerce clause was accepted in businesses such as railroads and water transportation since they traditionally crossed state boundaries. This philosophy changed during the New Deal when the Court refused to review appeals challenging government regulation of rights of employees, farm cultivation and the stock market. This change permitted the federal government to have a more regulatory role through a changed view of interstate commerce.

Over the years the commerce clause has continued to be interpreted more and more broadly, so that today, the national government regulates a wide range of commercial activities, including transportation, agriculture, labor relations, finance, and manufacturing. Almost no type of commerce is controlled exclusively by the states, and the current Court interpretation of commerce laws is extremely complex.

The Commerce Clause and Civil Rights

The Commerce clause also has been used to sustain legislation outside of commercial matters. In 1964 the Supreme Court upheld the 1964 Civil Rights Act forbidding discrimination based on race in public accommodations because

> "Congress's action in removing the disruptive effect which it found racial discrimination has on interstate travel is not invalidated because Congress was also legislating against what it considers to be moral wrongs."

Discrimination affects interstate commerce, so Congress constitutionally could legislate against discrimination. Again, many years later, Hamilton's loose interpretation of the Constitution insured that the principle of national supremacy prevailed over that of states rights.

Reining in the Commerce Power – Or Not

Since the 1990s, the Supreme Court has been limiting the national government's power under the commerce clause. In ***United States vs. Lopez*** (1995) the Court ruled that Congress had exceeded its authority when it banned possession of guns within one thousand feet of any school. The law was declared unconstitutional because it had "nothing to do with commerce." In ***United States v Morrison*** (2000) the Court held that the 1994 Violence against Women Act also overstepped the Constitution with the statement that violence against women had an adverse effect on interstate commerce.

While upholding these cases, the Supreme Court in 2005 took a stance that has enhanced federal power with regard to the commerce clause, indicating that each situation may be different. In 1996 California passed the Compassionate Use Act permitting medical marijuana use. This was in conflict with the federal Controlled Substances Act which banned the possession of marijuana (*Gonzales v Raich,* 2005.) While much of the marijuana was locally grown and used, the Court ruled that the federal law was appropriate because the local use affected the national supply and demand of the drug. The precedent to regulate local activities as part of a "class of activities" was "firmly established" making intrastate use "essential" to regulating the national market. In *Granholm v Heald*, (2005), the Court ruled that Michigan had permitted in-state wineries to ship their product to Michigan customers while prohibiting out-of-state wineries to ship into the state. The Court stated that this law favored in-state distributors. The 21st Amendment, which repealed Prohibition, gave states the ability to regulate alcohol importation, but the Court ruled that favoring one group over another was not the intent of the amendment. This case indirectly affects interstate commerce because it limits the power of the states to regulate out-of-state wine being shipped into its area.

The Court has distinguished a difference between economic activity and non-economic activity when applying the commerce clause. It ruled that *Lopez* and *Morrison* did not affect interstate commerce so that federal involvement was an interference of reserved powers. The Court felt that decisions regarding guns, school children, and acts of violence were best made at the local or state level.

TWO TYPES OF FEDERALISM

Until the 1930s, the relationship between the national and state governments was usually described as **dual federalism**, a system in which each remains supreme within its own sphere. However, as the commerce controversy in *Gibbons vs. Ogden* points out, separating national from state jurisdiction isn't always easy. With the New Deal programs of the 1930s the separation proved to be virtually impossible, ushering in the era of **cooperative federalism**. During this era state and federal governments cooperated in solving the common complex problems brought on by the Great Depression. The New Deal programs often involved joint action between the national government and the states. Cooperative federalism remains in place today, with the national government involved to some extent in virtually all public policymaking.

The two types of federalism are often compared by using an analogy with two types of cakes: the layer cake (dual federalism) with its clearly distinct separations, and the marble cake (cooperative federalism) where the two intertwine and swirl together.

THE POLITICS OF MODERN FEDERALISM

The structures of the federal system have not changed much since the Constitution was written, but modern politics have changed the relationship between national and state governments, especially over the past 50 years or so. Today a major aspect of federalism is the **grants-in-aid system**: the national government provides millions of dollars for federal grants to states. This is an example of **fiscal federalism** which involves the taxation and distribution of monies by the federal government to state and local government to fund projects. In this relationship most of the money comes from the federal government.

GRANTS-IN-AID

One of the national government's most important tools for influencing policy at the state and local levels is the federal grant. Congress authorizes grants, establishes rules for how grants may be used, and decides how much control the states have over federal funds. Federal grants fall into two general types:

- **Categorical grants** are appropriated by Congress for specific purposes – highway or airport building, welfare, or school lunches. These grants usually require the state to "match" (put up money for) the federal grants, although the matching funds can vary widely. There are hundreds of categorical grant programs, but a few, including Medicaid and Aid to Families with Dependent Children, account for almost 85 percent of total spending for categorical grants. State and local officials complain that these grants are often too narrow and cannot be adapted easily to local needs. The federal government may also apply **cross-over sanctions** which use federal funds in one program to influence state and local policy in another one. For example, the Reagan administration withheld money for highway construction to states that did not raise the drinking age to age 21. Another way for the federal government to influence state policy is in the use of **cross-cutting requirements** where the federal grant must be extended to all activities supported by federal funds. For instance, if a university discriminates illegally in one program such as athletics (violating the Civil Rights Act of 1964) it may lose federal monies that it receives for all of its programs.

- **Block grants** consolidate several categorical grants into a single "block" for prescribed broad activities, such as social services, health services, or public education. This type – promoted by Ronald Reagan – is referred to as "New Federalism" because it shifts responsibility for spending to the states. However, it has remained very similar to traditional federalism because while federal funding was reduced, particularly under President Reagan, much of the money for the programs still originated with the federal government. During the early 1980s Congress consolidated a number of categorical grants into block grants. Later presidents have advocated that more consolidation occur, but Congress has been reluctant to do so. Block grants give Congress less control over how the money is used, and representatives cannot take credit for grants to their particular districts. State governors generally have supported block grants, because they give states wide control of how and where the money is spent. City mayors have tended to oppose them because cities must rely on state governments to determine funding rules and amounts.

Today, even though block grants still exist, Congress is always tempted to add "strings" that set requirements for how federal grants are to be spent. As a result, block grants gradually become more categorical, a phenomenon known as **"creeping categorization."** The common belief is that the practice creates an electoral advantage for members of Congress who have more narrowly based grants. However, it can also be seen as a reaction to the misuse of block grants by states and local governments.

MANDATES

A recent federal control on the activities of state governments is a **mandate**, a rule that tells states what they must do in order to comply with federal guidelines. Often the mandates are tied to federal grants, but sometimes the mandates have nothing to do with federal aid.

Most mandates apply to civil rights and environmental protection. State programs may not discriminate against specific groups of people, no matter who pays for them. Today, anti-discrimination rules apply to race, sex, age, ethnicity, and physical and mental disabilities. States must comply with federal laws and standards regarding the environment, as well.

Mandates have been criticized strongly by state and local governments. One reason is the apparent "one size fits all" mentality of mandates. It may be hard for states to meet set standards. If federal regulations require states to improve an area of the environment, such as water, by a certain percentage it may be an impossible task within the time frame set by the law. Also, from their point of view, it is easy enough for Congress to pass mandates when the states must foot the bills. For example, the 1986 Handicapped Children's Protection Act provided federal regulations meant to assure equal access and opportunity for disabled children. Federal guidelines included requirements for public schools to build access ramps and elevators, provide special buses and personnel, and widen hallways, all with no federal money to help schools comply. These federal requirements have become known as **unfunded mandates**. The Handicapped Children's Protection Act was followed in 1990 by the Americans with Disabilities Act which required states to adjust facilities such as public buildings, state colleges and universities to make them accessible for those with disabilities. Environmentally the federal government had already held states responsible for national air quality standards determined by Congress under the Clean Air Act, 1970. In both cases adequate funds were not forthcoming from Congress for implementation.

Unfunded Mandate Reform

By the 1990s states, using the money given, were also burdened with regulations and little money to comply. In 1995, under the new Republican majority plan, Contract with America, limits to unfunded and under-funded mandates became a high priority. With President Clinton's support, the Unfunded Mandates Reform Act of 1996 was passed. It requires the Congressional Budget Office to estimate the costs of all mandates to state and local governments over $50 million. Only those requiring antidiscrimination measures were exempt from the law. However, after the attacks of 9/11/01 and the concerns over homeland security, new mandates have been passed forcing state compliance without cost consideration to the states.

Court Ordered Unfunded Mandates

In addition to legislative mandates federal courts have made decisions that forced states to spend tax dollars. Court-ordered prison reforms in construction, school desegregation and improvements in mental health facilities require states to spend money in order to meet court-ordered standards.

However, in 1997 the Court ruled against the provision in the Brady Handgun Violence Prevention Act of 1993 that forced state employees to check the backgrounds of those making handgun purchases. It stated that the 10th Amendment provision of "separate state sovereignty" had been violated.

States Try to Strike Back

States did not take all of these federal initiatives without reaction. Several states including California, Florida, Texas and New York filed suit against the federal government demanding reimbursement for the federally-required public services, such as education and health care, for illegal aliens. The states believed that the federal government was responsible because it did not adequately control the country's borders. While valid, the states lost this argument in the courts.

Examples of Federal Mandates for State and Local Governments

1983 – Social Security Amendments

1984 – Hazardous and Solid Waste Amendments

          Highway Safety Amendments

1986 – Asbestos Emergency Response Act

          Handicapped Children's Protection Act

          Safe Drinking Water Act Amendments

1988 – Drug-Free Workplace Acts

          Ocean Dumping Ban Act

1990 – Clean Air Act Amendments

          Americans with Disabilities Act

1996 – Personal Responsibility and Work Opportunity Reconciliation Act
          "Welfare Reform"

2001 – No Child Left Behind

2002 – Homeland Security Act

THE ADVANTAGES AND DISADVANTAGES OF FEDERALISM

Few Americans believe that the federalist system should be abandoned, but the nature of federalism is still a controversy today, and Americans still disagree about the balance of power between national and state governments.

ADVANTAGES	DISADVANTAGES
Mobilization of political activity The various levels of government provide many alternatives for a citizen to be heard regarding a concern. If a local official won't listen, a citizen may appeal to someone on the state or national level.	Confusion of political activity The various levels of government can be confusing to a citizen, so that he or she does not know which official to contact.
Interest groups cannot easily take over the government. Powerful interest groups cannot force their will upon less powerful groups because in order to control, they would have to take over not only the national government, but state and local governments as well. Small groups of people have a chance to be heard and influence legislation.	Small but motivated interest groups can block the will of the majority for extended periods of time. Sometimes small groups of people can impose their will for extended periods of time on the majority. For example, a relatively small group of southern senators blocked civil rights legislation for many years after most citizens favored such legislation.
Diversity of policies among states encourages experimentation and creativity. 50 different state governments tackle similar issues, and a good solution in one state can be modeled in another. For example, if a state finds a good way to finance public education, other states can mimic the plan, altering for special needs. On the other hand, if a state tries something that fails, at least it affects only one state, not all.	Diversity of policies among states creates inequality between citizens of different states. Because states provide different levels of support, citizens in some states have more advantages than those in other states. For example, welfare benefits vary widely among the states, as do funding levels for public education.
Diverse policies among states are good because uniform laws don't make sense in many areas. For example, speed limits on highways should be under state and local control, as should the minimum age for obtaining a driving license. Crowded New Jersey should not have the same speed limits as does wide-open Montana. Young people in farm states should be allowed to drive at early ages in order to help support the farm.	Diverse policies among states even for speed limits and driving ages creates confusion and inequality. Although speed limits obviously need to vary, arbitrary differences in state laws are confusing and outdated in this era of interstate highways. Differences in driving ages are not fair to young people in states with higher age requirements.

An individual's attitude about federalism depends partly on how much he or she values equality vs. freedom. Uniform laws passed by a unitary government tend to emphasize equal treatment of citizens. Diverse laws by their very nature allow a great deal of individual freedom.

THE "DEVOLUTION REVOLUTION"

Although the trend toward national supremacy has continued throughout most of American history, a movement has begun in recent years to devolve more responsibilities back to the states. The movement began as a Republican initiative shortly after the 1994 elections, when the Republicans became the majority party in both houses of Congress. The new conservative leadership looked for ways to scale back the size and activities of the national government. A major focus was the welfare system, and as a result, the "welfare to work" legislation passed in 1996 (Personal Responsibility and Work Opportunity Reconciliation Act) led to a major shift of responsibility for welfare programs from federal to state governments.

With the election of President George W. Bush and his "compassionate conservatism", the direction of this devolution process was changed by instituting programs that returned to the idea of **regulated federalism**. This type of federalism provided expansion of the national government by increasing the national standards on states by imposing rules at times with little, if any, funding. Through the No Child Left Behind Act, President Bush was criticized for imposing standards on states regarding education and increasing the Department of Education budget by 51%. Since President Reagan, this bureaucracy had been targeted by conservatives to be eliminated. The conservatives also demanded that control of schools be returned to local communities and states. President Bush did the opposite. Another example is the expansion of Medicare into prescription drug coverage. This policy has greatly increased federal government involvement and spending for welfare estimated to cost $534 billion. While the education requirements have been resented by many states as an intrusion, Medicare is an entitlement program that is traditionally regulated by the federal government and has been controversial primarily due to its cost.

Two events that account for the slowdown of the devolution revolution are:

- Terrorist attacks of September 11, 2001 created a need to guard against other attacks and protect the country from world terrorism, encouraging federal standardization to help guarantee protection.
- Hurricane Katrina demonstrated the need for federal agencies to aid states quickly in case of natural disasters. It also demonstrated the problems states have inadequately responding to the mass devastation brought about by natural disasters.

States always need help with transportation improvements as reflected in the $286 billion Transportation Act of 2006, which became very controversial because of the $24 billion included in the bill for "pork barrel projects" for favored congressional districts. However, it is just another example of how states depend upon the federal government funding to help with local projects.

Although the balance of power between national and state governments has varied over time, the federalist system is an essential building block of American government. In spite of this recent turn away from devolution, states still sponsor major programs to fund education, help distressed cities, and provide welfare. Local governments have wide controls over a myriad of services and regulations. The federalist system is rooted in the Constitution, and governmental powers certainly will continue to be shared among national, state, and local levels.

STATES' RELATIONS UNDER FEDERALISM

- **Full Faith and Credit** – While the 10th Amendment addresses the concept of reserved powers, the Constitution also is concerned with how states work with each other. The first paragraph in Article IV outlines relations among the states which involve respect for each other's acts and legal decisions. Known as the "full faith and credit" clause, it requires states to respect each other's public acts, records and court proceedings such as marriage licenses and birth certificates. There are limits, however. A divorce may not be recognized if a person goes to a state other than his/her residence in order to obtain that divorce.

- **Privileges and Immunities** – Citizens are afforded the same rights and privileges no matter the state. This applies to travel and change of residence.

- **Extradition** – A person accused of a crime in one state who flees to another must be returned to the state where the crime was committed.

- **State Compacts/Contracts** – States also work with each other to solve problems that cross state lines. Many of these deal with transportation such as highways and bridges, but they may also involve civil defense and environmental problems such as air and water pollution. Most compacts have occurred since World War II and are protected in the Constitution, Article I, Section 10, which prohibits laws that impair contracts. Congress and the courts may review these compacts if necessary. Congressional approval is necessary if the compacts affect delegated powers and the courts may order compliance of a state if necessary. State compacts are seen as the most effective way of ensuring interstate cooperation.

CONSTITUTIONAL BASIS OF FEDERALISM

Constitutional Provision	Effect on Federalism
Supremacy Clause Article VI	State laws, court decisions and constitutions must not be in conflict with the U.S. Constitution and the laws of the United States. This clause may affect the diversity with which states address problems.
Tenth Amendment Reserved Powers	This amendment allows states to take upon themselves the laws necessary to function, including health and safety. States have identified areas that are separate from the federal government such as education standards.
Elastic Clause Necessary and Proper Clause	This clause permits the power of Congress to be stretched to fit the times. However, it can also be used to intrude on reserved powers if the courts agree that it is "necessary and proper".
Powers Denied to States Article I, Sec. 10	These powers include practical matters such as coining money, declaring war, and taxing exports. These are national issues, not state concerns.
Amendment Procedures Article V	This article recognizes the need for the people, through their states, to ratify any changes to the Constitution. Whether it be through legislatures or state conventions, state approval is a necessary element of the procedures.
Full Faith and Credit Clause Article IV, Sec. 1	States must respect each other's laws, records, and court decisions with some exceptions.
Extradition Article IV, Sec. 2	Criminals may not flee to another state to avoid arrest. States cooperate with each other and return accused or escaped criminals to the state requesting help.
Privileges and Immunities Clause Article IV, Sec. 2	Citizens do not forfeit certain rights just because they cross state lines.

Commerce Clause Article I, Sec 8	States are able to control commerce within their boundaries, but Congress is permitted to control commerce that crosses state lines. This clause has been a constant area of review and changing interpretation throughout U.S. history.
***McCulloch v Maryland*, 1819**	This case recognizes "implied powers" of the federal government under the elastic clause and restricts state action against such powers. Its focus is the national bank, but the basic decision is still valid.
Eminent Domain Amendment V *Kelo v New London, Ct.*, 2005	This principle permits government, including state and local, to take property for "public use" but must provide "due process" and "just compensation" for the property. In the *Kelo* case, the Supreme Court ruled in favor of the local government stating that it was a local issue best settled at that level.

State Power – Significant or Weak?

The chart on the previous page demonstrates how the Constitution recognizes federalism in the United States by including state authority and the restrictions on it. However, states have also asserted their authority and diversity in various ways.

Gay Marriage – States have passed amendments or state laws regarding this issue either approving or disapproving gay marriage or civil unions. Many of these have come in the form of referenda. Massachusetts has provisions approving same-sex marriage while Vermont has endorsed civil unions. Hawaii provides benefits to same-sex couples. This issue is being challenged in various state courts.

Environmental Issues – Global Warming – California became the first state to cap greenhouse gas emissions. In 2004 Governor Arnold Schwarzenegger required state buildings to be 20% more efficient than the national standards by 2015. Governor Charlie Crist, Florida, asked the state legislature to allocate money to research alternative energy resources. Weather patterns that increase the number of hurricanes and rising water levels along the coast were stated as concerns of Governor Crist. Other states such as Arizona, New Mexico, Washington and Wisconsin plan to study the levels of carbon dioxide produced in their state.

Gay marriage and environmental issues are two examples of states taking the initiative regarding issues that they believe to be important. It enables their citizens' concerns to be addressed through state action when the federal government is seen as weak or conflicted in addressing them. State government is, therefore, still a vital element in the U.S. federal system.

IMPORTANT DEFINITIONS AND IDENTIFICATIONS

- block grants
- categorical grants
- the "commerce clause"
- concurrent powers
- confederal systems
- cooperative federalism
- creeping categorization
- cross-cutting requirements
- cross-over sanctions
- delegated powers
- devolution revolution
- dual federalism
- elastic clause
- eminent domain
- extradition
- federal systems
- federalism
- fiscal federalism
- "full faith and credit clause"
- *Gibbons v Ogden*
- grants-in-aid system

- *Kelo v New London, CT*
- loose construction
- mandate
- *McCulloch v Maryland*
- national supremacy
- necessary and proper clause
- nullification
- privileges and immunities
- regulated federalism
- reserved powers
- revenue sharing
- state compact/contract
- strict construction
- supremacy clause
- Tenth Amendment
- unfunded mandates
- unitary governments
- *United States v Lopez*
- *United States v Morrison*

UNIT ONE QUESTIONS

1. Which of the following political concepts is MOST associated with Enlightenment philosophy of the 17th and 18th century?

   (A) Authoritarian leadership
   (B) Powerful executive leadership
   (C) The elite theory
   (D) Consent of the governed
   (E) Pluralism

2. Which of the following is a central assumption of John Locke's social contract theory?

   (A) Humans are irrational.
   (B) Humans are self-interested.
   (C) Humans are immoral.
   (D) Rulers do not value individual liberty for their subjects.
   (E) Rulers grant life, liberty, and property to their subjects.

3. One reason that the founders were skeptical about using direct democracy as a model for the Constitution was that

   (A) direct democracy had not worked very well for the Ancient Greeks
   (B) direct democracy does not allow ordinary people much input into government decisions
   (C) they feared that direct democracy would lead to chaos and violence
   (D) they feared that representatives would be allowed too much political power
   (E) direct democracy allows minorities to be over-represented in the legislature

4. A principle in the Constitution designed to limit political authority was

   (A) a unitary form
   (B) the electoral college
   (C) 3/5 compromise
   (D) separation of powers
   (E) the elastic clause

5. Which of the following principles of the Constitution is most directly grounded in John Locke's concept of "consent of the governed"?

   (A) Popular sovereignty
   (B) Separation of powers
   (C) Checks and balances
   (D) Federalism
   (E) Limited government

6. Which of the following problems, under the Articles of Confederation, convinced many that the government needed to be changed?

   (A) Presidential powers exceeded legislative powers.
   (B) Central taxes were excessive and could not be challenged.
   (C) Both interstate and foreign trade had no centralized regulation.
   (D) States could not tax one another's trade goods.
   (E) The Supreme Court refused to rule in interstate matters.

7. Shay's Rebellion reinforced the founders' common belief that

   (A) state governments needed to be granted more powers
   (B) ordinary Americans had too many freedoms
   (C) the "excesses of democracy" needed to be checked
   (D) only property owners should have the franchise
   (E) small states were able to avert domination by the central government

8. The Great Compromise at the Constitutional Convention created a(n)

   (A) electoral college
   (B) presidency with separate powers from the legislature
   (C) independent judiciary
   (D) political party system
   (E) bicameral legislature

9. The principle of federalism is evident in all of the following provisions of the Constitution EXCEPT:

   (A) the amendment process
   (B) the electoral college
   (C) checks and balances
   (D) full faith and credit clause
   (E) 10th Amendment

10. The main purpose of the *Federalist Papers* was to

   (A) encourage states not to ratify the Constitution
   (B) limit the power of the central government
   (C) explain the rationale behind Constitutional provisions
   (D) encourage partisan support for the Federalist Party
   (E) promote the addition of the Bill of Rights to the Constitution

11. Unitary and federal systems differ in what important way?

    (A) A unitary system is generally not democratic; a federal system is.
    (B) Federalist systems have proven to be less effective in promoting civil rights than unitary systems.
    (C) Diffused authority is an important goal of federalist systems, whereas unitary systems are much more centralized.
    (D) Unitary systems tend to promote compromise in policy more than federalist systems do.
    (E) Executives in federal systems tend to have more power than executives in unitary systems.

12. Charles Beard believed that the framers' main interest in forming a new government in 1787 was

    (A) establishing stronger local authority
    (B) creating a stronger executive
    (C) protecting private property interests
    (D) clarifying the role of the judiciary
    (E) creating a bicameral legislature

13. Thomas Jefferson's view that the powers of the national government should be narrowly construed is called

    (A) consent of the governed
    (B) strict construction
    (C) the wall of separation
    (D) loose construction
    (E) national supremacy

14. John Marshall's ruling in *McCulloch vs. Maryland* that the "power to tax is the power to destroy" had the effect of establishing

    (A) state supremacy
    (B) national supremacy
    (C) strict construction of the Constitution
    (D) the policy of nullification
    (E) dual federalism

15. Which court case was most important in broadening the jurisdiction of the national government through the commerce clause?

    (A) *Marbury vs. Madison*
    (B) *McCulloch vs. Maryland*
    (C) *Gibbons vs. Ogden*
    (D) *United States vs. Lopez*
    (E) *Baron vs. Baltimore*

16. The marble cake analogy is often used to describe

    (A) dual federalism
    (B) national supremacy
    (C) sovereignty of the states
    (D) federal mandates
    (E) cooperative federalism

17. States usually prefer a form of fiscal federalism with few federal restrictions as evidenced in

    (A) cooperative grants
    (B) federal mandates
    (C) block grants
    (D) categorical grants
    (E) dual federal grants

18. Devolution of power in a federalist political system usually has the effect of

    (A) shifting more decision-making to the local level, closer to the people.
    (B) limiting the ability of judicial review to interfere with state law.
    (C) recognizing national authority over states rights.
    (D) permitting states to refuse to enforce federal laws hurtful to the states.
    (E) limiting the amount of federal regulation that can be forced on states.

19. Which of the following is a disadvantage of federalism?

    (A) Dual court systems that challenge each other result in confusion.
    (B) Few opportunities for leadership development result in elitism.
    (C) Confusion over responsibilities sometimes leads to a lack of public accountability.
    (D) Local governments become too independent of federal control.
    (E) Judicial review may overrule a presidential initiative.

State Welfare Benefits, 2000

Monthly Welfare Grants
Family of 3

State	Monthly Amount
Alaska	$923
Vermont	$708
California	$626
Kentucky	$262
Alabama	$164

Source: Ways & Means Committee, 2000

20. The chart above best reflects an important problem that results from federal devolution of welfare programs to the states as the

   (A) lack of bureaucratic ability to oversee state programs
   (B) level of diversity in relief provided by public assistance programs
   (C) ways in which states care about helping those in need of public assistance
   (D) length of time states provide public assistance
   (E) need for welfare programs in the United States

FREE RESPONSE QUESTION

As a way to organize government, federalism has both advantages and disadvantages.

a) Define federalism. *System of gov. — Shared sys. of gov. — Created at constitutional convention.*

b) Describe two (2) advantages of federalism. *provides unity stable economy. page 24*

c) For one advantage of federalism you identified in "b", give a specific example of how the advantage operates in the U. S. political system.

d) Describe two disadvantages of federalism. *page 24 — Confusion of responsibility*

e) For one disadvantage you identified in "d", give a specific example of how the disadvantage operates in the U.S. political system.

NO TESTING MATERIAL PRINTED ON THIS PAGE

GO ON TO THE NEXT PAGE

UNIT TWO

POLITICAL OPINIONS, BELIEFS, AND BEHAVIORS

CHAPTER THREE
POLITICAL CULTURE

Every country has a **political culture** – a set of widely shared beliefs, values, and norms concerning the ways that political and economic life ought to be carried out. The political culture defines the relationship of citizens to government, to one another, and to the economy. A good understanding of a country's political culture can help you make sense of the way a country's government is set up, as well as the political decisions its leaders make.

The American political culture may share beliefs, values, and norms, with those of other countries, but the sum and configuration of each political culture is unique. A **conflictual political culture** is one in which different groups (or subcultures) clash with opposing beliefs and values; a **consensual political culture** experiences less conflict. No matter how broadly the consensus is held, any culture contains values that overlap and conflict; the American political culture is no exception. Although many conflicts exist within the political system in the United States, American political culture is generally consensual because we have a broad base of shared political values. Most of our conflicts occur because we disagree on how these values should be implemented, not on the basic beliefs themselves.

ALEXIS DE TOCQUEVILLE

Alexis de Tocqueville – an early observer of American political culture – came to the United States during the 1830s to investigate why the American democracy seemed to be so successful, especially since his native France seemed to be having so much trouble with it. Tocqueville recorded his observations in *Democracy in America*, a book that remains today a classic study of American political values. He identified several factors that he believed to be critical in shaping America's successful democracy:

1. Abundant and fertile land
2. Countless opportunities for people to acquire land and make a living
3. Lack of a feudal aristocracy that blocked others' ambitions
4. An independent spirit encouraged by frontier living

Although many years have passed since Tocqueville made his famous observations about American political culture, these factors shaped our basic values of liberty, individualism, equal opportunity, democracy, rule of law, and civic duty.

SHARED VALUES

The values of the American political culture are grounded in the eighteenth century Enlightenment philosophy that so heavily influenced the founders. Over the years other values have been added, some supporting the original ones, some conflicting. American political beliefs and behaviors today reflect an accumulation of these values throughout United States history.

CORE VALUES

The following values have shaped the political culture since the founding of the country:

- **Liberty** – The value of liberty probably was the most important inspiration to the American Revolution, and it remains a core value today. Liberty was one of the natural rights first cited by John Locke and later by Thomas Jefferson: ...”that among these [rights] are life, liberty, and the pursuit of happiness..”
- **Equality** – Again, Thomas Jefferson refers to this basic value in the Declaration of Independence: “We hold these truths to be self evident, that all men are created equal..” Although most Americans don’t believe that everyone is equal in every sense of the word, the basic beliefs in equality of opportunity and equal treatment before the law have influenced the political system greatly.
- **Individualism** – The values of equality and liberty are complemented by a commitment to the importance and dignity of the individual. Under our system of government, individuals have both rights and responsibilities. **“Rugged individualism”** is a reflection of this value: the belief that individuals are responsible for their own well-being and that the strength of our system lies in the ability of individuals to be left alone to compete for success. This value is associated with the belief in the “common sense” of ordinary people and their ability to not only take care of themselves, but choose their government leaders as well.
- **Democracy** – Most Americans believe that government should be based on the consent of the governed, or that legitimacy ultimately lies in the hands of the people. We also believe in majority rule, but our emphasis on liberty and individualism causes us to believe that the rights of the minority should be protected as well.
- **Rule of law** – The belief that government is based on a body of law applied equally, impartially, and justly is central to American political culture. Rule of law stands in opposition to **rule by an individual**, which to many Americans implies following the whims of a dictator.
- **Civic duty** – Tocqueville noted that Americans of the early 19th century had a well-developed sense of community and individual responsibility to support community efforts. Although critics today observe that sense of community is not as strong in modern day, most Americans believe that they *ought to* be involved in local affairs and help out when they can.

Some international studies show that Americans by comparison tend to be more nationalistic, optimistic, and idealistic than people in other countries, although the scope of these studies is limited.

CHANGING AMERICAN VALUES

The firmly entrenched values of the late eighteenth and early nineteenth centuries were altered radically by the Industrial Revolution of the late 1800s. The most profound economic change was the increase in the inequality in the distribution of wealth and income. By the end of the century great wealth lay in the hands of a few people – the entrepreneurs or "robber barons." In a sense, the economic development brought out some inherent conflicts between the core values already established.

- **Capitalism** – Before the late 1800s, most personal wealth was based on land ownership. The commitment to **capitalism** – wealth based on money and other capital goods – became an additional shared political value during the Industrial Revolution, one that complements individualism and freedom.
- **Free enterprise** – During this same time period, American beliefs in freedom and individualism came to embrace **free enterprise** – economic competition without restraint from government.

These values reinforced the older emphasis on individualism. Just as early Americans had sought their fortune by claiming and farming new land by their own individual efforts, entrepreneurs of the late 19th century were flexing their muscles in the new industrial economy. However, the new commitment conflicted with the old value of equality, and tensions resulted. For example, robber barons were accused of exploiting workers and limiting competition in order to get ahead themselves, not only challenging equality, but other people's liberty as well. Monopolies also caused many to question equality of opportunity. The era illustrated inherent conflicts among the core values that had been in place for more than a century. The resolution was to legislate new government regulations to ensure fair treatment in the marketplace, and another belief was added to our political culture: government responsibility for the general welfare.

VALUE CHANGES SINCE THE 1930s

Although the Preamble to the Constitution states that **"promotion of the general welfare"** is a major purpose of government, the meaning of that value was transformed during the 1930s. The Great Depression brought about the near-collapse of capitalism, and the New Deal was an affirmation of the government's responsibility for the welfare of its people. In Roosevelt's 1944 inaugural address, he outlined a **"Second Bill of Rights"** that reflected his firm commitment to "economic security and independence." For example, he asserted everyone's rights to a useful job, food, clothing, a decent home, adequate medical care, and the right to a good education. These beliefs played a major role in the creation of the civil rights and social welfare legislation of the 1960s, and as recently as the early 1990s, President Clinton referred to Roosevelt's Second Bill of Rights when he said, "Health care is a basic right all should have." The defeat of his health care plan indicates that Americans don't always agree on the meaning of this value. Again, the movement created tension over the value of individualism, or the individual's responsibility to take care of himself. The government's responsibility for the general welfare became a major issue of the 2000 election campaign as candidates George W.

Bush and Al Gore debated the merits of a government-sponsored prescription plan for the elderly, and again in 2004, as President Bush supported privatization of Social Security programs, and challenger John Kerry did not. Health care continued to be an important issue in the presidential election of 2008 with both candidates, Barack Obama and John McCain, presenting health care reform proposals.

POLITICAL TOLERANCE

Another American value that is easily misunderstood is **political tolerance**. Democracy depends on citizens being reasonably tolerant of the opinions and actions of others, and most Americans believe themselves to be fairly tolerant. Studies show that political tolerance is much more complex a value than it appears on the surface. Among their findings are:

- The overwhelming majority of Americans agree with freedom of speech, religion, and right to petition – at least in the abstract.
- The overwhelming majority of Americans agree with freedoms of speech and religion, and people are not as politically tolerant as they proclaim themselves to be.
- The overwhelming majority of Americans agree with freedoms of speech and religion, and Americans are willing to allow many people with whom they disagree to do a great deal politically.
- The overwhelming majority of Americans agree with freedoms of speech and religion and Americans have become more tolerant over the last few decades.
- The overwhelming majority of Americans agree with freedoms of speech and religion and most people dislike one or another group strongly enough to deny it certain political rights, although people are not always inclined to act on their beliefs. As a general rule, people are willing to deny rights to people on the opposite end of the political spectrum. For example, liberals are most likely to deny right-wing groups, such as neo-Nazis or self-styled militia groups their rights, and conservatives are most likely to deny them to groups they may disapprove of, such as gays, atheists, or black militants. In conflict with popular opinion, research does not show that liberals are necessarily more tolerant than conservatives.

MISTRUST OF THE GOVERNMENT

A recent trend in changing American political values and beliefs is that of growing **mistrust of the government**. Although the trust reflected in the 1950s and early 1960s may have been artificially high, trust in government and its officials has declined significantly since the mid-1960s. Many scholars blamed the Vietnam War and Watergate for the initial, dramatic drops, but the trend is persistent into the early 21st century, with Americans in record numbers expressing disgust with politics and politicians.

Accompanying the mistrust of government has been a drop in political efficacy, a citizen's capacity to understand and influence political events. **Political efficacy** has two parts:

- **Internal efficacy** – the ability to understand and take part in political affairs.
- **External efficacy** – the belief of the individual that government will respond to his or her personal needs or beliefs.

Most studies find little difference over the last half-century in the levels of internal efficacy in the United States. However, there has been a big change in external efficacy, with most Americans believing that the government is not very responsive to the electorate. The levels dropped steadily during the 1960s and 70s, with many political scientists blaming the Vietnam War and Watergate for the growing belief that government officials operate without much concern for beliefs and concerns of ordinary people. The pattern continues until today, and may be one reason that incumbent presidents have had a difficult time getting reelected in recent years.

Americans seem to have come to the conclusion that government is too big and pervasive to be sensitive to individual citizens. However, international studies show that Americans feel significantly higher levels of political efficacy than do citizens of many European nations. Americans are less likely to vote than most Europeans, but they are more likely to sign petitions, work to solve community problems, and regularly discuss politics.

CULTURE WARS

Despite the fact that Americans share broad cultural and political values, some observers believe that conflict has increased since the mid-20th century, so that today we see two cultural camps in this country in constant combat with one another. The country has split on explosive political issues, such as abortion, gay rights, drug use, school prayer, terrorism, and the U.S. role in world affairs. On the one hand, some Americans believe that the United States is subject to relatively unchanging standards that are relatively clear – belief in God, laws of nature, and the United States in general as a force for good in the world. The opposite camp emphasizes that legitimate alternatives to these standards do exist, and that the U.S. has at times had a negative – or at best neutral – effect on world affairs.

The question is whether or not these differences of opinion actually amount to a big divide in the broad American political culture. One view is that they do because they strike at the very heart of the meaning of our democracy, but others believe that we are doing what we always have done – arguing about how our core values should be implemented.

IMPORTANT DEFINITIONS AND IDENTIFICATIONS:

- Alexis de Tocqueville
- capitalism
- conflictual political culture
- consensual political culture
- core American values
- free enterprise
- "general welfare"
- political culture
- political efficacy
- political tolerance
- rugged individualism
- rule by an individual
- rule of law
- Second Bill of Rights

CHAPTER FOUR
PUBLIC OPINION

Public opinion is the distribution of individual attitudes about a particular issue, candidate, or political institution. Although the definition is simple enough, public opinion encompasses the attitudes of millions of diverse people from many racial, ethnic, age, and regional groups. As a result, the study of American public opinion is especially complex, but also very important. For American government to operate democratically, the opinions of the American public must reach and become an integral part of the political process.

MEASURING PUBLIC OPINION

The measurement of public opinion is a complex process that involves careful interviewing procedures and question wording. To complicate the task further, people are often not well informed about the issues, and may comment on topics they know little about. Public opinion polls must be constructed and executed carefully in order to accurately reflect the attitudes of the American public.

Public opinion polling is a relatively new science, first developed by **George Gallup**, who did some polling for his mother-in-law, a candidate for secretary of state in Iowa in 1932. Gallup founded a firm that spread from its headquarters in Princeton, New Jersey, throughout the democratic world. Today, other well-known private firms conduct polls, and big television networks, magazines and newspapers, such as CNN, *Time*, and *The New York Times*, conduct their own polls. Pollsters are also hired by political candidates to determine their popularity, and the results of these polls often shape the direction of political campaigns. The national government even sponsors opinion polls of its own.

Polls generally start when someone wants a political question answered. For example, a candidate running for the House of Representatives may wonder, "What do people in the district need?" or "How strong a candidate do they think I am?" Or a newspaper may want to know, "How do people in this country feel about the threats of bioterrorism?" The candidate or publisher may commission a poll, and a reporter may base a story on the research findings. The pollsters then follow several important principles in gathering accurate statistics:

- **Representative sample** – The sample of those interviewed must be representative of the entire population. Every citizen cannot be polled regarding his or her opinion on a whole range of issues, but those selected must allow the pollster to make accurate assessments of public opinion. The most common technique employed is **random sampling**, which gives everyone in the population an equal probability of being selected. Most national surveys sample between one thousand and fifteen hundred persons. The pollster most commonly makes a list of groups, using criteria such as region, age, ethnic and racial groups, gender, and religion. From these groups, people are selected randomly for interviews. The disastrous Literary Digest Poll of 1936 provides a famous example of what can happen if the random sampling principle is ignored. That poll predicted that Alf Landon would beat Franklin Roosevelt by a landslide, but the results were the opposite. The Digest sample was biased because it was based on telephone books and club membership lists at a time when only well-to-do people had phones.

- **Respondent's knowledge** – People must have some knowledge of the issues they are asked about. If the issue is complex (such as American policy toward Afghanistan), people should be allowed to say, "I don't know", or "I haven't thought about it much." Still, people are often reluctant to admit a lack of knowledge about political issues, so pollsters always must allow for the fact that people often pretend to know things that they don't.

- **Careful and objective wording** – The structure and wording of the question is very important in obtaining an accurate response. "Loaded" or emotional words should not be used, and the pollster must not indicate what the "right" answer is. For example, consider a question like, "How much do you dislike leaders of Middle Eastern countries?" You could hardly expect an accurate answer. The categories of answers also determine the results of the poll. A yes or no question, such as, "Do you think the president is doing a good job?" will give very different results than a question that gives the interviewee a chance to rank the president's performance (excellent, very good, good, average, poor, very poor).

- **Cost efficiency v. accuracy** – Almost all polls have a budget, but accuracy should not suffer as a result. For example, a **straw poll** that asks television viewers to call in their opinions is not very expensive, but it generally is not very accurate either. The people that call in usually feel very strong about the issue. And some of them call in more than once.

- **Variances between samples** – The same poll conducted with a different random sample almost certainly will produce slightly different results. These slight variations are known as **sampling errors**. A typical poll of about fifteen hundred usually has a sampling error of plus (+) or minus (-) 3 percent. This means that 95% of the time the poll results are within 3 percentage points of what the entire population thinks. If 60% of the population supports a candidate for office, in actuality, 57-63% of the population supports him or her. Usually, the larger the sample in proportion to the population, the smaller the sampling error.

FACTORS THAT INFLUENCE POLITICAL ATTITUDES

When pollsters divide people into groups before they conduct random samples, they are acknowledging a well-proven fact: group identifications often influence political attitudes. Political attitudes are shaped by **political socialization**, a lifelong process through which an individual acquires opinions through contact with family, friends, coworkers, and other group associations. Today the media also plays a major role in political socialization, with political news and opinions widely available on TV, radio, and the internet. Political attitudes in turn determine how individuals participate, who they vote for, and what political parties they support. Many factors – including family, gender, religion, education, social class, race and ethnicity, and region – all contribute to American political attitudes and behavior.

FAMILY

The family is probably the most important source of political socialization, and so it plays a major role in shaping political attitudes, particularly of party identification. Polls show that the majority of young people identify with their parents' political party. The process begins early in life (by the age of ten or eleven), and even though individuals generally become more independent as they grow older, the correlation between adult party identification and the parents' party is still very high. A parallel trend, however, is a tendency for this correlation to be lower than it has in the past. This trend may be related to another trend: the growing number of voters who call themselves "independents" rather than Democrats or Republicans.

Logically, the more politically active your family, the more likely you are to hold the same beliefs. For example, most members of the extended Kennedy family are Democrats, and most Bush family members are Republicans. The relationship is weaker on specific issues – like gun control, school prayer, and government welfare programs – but still holds strong for overall political views and identifications.

GENDER

A person's gender also influences political views. For example, more women consider sexual harassment in the workplace to be a serious problem than do men, and more men than women tend to support military actions and spending in foreign affairs.

Party identification is also affected by gender, but the relationship has shifted through the years. In the 1920s when women first began to vote, they were more likely to support the Republican Party than were men. Some experts explain this correlation by pointing out that the Republicans tended to be more the party of "hearth and home" in the 20s. Whatever the explanation, the tendency for women to vote for Republicans continued through the 1930s. Although most women supported the Democrat Franklin Roosevelt over his Republican opponents, the percentage of women supporters was lower than the percentage of men who supported Roosevelt.

The trend held until the late 1960s, when the correlation reversed. Since that time women have been more likely than men to vote for Democrats. This "gender gap" has been explained by the advent of the modern women's rights movement and the Democrats' tendency to support points of view women support: equal opportunity for women, abortion rights, and welfare programs. On the other hand, some experts argue that Republicans are more concerned about defense issues, and thus they attract more men to their party. In the election of 2004, the gender gap appeared to be closing, with Republican George W. Bush garnering about 48% of all women's votes. However, Bush's support among men was significantly higher. According to Gallup, in 2008 women preferred the Democratic candidate by voting for Obama (57%) over McCain (43%). Men split evenly (50% - 50%) between the two candidates.

A more recent gender-related issue has to do with male vs. female support for women political candidates. Although common sense may tell us that women would be more likely to support women candidates, the research does not show a clear correlation. One problem is that relatively few women run for political office. Although their numbers have increased in recent elections, more women candidates run as Democrats than as Republicans, so it is difficult to know if the candidate's gender alone affects voting patterns of women and men.

One indicator that proves women are accepting the challenges of public office is the increased number of women governors. Women have served occasionally as state executives throughout the 20th century, but usually completed the terms of their husbands who had died in office. It wasn't until 1975 that Ella Grasso in Connecticut was elected to the job on her own merits. In 2009 women serve as governors from both parties and in all regions of the country such as Hawaii, Michigan, Kansas, North Carolina and Alaska. Hillary Clinton's campaign for the Democratic presidential nominee garnered support from both men and women in 2008. In spite of the fact that she lost the nomination to the first African American candidate, Barack Obama, the impact of her campaign was described by analysts as creating "18 million cracks in the glass ceiling," a reference to the number of votes she gained in the primary elections. Clinton was the first woman candidate to run a serious campaign for the presidency, indicating that men and women both are willing to support women candidates for high public offices.

Of course, Hillary Clinton was not the only female candidate in 2008. Sarah Palin's addition to the Republican ticket as the vice presidential candidate was both significant and precedent-setting for the party. As the first woman on the Republican ticket she immediately helped to organize the core Republican support that John McCain needed to help make him a more competitive presidential candidate. Her candidacy, as a conservative Republican, has forced a re-evaluation of women candidates. Although many Republican women have been elected to various levels of government, the question remains: will voters support a conservative woman for president?

MARRIED VS. UNMARRIED

Pollster John Zogby has pointed out that the gender gap (especially as evidenced in the 2004 presidential election) is not nearly so significant as the gap between married and unmarried voters. He found that on most issues single and married voters were often 25-30 points different, with singles more likely to vote for Democratic candidates, and married voters more likely to support Republicans. According to Gallup polling this trend continued in 2008, with unmarried voters supporting Barack Obama (65%) over John McCain (35%). Married voters preferred McCain by a margin of 56% to 44% for Obama.

RELIGION

An individual's religion is a factor in determining his or her political attitudes. Although the relationships are not as strong as they once were, these patterns still hold:

- Protestants are more conservative on economic matters (such as minimum wage and taxes) than are Catholics and Jews.
- Jews tend to be more liberal on both economic and social issues (such as civil liberties and rights) than are Catholics or Protestants.
- Catholics tend to be more liberal on economic issues than they are on social issues.

Some special research on fundamentalist Christians indicates that they tend to support more conservative candidates for public office, and that they are more likely to contribute to the Republican Party than to the Democratic Party. This more conservative tendency is stronger for attitudes about social issues (such as abortion, civil rights for minorities, and women's rights), than it is for foreign affairs and economic issues (such as government services and job guarantees).

In recent elections, a distinction has emerged between the political attitudes of those that attend religious services regularly and those that don't. The trend was particularly apparent in the election of 2004 and 2008 when churchgoers were more likely to vote for Republicans, and non-churchgoers were more likely to support Democrats. According to Gallup polling, this trend continued in 2008 when John McCain was given the edge by Protestant voters (53%) and those attending religious services weekly (55%). However, two exceptions to this assumption took place in 2008 as Barack Obama won the vote of Catholics (53%), and held a slight edge with voters that attend religious services monthly (51%).

EDUCATION

A person's level of education also affects political attitudes, but the evidence provides conflicting results. In general, the higher the individual's educational level, the more likely they are to hold conservative political points of view. However, many studies show that college education often influences individuals to have more liberal social and economic attitudes than they had before they started college. These studies show that the longer students stay in college and the more prestigious the institution they attend, the more liberal they become. The reasons for the correlation are unclear, but some experts believe that the liberal attitudes of professors may influence students. Others believe that the differences lie not in the schooling itself, but in the characteristics of people who attend college versus those that don't. In 2008 Barack Obama gained support from those with a grade school education (67%) while he also did well with those voters with a post-graduate degree (65%). The only category that John McCain won was those with a high school diploma (53%). (Gallup)

SOCIAL CLASS

A number of years ago, the relationship between social class and political attitudes was clear: the higher the social class, the more conservative the individual, and the more likely he or she was to belong to the Republican Party. Today, that relationship is much less clear, perhaps partly because of the correlation cited above between college education and liberalism. Even though the broad affiliations between blue-collar workers and the Democratic Party and businessmen and the Republican Party still have some credibility, those relationships have been much weaker than they once were. Union families continued their support of Democratic candidates by giving Barack Obama 64% of their vote in 2008. (Gallup)

RACE AND ETHNICITY

Much research has focused on the relationship between an individual's race and ethnicity and his or her political attitudes. The oldest and largest numbers of studies focus on black Americans, who tend to identify with the Democratic Party and are still the most consistently liberal group within that party. In recent presidential elections, blacks have voted in overwhelming numbers (close to 90%) for the Democratic candidate. This support increased in 2008 as Barack Obama, the first African American candidate and a Democrat, received 99% of the black vote.

Much less research has been conducted with Hispanic Americans, but preliminary results indicate that they too tend to be more liberal than the majority, with a tendency to affiliate with the Democratic Party. However, the correlation appears to be weaker than that of black Americans. In 2008, Hispanics, America's largest immigrant group, gave a significant amount of support to presidential candidate Democrat Barack Obama with 67% versus 31% of their vote for Republican John McCain. (Pew Research Center)

A very limited amount of research among Asian Americans indicates that they are more conservative than blacks or Hispanics, although attitudes of the various nationalities of Asians fluctuate widely. For example, preliminary research indicates that Korean Americans are more liberal than are Japanese Americans. Overall, more Asian Americans voted in the 2000 presidential election for Democrat Al Gore than for Republican George W. Bush, so the influence of Asian ethnicity on political attitudes is still not clear. In 2004 Asians also tended to favor Democratic candidate John Kerry. This support continued in 2008 with Asians supporting Barack Obama (62%) over John McCain (35%).

GEOGRAPHIC REGION

As a general rule, people on either coast tend to be more liberal than those in the middle of the country. However, there are many problems in defining that tendency because the rule is overbroad. For example, many Californians are very conservative, as are a number of New Englanders. However, part of the reason for the trend is probably an urban/rural differentiation, with coastal cities inhabited by minorities, recent immigrants, and members of labor unions. Cities in the "rust belt" of the Great Lakes region also tend to vote Democratic, partly because they have strong labor constituencies.

The Southeast presents some special problems with applying the rule, partly because party affiliations of Southeasterners have been changing over the past fifty years or so. Since the 1950s, many southerners have broken their traditional ties with the Democratic Party. From the time of Reconstruction until the 1950s, the "Solid South" always voted Democratic. Virtually all representatives, senators, governors, and local officials in the South belonged to the Democratic Party. Since the 1950s, more and more political leaders have affiliated with the Republicans, so that today, in most Southern states, both parties have viable contenders for public office. Some experts explain this phenomenon by pointing out that many southerners disagreed with the Democratic Party's support for the black civil rights movement starting in the 1950s, with the result that many white southerners changed their party affiliation.

 Although some research indicates that white southerners tend to be less liberal than others on social issues, such as aid to minorities, legalizing marijuana, and rights of those accused of crimes, southern attitudes on economic issues (government services, job guarantees, social security) are very similar to those from other regions. Although there is some evidence that southerners are more conservative than they were fifty years ago, political views today of white southerners are less distinct from those in other regions than they used to be.

In 2008, according to Gallup polling, all regions, except the South, gave a higher percentage of the vote to Democrat Barack Obama for president. However, Republican John McCain only managed a 50% - 50% split of the vote in the South.

AGE

Voters under 30 years old increasingly trended toward the Democratic Party in the elections of 2004, 2006 and 2008. The Pew Research Center reported that in presidential elections young voters supported John Kerry in 2004 (54%) and Barack Obama in 2008 (66%) while Al Gore in 2000 did not gain a majority of their vote (48%). In 2008, young voters tended to be more supportive of an activist government and were more anti-war with 77% disapproving of the war in Iraq versus a 63% overall disapproval of the war.

POLITICAL IDEOLOGY: LIBERALS AND CONSERVATIVES

A **political ideology** is a coherent set of values and beliefs about public policy. In U.S. politics, ideologies generally are thought to fall into two opposite camps: liberal and conservative. While there are general guidelines for determining the nature of liberalism and conservativism, the differences between the two are not always obvious. Following and describing ideologies is also complicated by the fact that they change over time, so that being "conservative" or "liberal" today is not necessarily the same as it was a few years ago.

How Ideological are American Citizens?

The classic study of the 1950s, *The American Voter*, investigated the ideological sophistication of the American electorate. The authors created four classifications of voters:

- **ideologues** – 12 % of the people connected their opinions and beliefs to policy positions by candidates and parties. In other words, only 12% of the American voting populations voted along primarily ideological lines.

- **group benefits voters** – 42% of the people voted for parties based on which one they thought would benefits groups they belonged to or supported. ("Democrats are more supportive of labor union members like me.")
- **nature of the times voters** – 24% of the people linked good times or bad times (usually based on economics) to one political party or the other and vote accordingly. ("The Republicans can get us out of this recession.")
- **no issue content** – 22% of the people could give no issue-based or ideological reasons for voting for a party or a candidate. ("_____ is better looking than the other candidate.")

Follow up studies conducted through 1988 reveal some variation in percentages among the groups, with ideologues faring somewhat better than they did in the 50s, but they remained a relatively small group (18% in 1988).

Liberalism vs. Conservatism

The terms **"liberal"** and **"conservative"** are confusing partly because their meaning has changed over the course of American history. In early American history, liberals disapproved of a strong central government, believing that it got in the way of ordinary people reaching their ambitions. They saw the government as a friend of business and the political elite. Conservatives, on the other hand, believed that government was best left to political elites, although they did not deny the rights of individual voters to contribute to the political system.

That trend reversed during the 1930s with Franklin Roosevelt's New Deal – big government programs to help ordinary people get back on their feet during the Great Depression. During that era, Democrats began to see the government as a friend to the "little people" – one that provided much needed support during bad economic times. Republicans came to support the belief in "rugged individualism" – the responsibility of all people to take care of themselves. Although Democrats are not always liberal and Republicans are not always conservative, liberals since Roosevelt have generally supported a larger, more active role for the central government than conservatives have. However, some observers believe that this distinction between liberals and conservatives may be changing in the early 21st century. Conservative President George W. Bush was often seen as supportive of "big government," a fact that more traditional conservatives criticized.

Even though the terms liberal and conservative are more meaningful for political activists than they are for the rank-and-file voter, the concepts are roughly, if inconsistently, understood by most Americans.

The following table summarizes some of the political beliefs likely to be preferred by liberals and conservatives:

ISSUE	LIBERALS	CONSERVATIVES
Health Care	Health Care should be more widely available to ordinary people and not necessarily tied to work; tendency to support a national health care system.	Health care is best handled by private insurance companies and most logically tied to work place benefits.
Crime	Cure the economic and social reasons for crime.	Stop coddling criminals and punish them for their crimes.
Business Regulation	Government should regulate businesses in the public interest.	Businesses should be allowed to operate under free market conditions.
Military Spending	Spend less.	Spend more.
Taxes	The rich should be taxed more; the government is responsible for reducing economic inequality.	Taxes should be kept low.
Welfare State	The government is responsible for helping the poor find employment and relieving their misery.	People are responsible for their own well-being; welfare takes away the incentive to take care of themselves.
Civil rights	Support for pro-active civil rights government policies	Limited government role in promoting social equality
Abortion	Pro-choice	Pro-life
Religion	Clear separation of church and state	Support for faith-based political initiatives
Same Sex Marriage	Legalize it, at least for civil unions. Should receive legal rights as couples.	Ban it. Marriage should be legally defined as between a man and woman. No civil unions.
ANWR Drilling & Offshore Oil Drilling	Prevent it. Consider the environmental costs.	Prefer it. Consider the cost of oil over the environment.

Individuals may have political beliefs that are a combination of liberalism and conservatism. Most commonly they may divide their opinions about economic and social issues. Americans that fit into this category are becoming identified more as moderates or centrists. The Pew Research Center reported after the November, 2008 election that, in all age groups, close to one third of voters identified themselves as moderates. Independents had a larger group identified as moderate with 45%, but those calling themselves moderate Republicans was much smaller with only 25%. However, as many as 37% of all Democrats claim to hold more moderate views. Generally moderates prefer not to accept a rigid ideology. For example a moderate may be an economically liberal, socially conservative person who believes in government support for health and welfare, but may oppose gay rights and/or equal opportunity programs for ethnic/racial minorities.

The "Neo-Cons"

After the terrorist attacks of September 11, 2001, the term **"neo-con"** began to emerge to describe the emergence of a post-Cold War conservative movement. Its main goal has been to counter global terrorism, especially as carried out by radical Islamists. Although neo-cons may be from either political party, they tend to affiliate as Republicans. Prominent neo-cons in the George W. Bush Administration were Vice-President Dick Cheney and Secretary of Defense Donald Rumsfeld, who led the drive to war in Iraq in 2003. Neo-cons advocate the breakup of global terrorist networks, and some endorsed the spread of President George W. Bush's "war on terrorism" to include Iran, Syria, and Saudi Arabia, as well.

ELECTION OF 2008 – NO REAL IDEOLOGICAL SHIFT

Just after the election of 2008, the Pew Research Center released a report stating the number of those who identified themselves as Democrats has increased recently, but the number of Americans describing themselves as conservative, moderate or liberal has remained relatively stable. A smaller percentage of Americans considered themselves liberal in 2008 (21%), and more Americans considered themselves either conservative (38%) or moderate (36%). These numbers have remained stable since President George W. Bush was first elected in 2000. Another factor that has not changed is that compared to older Americans, people under 30 years old are more likely to identify themselves as liberal (27%) and that older Americans, 65 years and older, are more likely to consider themselves conservative (45%). Moderate Americans remain a significant political group with approximately one-third of all age groups identifying with this group.

IMPORTANT DEFINITIONS AND IDENTIFICATIONS:

- *The American Voter*
- centrists
- conservatism
- George Gallup
- liberalism
- moderates
- neo-con
- political ideology
- political socialization
- public opinion
- random sample
- sampling error
- "Solid South"
- straw poll

CHAPTER FIVE
POLITICAL PARTICIPATION AND VOTER BEHAVIOR

Political participation encompasses the various activities that citizens employ in their efforts to influence policy making and the selection of leaders. People participate in politics in many ways. They may write their representative or senator, or work for a candidate or political party. They can make presentations to their local school board or city council, or call the police to complain about the neighbor's dog. Partly because of our system of federalism, people have many opportunities to participate in our democracy on national, state, and local levels. Some forms of participation are more common than others and some citizens participate more than others. Americans in general are comparatively active in politics, but the United States is notorious among modern democracies for its low voter turnout rates. Although the rates went up significantly in the election of 2004, the turnout for the previous two U.S. presidential elections was just about 50%. By contrast, most western democracies in Europe have voter turnout rates well above 70%.

TYPES OF PARTICIPATION

Researchers have found for years that American citizens most commonly participate in national politics by following presidential campaigns and voting in the presidential election. According to the National Election Studies from the Center for Political Studies at the University of Michigan, Americans reported the following types of political participation during the campaign for the election of 2004:

- 86% watched the campaign on television
- 77% voted in the election
- 48% tried to influence others how to vote
- 21% put a sticker on their car or wore a button
- 13% gave money to help a campaign
- 7% attended a political meeting
- 3% worked for a party or candidate

These statistics can be deceptive because they reflect how people say they participate. For example, despite the fact that 77% said they voted in the 2004 election, the real turn out was closer to 55%. One explanation is that people know that they should vote and don't want to admit it if they didn't.

WHO PARTICIPATES?

Experts have found several demographic characteristics to be strongly associated with high levels of political participation:

- **Education** – The single most important characteristic of a politically active citizen is a high level of education. Generally, the more education an individual has, the more likely he or she is to vote. Why? Perhaps because the well educated better understand complex societal issues, or maybe they better understand the importance of civic responsibility. However, it could just be that their occupations are more flexible in allowing them to take time to go to the polls.

- **Religious involvement** – As religious involvement increases, so does political participation. Regular churchgoers are more likely to vote than those that do not attend. Why? Some possibilities are that church involvement leads to social connectedness, teaches organizational skills, and increases one's awareness of larger societal issues.

- **Race and ethnicity** – If only race and ethnicity are considered, whites have higher voting rates than do blacks and Latinos. However, that tendency is somewhat deceptive. Some studies that control for income and education differences have found that the voting rates are about the same for whites, blacks, and Latinos. The 2008 presidential election saw an increase of both black and Hispanic voters. As a part of the total electorate, African American numbers went from 11% in 2004 to 13% in 2008 while Hispanic voters increased slightly from 8% to 9% for the same elections.

- **Age** – Despite the big push in the early 1970s to allow 18 year olds to vote, voting levels for 18-24 year olds are the lowest of any age category. Older people are more likely to vote than are younger people. The highest percentages of eligible voters who actually vote are in those groups 45 and above. In 2008 there was hope that young voters would turn out in larger numbers than in the past. This was expected because many had worked in the primaries and caucuses earlier in the year. Many were also drawn to the candidacy of the younger, charismatic Barack Obama. However, according to the Pew Research Center exit polls, in 2008 young voters were estimated to be only 18% of the total electorate which was only a slight increase from 17% in the 2004 election.

- **Gender** – For many years women were underrepresented at the voting booths, but in recent elections, they have turned out in at least equal numbers to men. In fact, since 1992, turnout among women voters has exceeded that of men. However, this trend is relatively new, so in general we can say that men and women vote at about the same rates.

- **Two-party competition** – Another factor in voter turnout is the extent to which elections are competitive in a state. More competitive elections generally bring higher turnouts, and voter rates increase significantly in years when presidential candidates are particularly competitive.

It is important to note that an individual is affected by many factors: his or her age, social class, education level, race, gender, and party affiliation. Thus factors form **cross-cutting cleavages**, making it very important to control for other factors that may produce a counter influence. For example, in order to compare gender differences in voter turnout rates, a researcher would have to compare men and women of similar ages, education level, race, and party affiliation. Otherwise, the voting behavior may be caused by a factor other than gender.

VOTING

Voting is at the heart of a modern democracy. A vote sends a direct message to the government about how a citizen wants to be governed. Over the course of American history, voting rights have gradually expanded, so that today very few individuals are excluded. And yet, expanding suffrage is countered by a recent trend: that of lower percentages of eligible voters in recent presidential elections actually going to the polls to cast their votes. For example, less than 50% of eligible voters actually voted in the 2000 presidential election. The trend did reverse itself in the election of 2004, when turnout increased to about 55%. That trend continued in 2008 when preliminary numbers indicated 56 – 60% of Americans turned out to vote. In the presidential elections of 2004 and 2008, both parties worked hard to get new voter registrations and to encourage their base of supporters to actually get to the polls to vote.

EXPANDING SUFFRAGE

Originally the Constitution let individual states determine the qualifications for voting, and states varied widely in their laws. All states excluded women, most denied blacks the franchise, and property ownership was usually required. The expansion of the right to vote resulted from constitutional amendment, changing federal statutes, and Supreme Court decisions. Changes in suffrage over American history include:

- **Lifting of property restrictions** – At first, all states required voters to be property owners, with varying standards for how much property a man had to own to merit the right to vote. During the 1830s when Andrew Jackson was president, most states loosened their property requirements to embrace **universal manhood suffrage**, voting rights for all white males. By the end of Jackson's presidency, all states had lifted property restrictions from their voting requirements.

- **Suffrage for black Americans and former slaves** – After the Civil War three important amendments intended to protect civil rights of the newly freed former slaves were added to the Constitution. The last of the three was added in 1870 – the **15th Amendment**, which said that the "right of citizens of the United States to vote shall not be denied or abridged by the United States or by any state on account of race, color, or previous condition of servitude." Despite the amendment, many state legislatures enacted **Jim Crow laws** – such as literacy tests, poll taxes, and the grandfather clause – that prevented many blacks from voting until well past the mid-20th century. During the Civil Rights movement of the 1950s and 60s, the Supreme Court declared various Jim Crow laws unconstitutional. The federal Voting Rights Act of 1965 and other federal laws prohibited states from using discriminatory practices, such as literacy tests. The 24th Amendment, ratified in 1964, banned the use of a poll tax.

- **Women's suffrage** – In contrast to black Americans, women were kept from the polls by law more than by intimidation. An aggressive women's suffrage movement began before the Civil War, but it brought no national results until social attitudes toward women changed during the Progressive Movement of the early 20th century. The result was the passage of the **19th Amendment**, which extended the vote to women in 1920. The 19th Amendment doubled the size of the electorate.

- **18-21-year-olds** – A final major expansion of voting rights occurred in 1971 when the **26th Amendment** changed the minimum voting age from 21 to 18. A few states – such as Georgia, Kentucky, Alaska, and Hawaii – had allowed younger people to vote before 1971. The increased political activism of young people, particularly on college campuses during the 1960s, almost certainly inspired this expansion of voting rights.

VOTER TURNOUT

Voter turnout can be measured in two different ways: by showing the proportion of the **registered voters** that actually voted in a given election, and by showing the percentage of the eligible voters that vote. According to recent figures, American statistics look much better if the first method is employed. If we take the proportion of registered voters, between 75 and 80% voted in recent presidential elections; if we take the percentage of the voting-age population, only about 50% actually voted in 1996 and 2000, a figure much lower than most other democracies. The figure increased significantly in 2004, but it still remained lower than those in many countries. For example, in Great Britain and Canada, about 3/4 of all eligible voters vote in major elections, and in Italy and Australia, approximately 90% vote.

Because the results of the two methods differ so widely in the U.S., many observers believe that the main problem with getting people to the polls is the cumbersome process of voter registration.

Voter Registration

Laws vary according to state, but all states except North Dakota require voter registration. Until a few years ago some states required voters to register as much as six months before the election. In other words, if someone moved into the state, forgot to register, or passed their eighteenth birthday, he or she would be ineligible to vote in any elections for six months. These rigid requirements were the result of voting abuses of the early 20th century (ballot box stuffing, people voting twice, dead people voting), but in recent times, they are believed to be responsible for low voter turnout. Federal law now prohibits any state from requiring more than a 30-day waiting period.

In 1993 Congress passed the National Voter Registration Act - the **"motor-voter"** bill – that allows people to register to vote while applying for or renewing a driver's license. The act also requires states to provide assistance to facilitate voter registration. Removal of names from voting rolls for nonvoting is no longer allowed. Supporters of the law claimed that it would add some 49 million people to the voting rolls; however, it is unclear whether or not motor-voter policies have actually affected voting patterns, since other factors – such as active voter recruitment by parties and candidates – may have affected the higher turnouts in 2004 and 2008. In general, Democrats were more supportive of the bills than Republicans because they believed that the demographics of new voters might favor the Democratic Party. However, the tremendous increase in voter registrations in 2004 did not particularly benefit the Democrats, as many of the new voters supported the Republicans.

Neither the 1996 nor 2000 presidential elections showed increases in voting percentages, with only some 50% of eligible voters actually voting, a figure even lower than those for most other recent elections. The voting increases in 2004 and 2008 were generally attributed to hard work by the political parties to get people registered and to the polls, and not to the motor-voter bills.

Congress passed the **Help America Vote Act** (HAVA) in 2002 to improve state voting systems and voter access by helping states to create state-wide voter registration databases. While the intent was to simplify access to voter records, the new databases caused some election-day problems. Elections workers had trouble accessing information, sites crashed under heavy election day demands and, in some cases, voter information was incorrectly posted. These problems caused delays resulting in long lines and frustrated voters. State elections officials became concerned about possible litigation because citizens have been deprived of their right to vote. The impact of the reform is yet to be determined.

Other Reasons for Low Voter Turnouts

Several other reasons are often cited for low voter turnout in the United States:

- **The difficulty of absentee voting** – Even if citizens remember to register ahead of time, they can only vote in their own precincts. If a voter is out of town on election day, he or she has to vote by absentee ballot. States generally have stringent rules about voting absentee. For example, some states require a voter to apply for a ballot in person.
- **The number of offices to elect** – Some critics argue that because Americans vote for so many officials on many different levels of government, they cannot keep up with all the campaigns and elections. As a result, they don't know who to vote for, and they don't vote. Americans vote for more public officials and hold more elections by far than any other modern democracy. In most states, primary elections, general elections, and special elections are held every year or two.
- **Weekday, non-holiday voting** – In many other democracies, elections take place on weekends. Others that hold elections on weekdays declare election day a national holiday so that no one has to go to work. By law, national general elections in the United States are held on the Tuesday after the first Monday in November in even-numbered years. Most state and local elections are also held during the week, and only a few localities declare election day a national holiday. Many people find it difficult to get off work in order to vote.

- **Weak political parties** – In many countries, parties make great efforts to get people to the polls. Even in earlier days in the United States, parties called their members to ensure that they register and that they vote. Parties also would often provide transportation to the polls. Although parties still stage "get-out-the-vote campaigns", parties today are not as strongly organized at the "grass roots" – or local – level as they used to be. However, this may be changing, since the parties did actively get out the vote in 2004 and 2008, and they were aided by groups known as "527s" (for the part of the tax code that allows them to be tax-free). These groups financed massive get-out-the-vote campaigns for both presidential candidates in each election.

In some studies that compare political participation rates in the United States with other countries, Americans tend to engage more frequently in non-electoral forms of participation, such as campaign contributions, community involvement, and contacts with public officials.

Does it really matter that the U.S. has a low voter turnout rate? Some say no because they think it indicates that Americans are happy with the status quo. On the other hand, others say that a low voter turnout signals apathy about our political system in general. If only a few people take the time to learn about the issues, we are open to takeover and/or manipulation by authoritarian rule. The higher voter turnout in 2004 did not result in a change of presidents, but may have resulted from a two-sided struggle over whether or not a change should take place. In 2008 the continued trend of higher voter turnout may have been caused by other factors, such as increased party and candidate efforts and the charismatic candidacy of Barack Obama. On the other hand, it may indicate that citizens are indeed becoming more interested in taking part in the political process.

Did the expansion of suffrage lead to lower voting rates by widening the voting base? Will the Motor-Voter Law eventually improve voting rates? Is voter registration still too difficult a process? Do we need to move elections to weekends? Do we need fewer elected positions? Or do low voter turnouts just indicate that people are happy with government and don't feel the need to vote? Do the higher voter turnout rates in the elections of 2004 and 2008 indicate a turnaround in political participation, or do they simply reflect an enthusiasm for a particular presidential race? Whatever the reasons, the United States today still has a lower voting rate than most other modern democracies.

IMPACT OF THE 2000 ELECTION

The 2000 presidential election demonstrated problems in the American electoral system. Many were a result of its federal design because states are responsible for choosing voting equipment and developing their voter registration procedures. In some instances, states permit local governments some discretion in these. This devolution of responsibility to the states has resulted in a variety of inconsistent practices, with some more reliable than others. The state of Florida's process came under scrutiny in the 2000 election when the close election results required a recount that cast the national spotlight on older punch-card voting machines used in some localities. Court challenges to Florida's recount laws and the difficulty of determining "voter intent" with the punch-card system resulted in a national discussion about the reliability of voting systems.   The Help America Vote Act (HAVA), of 2002 was passed by Congress to address some of the problems. It provided funding to help states update their voting equipment, and also created minimum election administration standards. The **Election Assistance Commission** was created to carry out the reforms.

NEW WAYS TO VOTE

Before the 2004 election there were two primary ways to vote; by absentee ballot or by ballots cast at local polls on election day. State restrictions on absentee ballots made it difficult for some voters to use this method, so HAVA encouraged states to be more creative in providing various voting procedures. Some new methods for voting include using provisional ballots, early voting, expanding same-day registration, and online voting.

- **Provisional ballots** – These ballots are used when it is not clear that a voter is officially registered. This system allows the voter to cast a ballot that will be counted after eligibility has been confirmed by an elections official. The provisional ballot will not be counted if the voter is not properly registered. HAVA required that the provisional ballot be used by states beginning with the presidential election of 2004. It was also used in the 2006 mid-term election and the presidential election of 2008. Provisional ballots are controversial because some question whether or not they are properly counted. Concerns center on the belief that states may not have the resources to adequately research records that may allow the vote to be counted. Another criticism is that varying methods that states use to count provisional ballots create inconsistencies that protect the voting rights of some citizens but not others. These concerns are particularly important in battleground states where the vote is expected to be close. In 2004 Ohio was a battleground state where a total of 5.7 million votes were cast with 157,000 provisional ballots cast. President Bush won the state by only 118,000 votes. Many believe that such situations prove that all efforts should be made to count legal provisional ballots and that federal guidelines regarding them should be developed. According to the Election Data Service the national rate of provisional ballots being counted in 2004 was 64.5%, and it is unclear why the remaining 35.5% were not counted.

- **Early voting** – This procedure permits people to vote before election day in person or by mail. States determine the specifics such as the dates of early voting and the hours the polls will be open. In 2008 this system was used by 34 states. Early voting began in states as early as September 25th and continued for two to four weeks. Preliminary reports state that about 30% of eligible voters in 2008 used this, an increase from 15% in 2004. Because this system has been successful, it is expected to spread to other states for future elections.

- **Same-day voter registration** – Under this system, people may register and vote on the same day rather than register at least a month before the election. This method was used by 10 states in 2008. Concerns about this method center on the difficulty of properly verifying voter information for on-the-spot voting. In spite of this problem, other states are looking into adopting same-day voter registration.

- **On-line voting** – People may vote by scanning, uploading and submitting the ballot on a computer. In 2008 Arizona used this system for the military and voters living overseas. While it has some advantages, many critics worry that on-line voting cannot be adequately protected from fraud.

IMPORTANT DEFINITIONS AND IDENTIFICATIONS

- 15th Amendment
- 19th Amendment
- 24th Amendment
- 26th Amendment
- cross-cutting cleavages
- early voting
- Election Assistance Commission
- "grass roots"
- Help America Vote Act (HAVA)
- Jim Crow Laws
- motor voter laws
- same-day voter registration
- political participation
- provisional ballots
- registered vs. eligible voters
- universal manhood suffrage

UNIT TWO QUESTIONS

Liberal-Conservative Self-Identification – 1972-2004						
	1972	**1980**	**1988**	**1996**	**2002**	**2004**
Liberal	18%	17%	17%	18%	23%	23%
Moderate	27%	20%	22%	24%	22%	26%
Conservative	26%	28%	32%	33%	34%	32%
Don't Know, Haven't thought	28%	36%	30%	25%	22%	20%

1. The data in the table above supports which of the following conclusions?

   (A) The percentage of people that don't know/haven't thought about their ideological leanings declined steadily during the years from 1972 to 2004.
   (B) The percentage of people identifying themselves as conservatives increased steadily from 1972 to 2002, then dropped slightly in 2004.
   (C) Liberalism has not gained support among American citizens because conservatives have created a negative image of liberals.
   (D) Most people identified themselves as moderates during the years from 1972 to 2004.
   (E) Many people who once identified themselves as moderates now consider themselves to be conservatives.

2. The Help America Vote Act, 2002 provided for

   (A) a uniform national ballot
   (B) a national data base listing all registered voters
   (C) federal funds to states for updating voting equipment
   (D) federal regulations covering voter registration procedures
   (E) federal regulations forcing states to purge their records of ineligible voters

3. Which of the following American values emerged later than the others in the history of the country?

   (A) individualism
   (B) equality of opportunity
   (C) rule of law
   (D) belief in government responsibility for the welfare of the people
   (E) civic duty

4. Which older American value was reinforced most directly by the new value of capitalism as it emerged in the late 19th century?

   (A) democracy
   (B) belief in government responsibility for the welfare of the people
   (C) equality
   (D) civic duty
   (E) individualism

5. The "Second Bill of Rights" most directly reflects Franklin Roosevelt's firm commitment to

   (A) capitalism
   (B) "rugged individualism"
   (C) rule of law
   (D) economic security
   (E) internationalism

6. Which of the following is an example of gerrymandering?

   (A) A state change from an open to a closed primary system
   (B) State voting districts that favor rural voters
   (C) State-legislature-drawn voting districts that favor one party over another
   (D) State-legislature-drawn districts that provide for fair representation of all interests
   (E) Voting districts drawn by an independent commission based on the newest census information

7. Which of the following is the best explanation for why incumbent presidents have had a difficult time getting reelected in recent years?

   (A) An increasingly educated electorate
   (B) A drop in levels of internal efficacy
   (C) A drop in levels of external efficacy
   (D) An increasing emphasis on the importance of international relations
   (E) A decline in the intensity of the culture wars

Public Officials Don't Care What People Think, 1988 - 2004					
	1988	1992	1996	2000	2004
Agree	51%	52%	61%	56%	50%
Disagree	37%	37%	24%	33%	34%
Neither	11%	10%	15%	10%	15%
Don't Know	0%	1%	0%	1%	0%

8. The data in the table above supports which of the following conclusions?

    (A) People felt that the government paid more attention to their opinions after 2000.
    (B) External political efficacy remained relatively low from 1988 – 2004.
    (C) External political efficacy dramatically increased in 2004.
    (D) More respondents were not sure if the government cared about public opinion from 1996 - 2004.
    (E) Many respondents probably did not understand the question.

9. George Gallup is best known for his work as

    (A) an early evaluator of the core values for the American political culture
    (B) a commentator on the current culture wars
    (C) a pollster
    (D) an advocate for the youth vote
    (E) an organizer of early presidential debates

10. Which of the following types of polls is least likely to be accurate?

    (A) a national poll based on random sample
    (B) a state-wide poll based on random sample
    (C) a straw poll that asks television viewers to call their views in
    (D) a poll conducted by an candidate for elected office
    (E) a poll conducted by selecting respondents randomly from a phone book

Trust the Federal Government 1958-2000								
	1958	**1964**	**1968**	**1972**	**1980**	**1988**	**1992**	**2000**
None of the time	0%	0%	0%	1%	4%	2%	2%	1%
Some of the time	23%	22%	36%	44%	69%	56%	68%	55%
Most of the time	57%	62%	54%	48%	23%	36%	26%	40%
Just about always	16%	14%	7%	5%	2%	4%	3%	4%
Don't know, depends	4%	1%	2%	2%	2%	1%	1%	1%

11. The data in the table above supports which of the following conclusions?

    (A) The growth of the national media has caused a significant decline in trust in the federal government.
    (B) Levels of trust in the federal government have changed very little since 1958.
    (C) The main reason that levels of trust in the federal government have declined in recent years is an unusually large number of public scandals.
    (D) Levels of trust in the federal government have declined significantly since 1958.
    (E) Levels of trust in the federal government increased during the 1970s, but have decreased since then.

12. Which of the following best describes the political culture of a country?

    (A) The view that foreign countries have of a neighboring state
    (B) The level of political efficacy that citizens have toward their government
    (C) The shared beliefs and values that a citizenry has within a country
    (D) The level of trust the citizens have in the nation's economic system
    (E) The level of trust a nation has in its political leaders

13. Which of the following is true about Americans who regularly attend religious services?

    (A) They generally turn out to vote more in local elections than in national ones.
    (B) They generally do not feel that political participation is necessary.
    (C) They tend to vote infrequently and are not an important factor in elections.
    (D) They tend to vote for independent candidates.
    (E) They are more likely to vote than those who do not regularly attend religious services.

14. Which of the following groups most consistently supports the Democratic Party?

(A) Catholics
(B) Blacks
(C) Latinos
(D) Southerners
(E) Labor union members

15. The "Solid South" is a reference to the tendency of southern voters to

(A) have very good voter turnouts on election day
(B) vote in recent elections for Democratic candidates on both state and national levels
(C) vote in recent elections for Republican candidates on both state and national levels
(D) vote for white, male, conservative candidates for public office
(E) consistently vote Democratic on both state and national levels until the 1950s

16. Which of the following states is most likely to support a Democratic presidential candidate?

(A) California
(B) Florida
(C) Texas
(D) Ohio
(E) Virginia

17. In the United States the terms liberal and conservative have

(A) remained fairly stable in their meaning throughout history.
(B) been unimportant to the development of the American political system.
(C) viewed government institutions as important instruments of change.
(D) traditionally applied more to political activists than to the average American voter.
(E) had more of an impact in social rather than economic policy in the United States.

18. Which of the following factors is most difficult to correlate clearly to political opinion?

(A) gender
(B) family
(C) social class
(D) race/ethnicity
(E) region

19. Which of the following is probably the best technique for a pollster to use to control the reluctance that most respondents have to admit a lack of knowledge on a topic?

(A) ask only easy questions that the most ordinary people can readily understand
(B) be sure that the sample accurately reflects the population
(C) conduct in-depth interviews rather than using questionnaires
(D) conduct a straw poll
(E) give "I don't know" or "I haven't thought about it" as an alternative answer

20. Which of the following is the best description of the effect that college education has on political attitudes?

(A) College educated people almost always support the Democratic Party.
(B) College educated people almost always support the more intelligent candidate.
(C) People who graduate from colleges in the Midwest are usually more liberal than those that graduate from colleges in the Northeast.
(D) The Northeast usually votes Democratic because it has more college educated people than other regions have.
(E) College education often has a liberalizing effect on an individual's political attitudes.

21. Citizens that believe the government listens and reacts to their political views when developing policy have a high level of external political

(A) legitimacy
(B) attachment
(C) effectiveness
(D) efficacy
(E) party loyalty

22. Which of the following is NOT a reason commonly presented by political scientists to explain lower voter turnouts in the U.S. than in other democracies?

(A) the larger numbers of offices to elect in the U.S.
(B) weekday, non-holiday voting in the U.S.
(C) weak political party effort in the U.S.
(D) the difficulty of voting caused by registration and absentee voting requirements
(E) lower participation rates among Americans for other types of political activities

23. Which of the following is traditionally a liberal point of view?

    (A) A limited role of the government in promoting social equality.
    (B) Promotion of a clear separation of church and state regarding policy.
    (C) More restrictions on the rights of those accused of criminal behavior.
    (D) Less support for welfare programs as it destroys personal incentive.
    (E) Promotion of a flat income tax system for American citizens.

24. The process in which an individual develops political opinions through family, friends and other groups is known as political

    (A) liberalization
    (B) association
    (C) affiliation
    (D) participation
    (E) socialization

25. The news source that Americans primarily use to help form their public opinions is

    (A) newspapers
    (B) the internet
    (C) news magazines
    (D) television
    (E) radio

26. Which of the following is the best reason why voter registration processes are cumbersome in most states?

    (A) The states rely on voter registrations for a great deal of public revenue.
    (B) Voter fraud has increased significantly in recent elections.
    (C) Most requirements were put in place in reaction to voting abuses of the early 20th century.
    (D) No federal laws have been passed that attempt to make the process any easier.
    (E) Both major political parties support strict voter requirements because they don't want to see any shifts in voter preferences.

27. Which of the following is true about the political participation of young people in the election of 2008?

    (A) The national percentage of young people voting increased by a small percentage.
    (B) For the first time young people turned out to vote in larger numbers than older voters.
    (C) Very few young people worked in campaigns, yet they still voted in record numbers.
    (D) The percentage of young voters did not change from the 2004 election.
    (E) The percentage of young voters was the lowest in recorded history.

28. "527s" became an important part of election campaigns in 2004 because they

    (A) allowed candidates to more easily accept government contributions to presidential campaigns
    (B) financed massive get-out-the-vote campaigns for both presidential candidates
    (C) encouraged third party candidates to compete successfully for seats in Congress
    (D) helped to close the loopholes that allowed large amounts of "soft money" to be used for political purposes
    (E) gave a great deal of money to the parties, who in turn contributed that money to candidates' individual campaigns

29. When compared to other countries the United States voter turnout is

    (A) about the same.
    (B) much more partisan.
    (C) higher, but only during presidential election years.
    (D) higher overall.
    (E) lower overall.

30. Which of the following groups was the LAST to gain voting rights in the United States?

    (A) non-property owning males
    (B) immigrants who are not citizens
    (C) blacks
    (D) 18-21 year olds
    (E) Women

FREE RESPONSE QUESTION

Many factors shape the political socialization experience of U.S. citizens.

    a)   Define political socialization.

    b)   Identify two factors that shape the political socialization experience of US citizens experience political socialization.

    c)   Explain how each of the factors identified in "b" shapes the political socialization experience of U.S. citizens.

NO TESTING MATERIAL PRINTED ON THIS PAGE

UNIT THREE

POLITICAL PARTIES,
ELECTIONS AND CAMPAIGNS,
INTEREST GROUPS,
AND MASS MEDIA

CHAPTER SIX
POLITICAL PARTIES

Today many Americans take pride in their status as "independent voters," partly because they see parties as lacking vision for the country. Since many people think that each of the major parties only cares about defeating or humiliating the other, they avoid identification as a "loyal Democrat" or a "staunch Republican." These negative attitudes toward parties are rooted in the roles that they play in American politics.

In most democracies political parties are important institutions that link citizens to their government. The founders of the U.S. political system hoped to avoid the "mischief" of political factions when they envisioned a government with enough points of influence to make parties unnecessary. James Madison reflected in his famous Federalist #10 that political factions are necessary evils to be controlled by federalism and separation of powers, but the founders still believed that political parties such as those that dominated British politics could and should be avoided at all costs. Of course, parties appeared almost as soon as the new government was created, with their origins in the disagreements between two of Washington's cabinet members, Thomas Jefferson and Alexander Hamilton.

Some observers believe that modern avoidance of political party labels may have been reversed by the election of 2004. Voter participation increased dramatically in that year, partly because of almost unprecedented efforts by both Republicans and Democrats, again reflecting that parties are an integral part of the American political system.

FUNCTIONS OF POLITICAL PARTIES

Political parties fulfill the following functions in the American political system:

- **Connecting citizens to their government** – Parties are one of several **linkage institutions** that connect people in a large democracy to the government. In any country with a population large enough to form a representative democracy, institutions that link the people to government are a necessity. Modern linkage institutions include interest groups, the media, elections, and political parties. Party ideology and organization increase **political efficacy** by helping citizens to make sense of government decisions and processes and to feel that government listens to them.
- **Running candidates for political office** – Parties pick policymakers and run campaigns. Most elected officials, whether at the local, state, or national level, run as nominees of a major political party. Whereas personal wealth certainly helps, most candidates rely on the party organization to coordinate and fund their political campaigns.

- **Informing the public** – Parties articulate policies and give cues to voters. Although both major parties are by necessity broadly based, they each convey an image and endorse policies that help voters decide which candidates to support.
- **Organizing the government** – Parties often coordinate governmental policy-making that would be more fragmented among the three branches and the local, state, and federal levels. Informal relationships between officials in different parts of government but with similar partisan ties can make policy-making go more smoothly.

WHY A TWO PARTY SYSTEM?

Most modern democracies have a multi-party system, so the United States is definitely in the minority with its two party system, one of only about fifteen in the world today. Even though a number of third parties have emerged in the course of U.S. history, none have endured, and with the exception of a short period in the early 1800s, two major political parties have always competed with one another for power in the system. Three important reasons for the American two-party system are:

- **Consensus of values** – It is easy to complain about petty bickering between Democrats and Republicans. What we sometimes forget is that Americans share a broad consensus, or agreement, of many basic political values. Both parties believe in liberty, equality, and individualism. Neither advocates that the Constitution be discarded, and both accept the election process by conceding defeat to the winners. In many countries with multi-party systems, the range of beliefs is greater, and disagreements run deeper.
- **Historical influence** – The nation began with two political parties – the Federalists and the Anti-Federalists. During early American history politicians tended to take sides, starting with the debate over the Constitution, and continuing with the disagreements within George Washington's cabinet. The tendency has persisted throughout American history.
- **The winner-take-all System** – The single most important reason for a two-party system is the **winner-take-all** or **pluralist** electoral system. This system contrasts to those with **proportional representation** where the percentage of votes for a party's candidates is directly applied as the percentage of representatives in the legislature. The winner in American elections is the one who receives the largest number of votes in each voting district. The winner does not need to have more than 50 percent, but only one vote more than his or her closest competitor. This process encourages parties to become larger, embracing more and more voters. So third parties have almost no hope of getting candidates into office, and their points of view tend to fall under the umbrella of one or both of the big parties.

ORGANIZATION OF THE TWO-PARTY SYSTEM

In contrast to most large economic organizations, such as corporations, the people at the top of the party organizations do not have a lot of power over those at the lower levels. Instead, the parties have strong "grass roots," or state and/or local control over important decisions. To be sure, each has a national committee that organizes a convention every four years to nominate a president. Each party has a national chairperson who serves as spokesperson, and at least nominally coordinates the election campaign for the presidential candidate. In reality, however, the candidate runs his own campaign, with the help of multiple advisers, including the party chairman.

Local party organizations are still very important in political campaigns because they provide the foot soldiers that hand out party literature and call on citizens to register and to come to the polls on election day. In 2004 and 2008 both parties ran active get-out-the-vote campaigns at the grass roots level, resulting in very high voter turnouts.

The organization of both parties looks very much the same on paper. Both have:

- a national committee composed of representatives from each state and territory.
- a full-time, paid national chairman that manages the day-to-day work of the party.
- a national convention that meets formally every four years during the summer before a presidential election in November.
- a congressional campaign committee that assists both incumbents and challengers.
- a broad, not always consistent, ideological base since they must appeal to a large number of voters.

HISTORICAL DEVELOPMENT OF THE PARTIES

Historically, the two-party system has been characterized by long periods of dominance by one party followed by a long period of dominance by the other. The eras begin and end with shifts in the voting population called **realignments** that occur because issues change, and new schisms form between groups.

THE EARLY YEARS

The first two political parties to emerge during Washington's term of office were the **Federalists** and the **Anti-Federalists**. The major issue in the beginning was the ratification of the Constitution, with the Federalists supporting it and the Anti-Federalist wanting guarantees of individual freedoms and rights not included in the original document. The issue was resolved with the addition of the Bill of Rights, but the parties did not disappear with the issue.

The Federalists were led by Alexander Hamilton, the Secretary of the Treasury, and they came to represent urban, business-oriented men who favored elitism and a strong central government. The Federalists supported Hamilton's establishment of the Bank of the United States because they saw it as forwarding their interests and beliefs. The Anti-Federalists came to be known as the **Democratic-Republicans**, led by Thomas Jefferson. They favored strong state governments, rural interests, and a weaker central government. They opposed the bank as an enemy of state control and rural interests.

With Hamilton's death and John Adams' unpopularity as president, Jefferson emerged as the most popular leader at the turn of the nineteenth century. As president he gradually became more accepting of stronger central government, and the two parties' points of view seemed to merge most notably in the "Era of Good Feeling" presided over by James Monroe, one of Jefferson's protégés. The Democratic-Republicans emerged as the only party, and their dominance lasted until the mid-1800s, though under a new name, the Democrats.

JACKSONIAN DEMOCRACY

The two-party system reemerged with the appearance of Andrew Jackson, who represented to many the expanding country, in which newer states found much in common with the rural southern states but little with the established Northeast. A new party emerged, the **Whigs**, who represented many of the interests of the old Federalist party.

Jackson's election in 1828 was accomplished with a coalition between South and West, forming the new Democratic Party. Jackson's Democrats were a rawer sort than Jefferson's, who were primarily gentlemen farmers from the South and Middle Atlantic states. With the Jacksonian Era's universal manhood suffrage, virtually all men could vote, so rural, anti-bank, small farmers from the South and West formed the backbone of the Democratic Party. During this era the Democrats initiated the tradition of holding a national convention to nominate a presidential candidate. Delegates selected from state and local parties would vote for the candidate, rather than a handful of party leaders who met in secret (called a caucus). The Whigs were left with not only the old Federalist interests, but other groups, such as wealthy rural southerners, who had little in common with other Whigs. The party was not ideologically coherent, but found some success by nominating and electing war heroes, such as William Henry Harrison and Zachary Taylor.

NORTH/SOUTH TENSIONS

As economic and social tensions developed between North and South by the 1840s and 50's, Whig party unity was threatened by splits between the southern and northern wings. As the Whigs were falling apart, a new **Republican Party** emerged from the issue of expansion of slavery into new territories. The election of 1860 brought the first Republican – Abraham Lincoln – into office, setting off the secession of southern states, and with them, many supporters of the Democratic Party. The Civil War, then, ended the era of dominance of the Democrats, and ushered in a new Republican era. Voters realigned, according to regional differences and conflicting points of view regarding expansion of slavery and states rights.

THE REPUBLICAN ERA: 1861-1933

With the exception of Grover Cleveland and Woodrow Wilson, all presidents from Abraham Lincoln (1861-1865) through Herbert Hoover (1929-1933) were Republicans. During most of that time, Republicans dominated the legislature as well. By 1876 all of the southern states had been restored to the Union, but their power, as well as that of the Democratic Party, was much diminished.

The Republicans came to champion the new era of the Industrial Revolution, a time when prominent businessmen, such as John Rockefeller and Andrew Carnegie, dominated politics as well as business. The Republican Party came to represent laissez-faire, a policy that advocated the free market and few government regulations on business. Ironically, laissez-faire, meaning "to leave alone", was the old philosophy of the Jacksonian farmers, who wanted government to allow them to make their own prosperity. The Republican philosophy of the late 1800s favored the new industrialists, not the small farmer of the earlier era.

THE SECOND DEMOCRATIC ERA: 1933-1969

The prosperous, business-oriented era survived several earlier recessions but not the Great Depression that gripped the country after the stock market crash of 1929. The cataclysmic economic downturn caused major realignments of voters that swung the balance of power to the Democrats. The Republican president, Herbert Hoover, was rejected in the election of 1932 in favor of the Democrat's Franklin Roosevelt. Roosevelt's victory was accomplished through forging the **"Roosevelt Coalition"** of voters, a combination of many different groups that wished to see Herbert Hoover defeated. The coalition was composed of eastern workers, southern and western farmers, blacks, and the ideologically liberal.

In their efforts to bring the country out of the depression, Roosevelt's Democrats established a government more actively involved in promoting social welfare. Ironically, the formerly states-rights-oriented Democrats now advocated a strong central government, but one dedicated to promoting the interests of ordinary people. Democrats dominated both legislative and executive branches. Even the Supreme Court had to rein in its conservative leanings, although it did check Roosevelt's power with the famous "court-packing" case. (In an effort to get more support for his New Deal programs from the Supreme Court, Roosevelt encouraged Congress to increase the number of justices from nine to fifteen and to require mandatory retirement of justices by the age of 70. Roosevelt eventually withdrew his plan).

Roosevelt was elected for an unprecedented four terms and was followed by another Democrat, Harry Truman. Even though a Republican, Dwight Eisenhower, was elected president in 1952, Congress remained Democratic. The Democrats regained the White House in 1960 and retained it throughout the presidencies of John F. Kennedy and Lyndon Johnson. But a new era began with the presidency of Richard Nixon in 1969.

THE ERA OF DIVIDED GOVERNMENT: 1969-2008

Richard Nixon's election in 1968 did not usher in a new era of Republican dominated government. Instead, a new balance of power between the Democrats and Republicans came into being. With a few exceptions, control of the legislature and the presidency has been "divided" between the two major political parties since the late 1940s. When one party holds the presidency, the other has dominated Congress, or at least the Senate.

The division brings with it the problem of **"gridlock"**, or the tendency to paralyze decision making, with one branch advocating one policy and the other another, contradictory policy. Scholars have various theories about the causes of the new division of power, but one cause may be the declining power of political parties in general.

The Republican Hold on the Presidency: 1969-1993

From 1969 through 1993, the Republicans held the presidency except during the Carter Presidency from 1977-1981. Starting in the late 1960's, Republicans began to pay more attention to the power of electronic media and to the importance of paid professional consultants. They converted into a well-financed, efficient organization that depended heavily on professionals to help locate the best candidates for office.

Some experts believe that these changes were largely responsible for Richard Nixon's victory in 1968. Nixon was carefully coached and his campaign was carefully managed to take advantage of electronic media. The campaign made extensive use of public opinion polls to determine party strategy. The new emphasis also influenced the party's choice of candidates in 1980 and 1984, with former television and film actor Ronald Reagan as master of the media. The party also took advantage of new technology and generated computerized mailings to raise large sums of money for campaigns. By the mid-1980's, the Republicans were raising far more money than the Democrats were.

During the same time period, the Democrats were changing in many almost opposite ways from the Republicans. The Democrats became more concerned with grass roots, or common man, representation. The Democrats were reacting at least partly to the break-up of the old Roosevelt Coalition, but also to the disastrous 1968 convention in Chicago that showed the party as highly factionalized and almost leaderless. As a result, they gained a reputation for being unorganized and disunited.

In 1969, the Democratic Party appointed a special **McGovern-Fraser Commission** to review the party's structure and delegate selection procedures. The commission determined that minorities, women, youth, and the poor were not adequately represented at the party convention. The party adopted guidelines that increased the representation and participation of these groups. The number of superdelegates, or governors, members of Congress, and other party leaders was reduced substantially. The 1972 convention selected as their candidate George McGovern, a liberal who lost in a landslide to Republican Richard Nixon. Although Democrat Jimmy Carter won the Presidency in 1976, he was defeated by Ronald Reagan in 1980, and the Republican Party held the presidency until 1993.

Divided Government Today

During the Reagan presidency, the Democrats began to adopt some of the Republican strategies, including computerized mailing lists, opinion polls, and paid consultants. The party managed to get their candidate, Bill Clinton, to the White House in 1993, a position that he held for two terms. However, government remained divided because the Republicans won both houses of Congress in 1994 and held them until 2001, when the

Senate regained a Democratic majority. By this time, Republican George W. Bush had been elected president, so the tradition of divided government – established in 1969 – continued. However, Republicans regained control of the Senate in the election of 2002, and they swept the presidency and both houses of Congress in the election of 2004. Although there was speculation that a new Republican era was beginning, the 2006 mid-term election brought a return of divided government when the Democrats took a majority in both houses of Congress. This short period of divided government ended in 2009 when the Democrats maintained control of the House and Senate and gained control of the presidency with the election of Barack Obama.

PERIODS OF DIVIDED GOVERNMENT SINCE 1992
(* Indicates periods of divided government)

ELECTION YEAR	PRESIDENT & PARTY AFFILIATION	HOUSE OF REPRESENTATIVES MAJORITY PARTY	SENATE MAJORITY PARTY
1992	William Clinton, Democrat	Democrat	Democrat
*1994	William Clinton, Democrat	Republican	Republican
*1996	William Clinton, Democrat (re-elected)	Republican	Republican
*1998	William Clinton, Democrat	Republican	Republican
*2000	George W. Bush, Republican	Republican	Democrat
2002	George W. Bush, Republican	Republican	Republican
2004	George W. Bush, Republican (re-elected)	Republican	Republican
*2006	George W. Bush, Republican	Democrat	Democrat
2008	Barack Obama, Democrat	Democrat	Democrat

The table indicates that there have been five periods of divided government out of the past nine Congressional election cycles. In spite of the fact that both President Clinton and President Bush gained enough electoral support to be re-elected to a second term, they each experienced periods of divided government while in office. Whether this trend will continue under President Obama is yet to be seen.

MINOR PARTIES

Whereas two parties have always dominated the American system, **minor** or **third parties** have also played a role. Minor parties may be divided into two categories:

- **Those dominated by an individual personality,** usually disappearing when the charismatic personality does. One example is Theodore Roosevelt's Bull Moose, or Progressive Party, that was largely responsible for splitting the Republicans and throwing the 1912 election to the Democrats. Another example is George Wallace's American Independent Party in 1968 and 1972, starting as a southern backlash to the civil rights movement, but eventually appealing to blue collar workers in other parts of the country.

- **Those organized around a long-lasting goal or ideology.** Examples are the Abolitionists, the Prohibitionists, and the Socialists. The Abolitionists and Prohibitionists disappeared after their goals were accomplished. The Socialists have remained a minor ideological party throughout the twentieth century, winning almost a million votes in the election of 1912.

Probably the most influential third party in American history was the **Populist Party** of the late nineteenth and early twentieth centuries that first represented the interests of farmers, but was responsible for wide-ranging democratic reforms. The Populists' best known leader was William Jennings Bryan, who was enticed to accept the nomination of the Democratic party first in 1896. The fate of the Populists was the same as for most other third parties: their goals were adopted by a major party, deferring to the "winner-take-all, or pluralist system, that supports a two party system.

In 1992 Ross Perot, a wealthy Texas businessman, tried to defy the two party system by running for president as an independent without the support of a political party. He hired professional campaign and media advisers, created a high profile on national television interviews, bought a massive number of TV ads, and built a nationwide network of paid and volunteer campaign workers. In the election, he gained 19% of the vote, but did not capture a single electoral vote. In 1996, he again entered the race, but also announced the birth of a third party that fizzled when he received less than half as many votes as he did in 1992. In 2000 Ralph Nader ran for the Green Party, but he won only about 3% of the vote. In 2004 and 2008 Nader ran as an independent, and the Green Party fielded their own candidates for office, but neither managed to garner many votes.

Minor parties have sometimes had a big impact on American politics when their platforms have been taken over by major parties. For example, Populist reforms for 8-hour workdays for city workers and farm subsidies for rural areas were later pushed forward by the Democratic Party. Third parties have almost certainly affected election outcomes, most obviously in 1912, when Theodore Roosevelt ran for the Progressive Party, splitting the Republican vote and throwing the election to Democrat Woodrow Wilson. Many Democrats believe that Al Gore would have won the election of 2000 had Ralph Nader not run. Likewise, some Republicans claim that Ross Perot was responsible for George H. Bush's loss of the election of 1992. Minor party candidates participated in the 2008 presidential campaign, but they did not play a significant role in the outcome of the election.

PARTY POWER: THE EFFECTS OF DEALIGNMENT

In the modern era voter realignments do not appear to be as clear-cut as they once were, partly because of the phenomenon of **dealignment**. Over the past fifty years party identification appears to be weakened among American voters, with more preferring to call themselves "independents." Not only have ties to the two major parties weakened in recent years, but voters are less willing to vote a **straight ticket**, or support all candidates of one party for all positions. In the early 1950s only about 12% of all voters engaged in **ticket splitting**, or voting for candidates from both parties for different positions. In recent years, that figure has been between 20 and 40%. If dealignment indeed is occurring, does this trend indicate that parties are becoming weaker forces in the political system? Many political scientists believe so.

EARLY 20TH CENTURY REFORMS

During the late 1800s party machines, organizations that recruited members by the use of material incentives – money, jobs, places to live – exercised a great deal of control by party "bosses." These machines, such as Tammany Hall in New York City, dictated local and state elections and distributed government jobs on the basis of support for the party, or patronage. The reforms of the early twentieth century Progressive movement, first inspired by the Populist movement, took control of nominations from party leaders and gave it to the rank-and-file. Several important changes – the establishment of primary elections in many states, the establishment of the civil service, the direct election of senators, and women's suffrage – all gave more power to voters and less to the parties.

LATE 20TH CENTURY DEVELOPMENTS

The growing emphasis on electronic media campaigns, professional consultants, and direct-mail recruitment of voter support also may have decreased the importance of parties in the election process. In addition, partly as a result of media influence, candidate organizations, not party organizations, are the most powerful electoral forces today. Office seekers, supported by consultants and media, organize their personal following to win nominations. If they win office, they are more responsive to their personal following than to the party leadership. The result is less party clout over politicians and policy.

On the other hand, the national party organizations are significantly better funded than they were in earlier days and make use of electronic media and professional consultants themselves. They often function as advisers and all-important sources for campaign funds. Moreover, parties are deeply entrenched organizational blocks for government, particularly Congress. Although they may not be as strong an influence as they once were, parties form a basic building block for the American political system, and they still give candidates labels that help voters make decisions during election time.

THE REALIGNMENT OF 2008?

The Republican sweep of the presidency and Congress in 2004 was seen as a possible major realignment of Americans. The split between the "Red States" (Republican) and the "Blue States" (Democrats) separated states along the west coast, the Northeast, and the Midwest (blue states) from the rest of the country that supported Republican George W. Bush. Voters of both parties appeared to have stronger party loyalties than in recent years, and divisions were especially apparent between rural (Republicans) and urban voters (Democrats). The breakup of the Solid South also appeared to be complete, with long-time Democratic senators resigning and being replaced by Republicans. However, in 2008 presidential candidate Democrat Barack Obama gained the support of states that either leaned toward or had strongly supported Republicans in previous elections. In the South he gained Florida, North Carolina ,and Virginia. In the Midwest, Obama took Ohio and Indiana, and in the West he won the electoral votes of New Mexico, Colorado, and Nevada. Probably the most surprising party changes were in Indiana and Virginia. Neither of these states had supported a Democratic presidential candidate since 1968. However, it is too soon to know whether or not this election indicates that a new realignment has occurred. Exit polling indicated that young voters may have given Obama the edge in both Indiana (young voters up by 5 points) and North Carolina (young voters up by 4 points). Democrats also gained strength in Congress. If a new realignment is to take place it may depend on the loyalty and dependability of these new voters.

IMPACT OF MINORITY AND YOUNG VOTERS IN 2008

The election of 2008 saw an increase in the number of minority and young voters. Many of these were first-time voters. Presidential candidate Democrat Barack Obama benefited more from these new voters than did Republican John McCain, since they were credited with giving Obama the edge in several states.

- **Young Voters** – While the percentage of young voters in the national electorate appeared to increase by only 1% (17% in 2004 to 18% in 2008), they overwhelmingly supported Barack Obama. Exit polls conducted by the Pew Research Center indicated that 66% of voters under 30 years old supported Obama compared to 32% for McCain. This was 13 points higher than the support Obama received from the general population. This trend has been in place since 2004 when John Kerry received 60% of young voters. As recently as the 2000 election young voters were evenly split between the two parties. Polling also indicates that young people consider themselves more liberal than older groups. They generally see the government as an agent of change for solving problems such as global warming, and they appear to believe the Democratic Party will bring about the reforms they seek. This support may be temporary since young voters have become political during a time when Republicans have been criticized for their handling of the Iraq War, Hurricane Katrina in 2005, and the financial crisis beginning in 2008. With Republicans in control much of that time, young people may be supporting the Democratic Party as a temporary alternative.

• **Minority Voters** – The election of 2008 saw an increase in numbers of both African American and Hispanic voters. African American turnout increased from 11% of the electorate in 2004 to 13% in 2008. It was reported that 99% of African American voters supported Barack Obama for president. Participation by Hispanics increased slightly from 8% of the electorate in 2004 to 9% in 2008. Hispanics also gave a large percentage (66%) of their vote to Obama. This was up 13 points from the support given to Kerry in 2004. Generally, this may indicate a shift of Hispanic voters identifying more with the Democratic Party. President George W. Bush received 40% of the Hispanic vote in 2004, but more current polling by the Pew Hispanic Center indicates that almost 60% of Hispanic voting-age adults identify strongly with the Democratic Party, perhaps because Hispanics prefer the more lenient immigration policies of the Democrats.

IMPORTANT DEFINITIONS AND IDENTIFICATIONS:

- Anti-Federalists
- dealignment
- Democratic-Republican Party
- divided government
- Era of Good Feeling
- Federalist Party
- grass-roots organization
- gridlock
- laissez faire
- linkage institutions
- McGovern-Fraser Commission
- minor/third parties

- political efficacy
- Populist Party
- proportional representation
- realignment
- Republican Party
- Roosevelt Coalition
- straight ticket
- superdelegates
- ticket splitting
- universal manhood suffrage
- Whig Party
- winner-take-all electoral system

CHAPTER SEVEN
ELECTIONS AND CAMPAIGNS

Elections form the foundation of a modern democracy, and more elections are scheduled every year in the United States than in any other country in the world. Collectively on all levels of government, Americans fill more than 500,000 different public offices. Campaigns – where candidates launch their efforts to convince voters to support them – precede most elections. In recent years campaigns have become longer and more expensive, sparking a demand for campaign finance reform. No one questions the need for campaigns and elections, but many people believe that the government should set new regulations on how candidates and parties go about the process of getting elected to public office.

FUNCTIONS OF ELECTIONS

Elections serve many important functions in the United States. Most obviously, elections choose political leaders from a competitive field of candidates. But elections are also an important form of political participation, with voting in presidential elections one of the most common types of participation by the American public in the political process. Elections give individuals a regular opportunity to replace leaders without overthrowing them, thus making elected officials accountable for their actions. Elections legitimize positions of power in the political system because people accept elections as a fair method for selecting political leaders.

GUIDELINES FOR ELECTIONS IN THE UNITED STATES

The Constitution sets broad parameters for election of public officials. For example, the Constitution provides for the election of members of the House of Representatives every two years, and it creates and defines the electoral college. By law Congress sets the date for national elections – the Tuesday after the first Monday in November. However, most electoral guidelines and rules are still set by the individual states.

ROLE OF POLITICAL PARTIES

Candidates for political office almost always run with a political party label; they are either Democrats or Republicans, and they are selected to run as candidates for the party. The party, however, is not as important as it is in many other democracies. Running for the presidency or Congress requires the candidate to take the initiative by announcing to run, raising money, collecting signatures to get his or her name on the ballot, and personally appealing to voters in primary elections.

In many other democracies, the party controls whether to allow candidates to run and actually puts their names on the ballot. Campaigns become contests between political parties, not individuals. In United States history, parties once had much more control over elections and campaigns than they do today. In the nineteenth century, the Democratic and Republican members of Congress would meet separately to select their nominees for the presidency. Congressional candidates were often chosen by powerful local party bosses, and citizens were more likely to vote a "straight party ticket" than they do now. The power of the party has dwindled as campaign techniques have changed.

WINNER-TAKES-ALL

In most American elections, the candidate with the most votes wins. The winner does not have to have a majority (more than 50%), but may only have a **plurality**, the largest number of votes. Most American elections are based on **single-member districts**, which means that in any district the election determines one representative or official. For example, when the U.S. Census allots to each state a number of representatives for the U.S. House of Representatives, virtually all state legislatures divide the state into several separate districts, each electing its own single representative.

This system ensures a two-party system in the U.S., since parties try to assemble a large coalition of voters that leads to at least a plurality, spreading their "umbrellas" as far as they can to capture the most votes. The winner-take-all system contrasts to proportional representation, a system in which legislative seats are given to parties in proportion to the number of votes they receive in the election. Such systems encourage multi-party systems because a party can always get some representatives elected to the legislature.

PRIMARIES AND GENERAL ELECTIONS

Political leaders are selected through a process that involves both primary and general elections.

Primaries

The **primary** began in the early part of this century as a result of reforms of the Progressive Movement that supported more direct control by ordinary citizens of the political system. A primary is used to select a party's candidates for elective offices, and states use three different types:

- **closed primaries** – A voter must declare in advance his or her party membership, and on election day votes in that party's election. Most states have closed primaries.
- **open primaries** – A voter can decide when he or she enters the voting booth which party's primary to participate in. Only a few states have open primaries.
- **blanket (or free-love) primaries** – A voter marks a ballot that lists candidates for all parties, and can select the Republican for one office and a Democrat for another. Very few states have primaries of this type.

Blanket primaries have been challenged more recently in the courts resulting in changes to their forms.

- *California Democratic Party v Jones,* 2000 – The federal Supreme Court struck down the California blanket primary because it forced parties to have their nominees for office determined by those who did not associate with the party, or worse, "have expressly affiliated with a rival." The Court felt that the blanket primary did not accomplish the purpose of primaries: that of political partisans choosing political candidates. Under blanket primaries citizens may choose to vote in a party primary no matter what the voter's declared party affiliation is. The outcome may be a candidate that the party does not feel best reflects its ideology or will be difficult to support in the general election. The decision subsequently seemed to affect the few blanket primaries that existed.
- *Washington State Grange v Washington State Republican Party,* 2008 – In 2003 the 9th District Court ruled that the Washington State primary system was unconstitutional, using the 2000 *California* decision as a precedent. Washington voters then approved Initiative 872, which created a modified blanket primary. It permitted each candidate on the ballot to associate with a preferred party regardless of whether the party approved of the candidate. In 2008 the Supreme Court ruled that the law did not violate the parties' rights to control their own candidates since nominees only indicated what party was preferred. No endorsement by the party was implied. This decision allowed blanket primaries to continue to exist in some form.
- **Louisiana Blanket (Cajun) Primary** – Louisiana practiced a different form of blanket primary that permitted a run-off ballot if no candidate won a majority in the first round of voting. The top two candidates, regardless of party affiliation, were on the run-off ballot. However, in June, 2006, the Louisiana legislature changed its Congressional primaries to a closed system while the state and local races remained as a non-partisan blanket primary system.

The state of Iowa has a well-known variation of a primary – a **caucus**. Under this system, local party members meet and agree on the candidate they will support; the local caucuses pass their decisions on to regional caucuses, who in turn vote on candidates, and pass the information to the state caucus, who makes the final decision. In both the primary and caucus, the individual party member has a say in who the party selects to run for office. A number of other states make at least limited use of the caucus to choose their candidates.

Both primaries and caucuses vary state by state. Some states permit political parties to determine if the primary is open or closed while others permit voters to declare their party affiliation when they vote or participate in the caucus.

General Elections

Once political parties select their candidates, they campaign against one another until the general election, in which voters make the final selection of who will fill various government offices. More people vote in a general election than in the primary, with about 55% voting in recent presidential year elections, as compared to about 25% in primary elections.

CONGRESSIONAL VS. PRESIDENTIAL CAMPAIGNS AND ELECTIONS

Presidential and congressional races follow the same basic pattern: candidates announce for office, the people select the party candidates in primary elections, party candidates campaign against one another, and the official is chosen in the general election. But presidential and congressional elections differ in many ways.

- Congressional elections are regional (by state for senators and by district for representatives); presidential elections are national.
- Elections to the House of Representatives are less competitive than are those for the Senate or for the presidency. Between 1932 and 1992, incumbents typically won with over 60 percent of the vote. In contrast, the presidency is seldom won with more than 55 percent, with George W. Bush winning with less than 49% of the vote in 2000 and 51% in 2004. Barak Obama was 53% of the vote in 2008. During the 1990s, a record number of new freshmen were elected to the House, but the incumbency tradition is still strong.
- Fewer people vote in congressional elections during off years (when there is no presidential election). The lower turnout (about 36%) means that those that vote are more activist, and thus more ideological, than the average voter during presidential years.
- Presidential popularity affects congressional elections, even during off years. This tendency is known as the **coattail effect**. In recent years, presidential popularity does not seem to have as much effect as it used to, with the Democrats suffering a net loss of ten seats when Bill Clinton won the 1992 election. Two years later in 1994 the Republicans retook majorities in both the House and Senate, proving Bill Clinton's coat to have no tails at all. In 2000 Republican George W. Bush narrowly won the White House, but Republicans lost seats in both House and Senate in that election year. However, in 2004, Bush's coattails were substantial, with Republicans gaining seats in both the House and the Senate. The **mid-term election** in 2006 brought an end to Republican control of both houses, signaling an end to the president's coattails. In the 2008 presidential election Republican candidate John McCain did not use the president in his campaign, preferring to articulate his own agenda.
- Members of Congress can communicate more directly with their constituents, often visiting with many of them personally and making personal appearances. The president must rely on mass media to communicate with voters and can only contact a small percentage of his constituents personally.
- A candidate for a congressional seat can deny responsibility for problems in government even if he or she is an incumbent. Problems may be blamed on other members of Congress or better still the president. Even though the president may blame some things on Congress, he must take responsibility ultimately for problems that people perceive in government.

THE ROAD TO THE PRESIDENCY

Campaigns may be very simple or very complex. If you run for the local school board, you may just file your name, answer a few questions from the local newspaper, and sit back and wait for the election. If you run for president, that's another story. Today it is almost impossible to mount a campaign for the presidency in less than two years. How much money does it take? That is currently an open question, but it certainly involves millions of dollars.

Step 1: Deciding to Announce

Presidential hopefuls must first assess their political and financial support for a campaign. They generally start campaigning well before any actual declaration of candidacy. They may be approached by party leaders, or they may float the idea themselves. Many hopefuls come from Congress or a governorship, but they almost never announce for the presidency before they feel they have support for a campaign. Usually the hopeful makes it known to the press that he or she will be holding an important press conference on a certain day at a certain time, and the announcement serves as the formal beginning to the campaign.

Step 2: The Presidential Primaries

Candidates for a party's presidential nominees run in a series of presidential primaries in which they register to run. The first primary traditionally has been held in February of the election year in New Hampshire. States hold individual primaries through June on dates determined ahead of time. Technically, the states are choosing convention delegates, but most delegates abide by the decisions of the voters.

Delegates may be allocated according to proportional representation, with the Democrats mandating this system. The Republicans endorse in some states a winner-take-all system for its delegates. In several states, the delegates are not pledged to any certain delegate. No matter what the system, however, the candidates who win early primaries tend to pick up support along the way, and those who lose generally find it difficult to raise money, and are forced to drop out of the race. The tendency for early primaries to be more important than later ones is called **frontloading**. By the time primaries are over, each party's candidate is almost certainly finalized. But frontloading came under scrutiny in the 2008 presidential primary system when the Democratic National Committee created a new primary election calendar. Iowa and New Hampshire were permitted to keep their prominence as the first caucus and primary respectively, but in order to bring more diversity to the early contests, the committee approved early primaries in Nevada and South Carolina. Other states would be able to hold their primaries any time after February 5, 2008. This resulted in states frontloading their primaries in order to gain more influence in the selection of the party nominee; sixteen of them (including California and New York) choosing February 5th as Election Day. While the Republican and Democratic leadership were concerned about the number of early primaries, Florida and Michigan scheduled January primaries in violation of party rules. This forced the parties to decide how to handle convention delegates from the two states. With so many early primaries, candidates had to rethink their strategies in order to properly cover so many states. Party leaders also feared that the party presidential nominee would be chosen so early that voters in many states would feel alienated; however, that did not occur. In fact, the Democratic Party had a long and somewhat divisive primary between Barack Obama and Hillary Clinton that was not settled until June 3, 2008. As a result, at least for Democrats, states that had later primaries played a very important role in choosing the nominee.

Because the Democratic candidate was undecided for so long, the primary process came under closer scrutiny than ever before. Unlike the Republican Party, which promotes a "winner-take-all" delegate system, the Democratic proportional system provided for a closer race between the top two candidates, Obama and Clinton. In order to counter this and other problems the Democratic Party also counts the votes of **super delegates**. Super delegates are current or former officials such as governors, presidents, and members of Congress who attend the Democratic National Convention. As party delegates they are free to vote their conscience, which means their vote does not have to reflect the results of their state primary. Many feared that this practice would be perceived as unfair, and as a result, party unity would be damaged. However, this did not happen since Barack Obama won the necessary number of delegates before the convention. Adding to all this confusion was the fact that primary systems can vary state-by-state. One of the most complicated is the Texas system that chooses convention delegates based on results from both a primary and a series of caucuses. This system gave a significant number of delegates to both Hillary Clinton (from the primary) and Barack Obama (from the caucuses).

The problems that surfaced during the 2008 primary campaign have led many critics to demand a review of the system before the 2012 campaign. One proposal takes a regional approach to the elections. The nation would be divided into four regions voting in sequence. The sequence would change every four years so that one region did not gain a permanent advantage. The regional plan does permit Iowa and New Hampshire to maintain their status as the first of the primaries. Another idea is the **"American Plan"** that would start the primaries in the small states and move on to the larger ones. It is believed that this idea would give long-shot candidates a chance to build support. Supporters of this system feel that voters in all states would have a reasonable opportunity to influence the primary results.

Step 3: The Conventions

The first party convention was held during the presidency of Andrew Jackson by the Democratic Party. It was invented as a democratic or "grass roots" replacement to the old party caucus in which party leaders met together in "smoke-filled rooms" to determine the candidate. Today national party conventions are held in late summer before the general election in November.

Before primaries began to be instituted state by state in the early part of this century, the conventions actually selected the party candidates. Today the primaries determine the candidate, but the convention formally nominates them. Each party determines its methods for selecting delegates, but they generally represent states in proportion to the number of party members in each state.

Even though the real decision is made before the conventions begins, they are still important for stating party platforms, showing party unity, and highlighting the candidates with special vice-presidential and presidential candidates' speeches on the last night of the convention. In short, the convention serves as a pep rally for the party, and it attempts to put its best foot forward to the voters who may watch the celebrations on television.

Step 4: Campaigning for the General Election

After the conventions are over, the two candidates then face one another. The time between the end of the last convention and Labor Day used to be seen as a time of rest, but in recent elections, candidates often go right on to the general campaign. Most of the campaign money is spent in the general campaign, and media and election experts are widely used during this time. Because each party wants to win, the candidates usually begin sounding more middle-of-the-road than they did in the primaries, when they were appealing to party loyalists.

Since 1960 **presidential debates** are often a major feature of presidential elections, giving the candidates free TV time to influence votes in their favor. In recent campaigns, the use of electronic media has become more important, and has had the effect of skyrocketing the cost of campaigns.

CAMPAIGN AND ELECTION REFORM

Two major types of criticisms have emerged in recent years concerning U.S. campaigns and elections: campaign spending and local control of the voting process.

CAMPAIGN SPENDING

Spending for campaigns and elections are criticized for many reasons. Major reforms were passed in 1974 largely as a result of abuses exposed by the Watergate scandal. Other important milestones have been the **1976 Amendments,** *Buckley vs. Valeo*, and the **Bipartisan Campaign Reform Act of 2002**.

The Reform Act of 1974 has several important provisions:

- A six-person **Federal Election Commission** was formed to oversee election contributions and expenditures and to investigate and prosecute violators.
- All contributions over $100 must be disclosed, and no cash contributions over $100 are allowed.
- No foreign contributions are allowed.
- Individual contributions are limited to $1,000 per candidate, $20,000 to a national party committee, and $5,000 to a political action committee.

- A corporation or other association is allowed to establish a PAC, which has to register six months in advance, have at least fifty contributors, and give to at least five candidates.
- PAC contributions are limited to $5,000 per candidate and $15,000 to a national party.
- Federal matching funds are provided for major candidates in primaries, and all campaign costs of major candidates in the general election were to be paid by the government.

The **1976 Amendments** allowed corporations, labor unions, and special interest groups to set up **political action committees (PACs)** to raise money for candidates. Each corporation or labor union is limited to one PAC.

Also in 1976 the Supreme Court ruled in ***Buckley vs. Valeo*** that limiting the amount that a candidate could spend on his or her own campaign was unconstitutional. "The candidate, no less than any other person, has a First Amendment right to engage in the discussion of public issues and vigorously and tirelessly to advocate his own election."

After the election of 1996 criticisms of campaigns became so strong that special congressional hearings were called to investigate them. Among the criticisms was the overall expense of both Democratic and Republican campaigns, since more money was spent in 1996 than in any previous campaign. President Clinton and Vice-President Gore were criticized for soliciting campaign funds from their offices and the White House, and Attorney General Janet Reno was called on to rule on the legality of their activities. Another major accusation was that contributions were accepted from foreigners, who were suspected of expecting favors for themselves or their countries in return.

Election finance reform was the major theme of Senator John McCain's campaign for the presidency in 2000. McCain particularly criticized **soft money** – funds not specified for candidates' campaigns, but given to political parties for "party building" activities. McCain and many others claimed that this money made its way into campaigns anyway.

Although McCain did not win the Republican nomination, he carried his cause back to the Senate where he had championed the cause for several years previous to the election. Partly as a result of the publicity during McCain's campaign, a major reform bill passed in 2002.

The Bipartisan Campaign Reform Act of 2002 banned soft money to national parties and placed curbs on the use of campaign ads by outside interest groups. The limit of $1000 per candidate contribution was lifted to $2000, and the maximum that an individual can give to all federal candidates was raised from $25,000 to $95,000 over a two-year election cycle. The act did not ban contributions to state and local parties, but limited this soft money to $10,000 per year per candidate.

The Honest Leadership and Open Government Act of 2007, concerned the bundling of campaign funds. Bundling is the combining of individual campaign funds organized by a lobbyist for the benefit of a federal candidate. Because the amount of bundled money is significantly more than normal campaign contributions, the bundler may gain undue influence over the candidate once he or she is elected to office. The Honest Leadership and Open Government Act increased public disclosure regarding lobbying activity and funding of campaigns including bundling. As a result the Federal Elections Commission (FEC) developed regulations that require political committees to name the lobbyists that bundle money for campaigns. It is yet to be seen how the 2008 election was affected by the law and FEC regulations.

ELECTION 2000: LOCAL CONTROL OF THE VOTING PROCESS

The problems with counting the votes in Florida during the 2000 presidential election led to widespread criticism of a long accepted tradition in American politics: local control of the voting process. When Florida's votes were first counted, Republican George W. Bush received only a few hundred more votes than did Democrat Al Gore. An automatic recount narrowed the margin of victory even further. Since the outcome of the election rested on Florida's vote counts, the struggle to determine who actually won was carried out under a national spotlight.

America watched as local officials tried to recount ballots in a system where local voting methods and regulations varied widely. Some precincts had electronic voting machines known for their accuracy and reliability. Others used paper punch ballots that often left "hanging chads" that meant that those ballots might not be counted by the machines that processed them. The recount process was governed by the broad principle of determining "intent to vote" that precincts interpreted in different ways. Important questions were raised. Are all votes counted? Are votes in poor precincts that cannot afford expensive voting machines less likely to be counted than are those in affluent areas? Do variations in voting processes subvert the most basic of all rights in a democracy – the right to vote?

The fact that these problems exist in most states across the country caused many to suggest national reform of the voting process. Some advocated nationalizing elections so that all voters use the same types of machines under the same uniform rules. Others pressured Congress to provide funds for poor precincts to purchase new voting machines. Even the Supreme Court – in its *Bush v. Gore* decision that governed the outcome of the election – suggested that states rethink their voting processes.

THE "527s" OF THE ELECTION OF 2004

The 2002 restrictions of contributions to parties led to the "527" phenomenon of the 2004 presidential campaign. These independent but heavily partisan groups gathered millions of dollars in campaign contributions for both Democratic and Republican candidates. So named because of the section of the tax code that makes them tax-exempt, the 527s tapped a long list of wealthy partisans for money, and so set off a debate as to their legality. The Democrats were the first to make use of the 527s, largely because George W. Bush had a much larger chest of hard money for his campaign. However, the Republicans eventually made use of the 527s too. The groups included America Coming Together and the Media Fund on the Democratic side, and Swift Vets and POWs for Truth and Progress for America Voter Fund for the Republicans. In 2004 court action forced the Federal Elections Commission (FEC) to review its regulations as they were applied to 527s. In 2006 the FEC began to view 527s much like PACs with regard to campaigns. While 527s were somewhat involved in the 2008 elections, both presidential candidates, John McCain and Barack Obama, publicly distanced themselves from 527 groups and their campaign strategies.

2004-2008 CHANGES IN ELECTIONS AND CAMPAIGNS

Although states are still in control of their elections procedures Congress has provided some guidelines and help with upcoming elections.

- **Help America Vote Act** – Congress passed the **Help America Vote Act** (HAVA) in 2002 to improve state voting systems by providing funds for updated equipment and mandating state-wide voter registration databases. New equipment and databases have caused some confusion at the polls that has resulted in long delays in some areas. Confusion at the polls has caused some state elections officials to be concerned about possible litigation over violations of rights of citizens who could not vote. It may be best to judge the system after a few more election cycles as the voters and government officials make the necessary adjustments.
- **New voting procedures** – States began experimenting with early voting, same day registration, and absentee balloting to enable more voters to participate. Early voting was used in some states between 2004 and 2008 in both the general and primary elections. In 2008 it was estimated that almost one-third of voters participated in this type of voting. With the acceptance of early voting, candidates must now consider adjusting their campaign strategy, such as planning appearances just before early voting begins. This would be particularly important in swing states or those states that are divided in their support of the candidates.

CRITICAL REALIGNING ELECTIONS

Elections may be important milestones in political history, either marking changes in the electorate, or forcing changes themselves. The strength of one political party or another may shift during critical or realigning periods, during which time a lasting shift occurs in the popular coalition supporting one party of the other. A **critical realigning election** marks a significant change in the way that large groups of citizens votes, shifting their political allegiance from one party to the other.

Realignments usually occur because issues change, reflecting new schisms formed between groups. Political scientists see several realignments from the past, during or just after an election, with the clearest realignments taking place after the elections of 1860, 1896, and 1932.

- **The election of 1860** – The Whig party collapsed due to strains between the North and South and the Republicans under Lincoln came to power. Four major candidates ran for the presidency, but the country realigned by region: North vs. South.
- **The election of 1896** – The issue was economically based. Farmers were hit hard by a series of depressions, and they demanded reforms that would benefit farmers. The Democrats nominated William Jennings Bryan, a champion of the farmers, and in so doing, alienated the eastern laborers, and creating an East/West split rather than the old North/South split of the post Civil War Era.
- **The election of 1932** – The issues surrounding the Great Depression created the New Deal coalition, where farmers, urban workers, northern blacks, southern whites, and Jewish voters supported the Democrats. As a result, the Democrats became the dominant party.

Since 1932 political scientists agree on no defining realignments, but a **dealignment** seems to have occurred instead. Rather than shifting loyalties from one party to another, people recently have seemed less inclined to affiliate with a political party at all, preferring to call themselves "independents." The trend may have reversed with the election of 2004, when voters lined up according to "red states" (Republicans) and "blue states" (Democrats). In that election the alignments were not only regional, but also urban vs. rural. Many analysts believe that a new alliance may have formed among highly religious people that cuts across traditional faiths, drawing from fundamentalist Protestantism, Catholicism, and even Judaism. These voters identified themselves through their regularly church-going habits, and tended to support Republican candidates for office in 2004. However, in 2006 the Democrats took control of both the House and Senate. The election of 2008 not only continued Democratic control of Congress but also brought Democrat Barack Obama to the White House. These changes were anticipated by many political analysts because of the unpopular war in Iraq and the economic downturn in 2008. In both of these situations polls indicated that the voters blamed these problems on the Republicans and the Bush Administration, continuing the trend toward dealignment. Voters do not appear to be voting according to party loyalties, but instead seem to be reacting to conditions of the time.

The expense and length of modern American elections and campaigns have become major issues in politics today. Some recommend that political party spending be more closely monitored, and others believe that overall spending caps must be set. Still others advocate national, not state, control of the primary process in order to reduce the length and expense of campaigns. Whatever the criticisms, American elections and campaigns represent a dynamic and vital link between citizen and government.

THE 2008 ELECTION

Several aspects of the 2008 election made it a historic one. Barack Obama was the first African American candidate, John McCain was the oldest candidate, and Sarah Palin was the first woman to be on the Republican ticket. Whoever won, election precedents would be broken. The serious presidential candidacy of a female – Hillary Clinton – was also a unique feature of this election.

Once the campaign was underway there were lingering racial questions about the Obama candidacy. Would white and Hispanic voters be reluctant to vote for a black man? The issue of the Hispanic voter remained a focus of discussion in states with a high Hispanic population, but the concern of white voter preference was a focus of national political analysts. Many were concerned about a possible "Brady Effect" named for Thomas Brady who seemed poised to become the first African American Mayor of Los Angeles in 1982. Polls generally had him winning by 10% points, but he lost the race. After the race the belief was that white voters did not want to appear to be racist so they said they would vote for Brady, but in the privacy of the polling station they did not. Would the same situation apply to Obama? Barack Obama was a different candidate because he was bi-racial, but the question remained: were Americans ready for an African American president?

The election of Barack Obama may be credited to several factors. One, not having anything to do with race, may have had more to do with public frustration with the Bush administration because of its handling of the economy and the war in Iraq. Obama's message of "Change" and "Hope" may have resonated with voters wanting a new direction. Another non-racial factor may have been John McCain's age (72 years old) and the fact that he had some health problems (skin cancer). However, those reasons would account for negative votes, those voting against a candidate. In examining the racial question, some analysts focused on the changes in American culture since Tom Brady's run for mayor in 1982. Changes in popular culture are referred in the media, such as the popular television program, *24*, which had a black president with actor Dennis Haysbert, and Morgan Freeman also played the president in the movie, *Deep Impact*. While these may seem minor, analysts combine these fictional characters with Colin Powell and Condolessa Rice, both African Americans who served in the high profile cabinet post of Secretary of State. These examples may have prepared Americans to see African Americans in positions of authority and so were more accepting of the idea of a black man as president. However, President Obama ran a campaign that emphasized inclusion rather than race. Although he did not ignore his identity as an African American, he did not run as a black candidate but emphasized he was an American running for the presidency. The fact that voters in traditionally Republican southern states – such as North Carolina, Virginia and Florida – voted for Obama demonstrates that white voters were able to accept an African American as president.

IMPORTANT DEFINITIONS AND IDENTIFICATIONS:

- 527s
- "American Plan"
- Bipartisan Campaign Reform Act of 2002
- blanket primaries
- *Buckley vs. Valeo*
- bundling
- California Democratic Party v Jones, 2000
- Campaign Reform Act of 1974
- caucuses
- closed primaries
- coattail effect
- critical realigning election
- dealignment
- Federal Election Commission
- frontloading

- general election
- Help America Vote Act, 2002
- Honest Leadership and Open Government Act, 2007
- mid-term election
- open primaries
- PACs
- plurality
- presidential debates
- single-member districts
- soft money
- super delegates
- swing states
- *Washington State Grange v Washington State Republican Party, 2008*
- winner-take-all system

CHAPTER EIGHT
INTEREST GROUPS

Imagine a person with an intense devotion to a social cause. Let's say that he or she believes strongly in animal rights, or is distressed about the deteriorating earth environment. Or think of someone else whose work is seriously undervalued, who works very hard but is paid very little money. What can any of these imagined people do to improve their situations? One solution is to start or join a group with similar interests, with the idea that people together can do more to bring about change than people alone. They could organize an **interest group** to put pressure for change on elected officials and policy makers on all levels of government.

An interest group is an organization of people who enter the political process to try to achieve their shared goals. Almost from the beginning, Americans have joined political groups, as noted by Alexis de Tocqueville in 1834, "In no country of the world has the principle of association been more successfully used…than in America." Today about 2/3 of Americans belong to such groups. However, Americans historically have distrusted the motives and methods of interest groups. James Madison called interest groups and political parties factions, and he saw federalism and separation of powers as necessary to control their "evils." Since the number of interest groups and the people who participate in them have increased greatly over the past half century, they appear to be even more important today than they have been in the past.

PARTIES, INTEREST GROUPS, PACS, AND 527S

Interest groups, like political parties, are organizations that exist outside the structure of government, but they interact with government in such a way that it is impossible to separate them. Policy making is intertwined with both parties and interest groups so that government would operate very differently without them. In recent years two other type of outside organizations, **political action committees (PACs)** and **527s**, have joined parties and interest groups as major influences on policy making in this country.

PARTIES VS. INTEREST GROUPS

Parties and interest groups have a great deal in common because they represent political points of view of various people who want to influence policy making. This similarity has led some observers to suggest that interest groups may someday even replace parties as linkage institutions to the electorate. However, some significant differences still exist.

- Parties influence government primarily through the electoral process. Although they serve many purposes, parties always run candidates for public office. Interest groups and PACs support candidates, but they do not run their own slate of candidates.
- Parties generate and support a broad spectrum of policies; interest groups support one or a few related policies. So, whereas a party may take a position on gun control,

business regulations, campaign finance reform, and U.S. involvement in conflicts abroad, an interest group almost always focuses on one area.

PACS AND 527S

Political action committees (PACs) are the political arms of interest groups, legally entitled to raise voluntary funds to contribute to favored candidates or political parties. Like political parties, PACs focus on influencing election results, but their interest in the candidates is narrowly based because they are almost always affiliated with particular interest groups. The number of PACs has mushroomed over the past 30 years, especially since the Campaign Reform Act of 1974, which limited individual contributions to campaigns. The act did allow PACs to exist, and most large interest groups formed them as ways to funnel money to their favorite candidates for office. **Emily's List** is an example of a PAC that helps elect pro-choice female candidates by providing them with campaign funds. Emily's List, which stands for "early money is like yeast", recognizes that it may be difficult for women to raise campaign funds and provides a way for supporters to help elect women even if there are no female candidates in their own areas. Individual politicians have also set up their own PACs to aid issues and candidates they support. Sarah Palin, 2008 Republican vice presidential candidate, started her own PAC after the election. This practice also allows politicians to form support groups for themselves should they run for office again. Today more than 4000 PACs represent corporations, labor unions, and professional and trade associations, but the biggest explosion has been in the business world, with more than half of them representing corporations or other business interests.

527 groups, named after a section of the United States tax code, are tax-exempt organizations created primarily to influence the nomination, election, appointment, or defeat of candidates for public office. Although PACs were also created under Section 527 of the Internal Revenue Code, 527s are not regulated by the Federal Election Commission and not are subject to the same contribution limits as PACs. During April of 2004, the Federal Election Commission (FEC) held hearings to determine whether or not 527s should be regulated under campaign finance rules, but they decided to delay any ruling until after the 2004 presidential election. During that election 527s, such as Swift Boat Veterans for Truth, Texans for Truth, The Media Fund, America Coming Together, and Moveon.org Voter Fund, raised large sums of money for both parties.

THE FEDERAL ELECTION COMMISION AND INTEREST GROUPS

In October, 2004 a Federal District Court decision denied a FEC request to temporarily stay an order striking down several FEC campaign rules. *Shays v Federal Elections Commission* (2004) stated that the FEC failed to properly interpret the **Bipartisan Campaign Reform Act** (BCRA), 2002, also known as the **McCain-Feingold Act**. The basic purpose of the law was to control the money that comes into federal campaigns and provide transparency for the money collected. The Supreme Court had upheld most of the provisions of the law in *McConnell v Federal Elections Commission* (2003) so that *Shays* supported the belief that the FEC should better enforce the law. There were three areas of concerns involving 527 groups:

- The FEC had permitted 527groups to raise large amounts of campaign funds in spite of the fact that they violated FEC rules by spending money on issue ads in support of federal candidates.
- The FEC also allowed substantial leeway for groups involved with get-out-the-vote drives that advocated certain issues. However, critics noted that promoting an issue also usually resulted in support for one candidate over another.
- The FEC had permitted internet advertising to be free of any legal restrictions. *Shays* argued that BCRA intended to control this type of activity. The court agreed that internet ads should be regulated in some instances.

Supporters of the decision believed that it forced the FEC to carry out BCRA in order to prevent loopholes, forcing the FEC to re-examine its current regulations regarding 527s.

In December, 2006 the FEC fined three 527 groups stating that their actions were similar to those of political action committees. The fines totaled $630,000, and included Swift Boat Veterans for Truth, Moveon.org Voter Fund, and Americans Coming Together. In March, 2007 the FEC also fined the Progress for America Voter Fund for acting like a PAC in the 2004 election without having registered as one. The FEC appeared to be serious about enforcing the BCRA but stated that it preferred to do so on a case-by-case basis rather than to develop a new set of rules and regulations. Critics of the FEC's actions felt that the fines were too small when compared to the amount of money raised by the political groups and also noted that the impact of the fines was weak because they occurred two years after the election. However, the FEC recognized that groups probably did not knowingly defy the law and, therefore, the FEC gave only minimal fines for their actions.

In 2007, Congress passed the **Honest Leadership and Open Government Act**, which focused on the bundling of campaign funds. **Bundling** is the combining of individual campaign funds which are organized by a lobbyist for the benefit of a federal candidate. In response, the FEC developed regulations that required political committees to name the lobbyists that bundle the money for campaigns. The laws and regulations are new and it remains to be seen how they will affect this new way of raising campaign contributions from groups. A current challenge for the FEC is the handling of expenditures during the 2008 election campaign. With over $1 billion spent in the presidential and congressional elections, it may be difficult for the FEC to apply the rules on a case-by-case basis. In the 2008 presidential campaign the impact of interest groups, PACs and 527s appeared to be more limited than in the 2004 campaign. Both candidates, John McCain (the co-sponsor of the McCain-Feingold Law) and Barack Obama, discouraged their involvement and distanced themselves from such groups during the campaign.

THEORIES OF INTEREST GROUP POLITICS

Are interest groups good or bad for American politics? Different points of view may be separated into three theories with different answers to that question.

ELITIST THEORY

Elitist theory argues that just a few interest groups have most of the power. Although many groups exist, most of them have no real power. The government is run by a few big groups trying to preserve their own interests. Furthermore, an extensive system of interlocking directorates (the same people sitting on several boards of corporations, foundations, and universities) fortifies the control. Elitists believe that corporate interests control a great many government decisions.

PLURALIST THEORY

Pluralist theory claims that interest groups benefit American democracy by bringing representation to all. According to pluralists, some of the benefits of interest groups are:

- Groups provide linkage between people and government. They allow people's voices to be heard in ways that otherwise would be lost.
- The existence of many groups means that any one group can't become too powerful because others counterbalance it.
- Groups usually follow the rules, and those that don't get bad publicity that helps to keep them in line.
- No one set of groups dominates because those weak in one resource are strong in others. So although business interest groups usually have more money, labor groups have more members.

HYPERPLURALIST THEORY

Hyperpluralist theory says that too many groups are trying to influence the political process, resulting in political chaos and contradiction among government policies. Hyperpluralists argue that the political system is out of control because the government tries to please every interest and allows them to dictate policy in their area. Since all interest groups try to protect their self-interest, the policies that result from their pressure are haphazard and ill-conceived.

THE GROWTH OF INTEREST GROUPS

Interest groups have been a part of American politics since the beginning, but their numbers have grown incredibly in recent years. Some well-known groups, such as the Sierra Club and the National Association for the Advancement of Colored People have existed for a century. Many interest groups, however, are relatively new, with more than half forming after World War II.

Interest groups seem to exist for everyone. Some are broad-based, like the National Association of Manufacturers, but others are almost unbelievably specific, such as the American Cricket Growers Association. Many groups base their organization on economics. More than three-fourths originated from industrial, occupational, or professional membership. In recent years more groups have moved their headquarters to

Washington to be as close to the source of power as possible. Today very few occupations or industries go without interest groups to represent them in Washington.

TYPES OF MEMBERSHIP

Membership in interest groups may be classified in two ways: institutional and individual. A group's members may be composed of organizations, such as businesses or corporations, or they may be composed of individuals.

- **Institutional interests** – The most usual organization represents a business or corporation. Over five hundred firms have lobbyists, public-relations experts, and/or lawyers in Washington, most of them opening offices since 1970. Other institutions represented in Washington are universities, foundations, and governments. For example, city governments are represented through the National League of Cities, and counties through the National Association of Counties. The National Council on Education speaks for institutions of higher learning.

- **Individual interests** – Individual Americans are much more likely to join religious and political associations than are citizens in other democracies. Many of the organizations they join are represented in Washington and lobby the government for favorable policies for their interest. Many of the largest interest groups have individual, not institutional, membership. For example, the American Federation of Labor - Congress of Industrial Organizations (AFL-CIO), one of the most powerful labor unions, represents 11 million workers. Other well-know groups, such as the NAACP, the Sierra Club, and the National Organization for Women (NOW), have very large memberships. Religious organizations are also well-represented, such as the influential Christian Coalition.

TYPES OF INTEREST GROUPS

Interest groups may be divided broadly into three general types: economic interests, consumer and public interests, and equality and justice interests. Every interest group does not fit easily into this classification, but many do.

ECONOMIC INTERESTS

Economic groups are concerned primarily with profits, prices, and wages. Although government does not set them directly, government can significantly effect them through regulations, subsidies and contracts, trade policy, and tax advantages.

- **Labor unions** focus on better working conditions and higher wages. To ensure their solidarity, unions have established the **union shop**, which requires new employees to join the union representing them. Employers, on the other hand, have supported right-to-work laws, which argue that union membership should be optional. Some, but by no means all, states have adopted right-to-work laws, but many union members today work in a union shop. In 1970 about 25 percent of the work force belonged to a union, but membership has been declining over the past decades. By 2000 unions were losing support among the general population, and many strikes were proving to be unsuccessful. According to the U. S. Department of Labor in January, 2009, labor unions represent approximately 12.4% of the labor force in the U. S. However, national labor unions remain today as powerful lobby groups in Washington. One important contribution of labor unions is in voter mobilization drives and their ability to make an electoral difference in states with high union membership, such as Michigan.

- **Agriculture groups** were once more powerful than they are today, since this once most usual occupation now employs only a small fraction of the American public. For many years, government policies that deal with acreage controls, price supports, and import quotas have been important to farmers. There are several broad-based agricultural groups, such as the National Farmers' Organization and the American Farm Bureau Federation, but equally important are the specialized groups. Different crops have different groups, such as the National Potato Council, the National Peanut Council, and the American Mushroom Institute. As proof of the lobby power of agricultural groups, in May 2002, President George W. Bush signed the Farm Security and Rural Investment Act, which authorized the largest agricultural subsidy in U.S. history to date. This law was followed by an even larger program with the Food, Conservation and Energy Act of 2008. Passed by overriding President Bush's veto, the law addressed several agricultural issues such as land conservation, ethanol development, and pest research.

- **Business groups** are by far the best represented, with more than half of all interest groups representing businesses. Large corporations, such as General Motors and AT&T, exercise considerable political influence, as do hundreds of smaller corporations. Since the late 1800s government has regulated business practices, and those regulations continue to be a major concern of business interest groups. A less visible type represents trade associations, which are as diverse as the products and services they provide. Examples are life insurance groups, tire manufacturers, restaurants, realtors, and moviemakers. The broadest trade association is the Chamber of Commerce of the United States, a federation of several thousand local chambers of commerce representing more than 200,000 of business firms. The pharmaceutical lobby, which represents many drug manufacturers is one of the most powerful business lobbies with over 600 registered lobbyists. The industry spent close to $200 million in 1999-2000 for lobbying and campaign purposes. The Medicare Prescription Bill, 2003, is an example of the influence of the pharmaceutical lobby, since the bill included a provision that prevented the federal government from directly negotiating lower drug prices from pharmaceutical companies. The Veterans Administration is permitted to negotiate with the drug companies to lower prices for veterans. The Center for Public Integrity also speculated that the 2008 federal government bailout of the "Big Three" in the auto industry (GM, Chrysler and Ford) was a result of the influence of business lobby groups.

- **Professional groups** – Some of the most powerful interest groups are **professional groups** that represent various occupations. Some well-known ones are the American Medical Association, the American Bar Association, the American Association of University Professors, and the National Education Association. These groups are interested in the many government policies that affect their professions. For example, lawyers are licensed by states, which set up certain standards of admission to the state bar. The American Bar Association is interested in influencing those standards. Likewise, the American Medical Association has been very involved in recent government proposals for nationally sponsored healthcare reforms, especially as they affect doctors.

CONSUMER AND PUBLIC INTEREST GROUPS

Today over two thousand groups champion causes "in the public interest." They differ from many other interest groups in that they seek a collective good or benefits for everyone, not just the members of the interest groups themselves.

- **Public interest groups** began during the 1960s under the leadership of consumer advocate Ralph Nader. Nader first gained national attention with his book, *Unsafe at Any Speed*, which attacked General Motors' Corvair as a dangerous and mechanically deficient automobile. Public Interest Research Groups (PIRGS) actively promote environmental issues, safe energy, consumer protection, and good government. PIRGS have a national membership of more than 400,000, making them one of the largest individual membership organizations in the country. Another well known public interest group is Common Cause, founded in 1970 to promote electoral reform and a political process that is more open to the public. The League of Women Voters, a nonpartisan public interest group, sponsored presidential debates until 2000, when the candidates did not agree with debate rules set by the League.

- **Environmental interests** – A special type of public interest group focuses on **environmental interests**. A few, like the Sierra Club and Audubon Society, were founded in the late 19th century, but most were created after 1970. Environmental groups promote pollution control, wilderness protection, and population control. They have opposed strip-mining, oil pipelines, offshore oil drilling, supersonic aircraft, and nuclear power plants. Their concerns often directly conflict with those of corporations whose activities they wish to control. Energy producers argue that environmentalists oppose energy projects necessary to keep our modern society operating. Perhaps as a result of the increased visibility of environmental issues provided by former Vice President Al Gore's book and Oscar-winning documentary, *An Inconvenient Truth*, environmental groups have become more visible. A website based on the book helps individuals and groups learn what they can do to reduce global warming, and conserve energy. It also provides teachers with lesson plans. Many environmental groups have emerged since the 1970s, including the Environmental Law and Policy Center, a Midwest group that conducts advocacy campaigns to improve environmental quality and protect the natural heritage of the United States. Other groups are The Yale Center for Environmental Law and Policy, which focuses on the reduction of energy use, and Earth Justice, which believes that the earth "needs a good lawyer" to track government policy and update the public on environmental issues.

EQUALITY AND JUSTICE INTERESTS

Interest groups have championed equal rights and justice, particularly for women and minorities. The oldest and largest of these groups is the National Association for the Advancement of Colored People (NAACP). The NAACP has lobbied and pressed court cases to defend equal rights in voting, employment, and housing. The most prominent women's rights organization is the National Organization for Women (NOW) that pushed for ratification of the Equal Rights Amendment (ERA) in the 1970s. Although the amendment did not pass, NOW still lobbies for an end to sexual discrimination. Other organizations that support equal rights are the National Urban League and the National Women's Political Caucus. The Gay and Lesbian Alliance Against Defamation (GLAAD) is dedicated to promoting and ensuring fair, accurate, and inclusive representation of gays in the media to eliminate homophobia. The Gay and Lesbian Leadership Institute helps to prepare future leaders for politics, government, business, and advocacy.

HOW INTEREST GROUPS WORK

Interest groups generally employ four strategies for accomplishing their goals: lobbying, electioneering, litigation, and appealing to the public for support.

LOBBYING

To **lobby** means to attempt to influence government policies. The term was originally used in the mid-seventeenth century to refer to a large room near the English House of Commons where people could plead their cases to members of Parliament. In early United States history, lobbyists traditionally buttonholed members of Congress in the lobbies just outside the chambers of the House or Senate. In the nineteenth century lobbyists were seen as vote buyers who used money to corrupt legislators. Today lobbying is regarded less negatively, but the old stereotypes still remain.

Lobbyists today influence lawmakers and agency bureaucrats in many different ways than cornering them outside their work places. Some of their activities include:

- contacting government officials by phone or letter
- meeting and socializing at conventions
- taking officials to lunch
- testifying at committee hearings

Members of Congress have learned to rely on lobbyists for information and advice on political strategy. How effective is lobbying? Lobbying clearly works best on people already committed to the lobbyist's point of view, so much of it is directed at reinforcing and strengthening support.

ELECTIONEERING

In order to accomplish their goals, interest groups need to get and keep people in office who support their causes. **Electioneering**, then, is another important part of the work that interest groups do. Many groups aid congressional candidates sympathetic to their interests by providing money for their political campaigns.

Today PACs do most of the electioneering. As campaign costs have risen, PACs have helped pay the bills. About half of the members of the House of Representatives get the majority of their campaign funds from PACs. PACs overwhelmingly support incumbents, although they sometimes play it safe by contributing to the campaigns of challengers as well. Incumbents, however, have voting records to check and also are likely to be reelected. Most candidates, including incumbents, readily accept PAC money.

LITIGATION

If interest groups cannot get what they want from Congress, they may sue businesses or the federal government for action. Environmentalist groups have used this tactic successfully to force businesses to follow government regulations. Even the threat of lawsuits may force businesses to change their ways.

Lawsuits were used successfully during the 1950s by civil rights groups. Civil rights bills were stalled in Congress, so interest groups, such as the National Association for the Advancement of Colored People, turned to the courts to gain a forum for school desegregation, equal housing, and labor market equality.

Interest groups may influence court decisions by filing **amicus curiae** ("friends of the court") briefs, which consist of written arguments submitted to the courts in support of one side of a case or the other. In particularly controversial cases, many briefs may be filed on both sides of the issue. For example, in the case of *Regents of the University of California v. Bakke* (1978), which challenged affirmative action programs as reverse discrimination, over a hundred different groups filed amicus briefings.

Groups may also file **class action lawsuits**, which enable a group of similar plaintiffs to combine their grievances into a single suit. A famous example is *Brown v. the Board of Education of Topeka* in 1954, which not only represented Linda Brown in Topeka, Kansas, but several other children similarly situated around the country.

APPEALING TO THE PUBLIC

Interest groups sometimes may best influence policy making by carefully cultivating their public image. Labor interests may want Americans to see them as hard-working men and women, the backbone of the country. Farmers may favor an image that represents old-fashioned values of working close to the earth in order to feed everyone else. Groups that suffer adverse publicity, like meat and egg producers whose products have been criticized for their high cholesterol and fat content, often advertise to defend their products. Their goal may be not only to promote business and sell their products, but to keep a favorable position among lobby groups in Washington. Because these ads do not directly affect the lobbying process, it is difficult to tell just how successful they are, but more and more groups are turning to high-profile ad campaigns.

THE "RATINGS GAME"

One well-known activity of interest groups is "rating" members of Congress in terms of the amount of support they give to legislation that is favorable to their causes. Many interest groups use these rating systems to describe members' voting records to interested citizens, and other times they use them to embarrass members. For example, environmental groups identified the twelve representatives that were most likely to vote against environmental bills, and named them "the Dirty Dozen." The typical scheme ranges from 0 to 100 percent, reflecting the percentage of times the member supports the group's legislative agenda.

WHERE DO INTEREST GROUPS GET THEIR MONEY?

Most interest groups have to work hard to raise money, but individual membership organizations have more trouble than most. In addition to dues collected from members, groups receive money from three important sources: foundation grants, federal grants and contracts, and direct mail.

- **Foundation grants** – Public interest groups particularly depend on **foundation grants**, funds established usually by prominent families or corporations for philanthropy. The Ford Foundation, for example, contributes to liberal public-interest groups, and the Rockefeller Family Fund almost single-handedly supports the Environmental Defense Fund. The Bill and Linda Gates Foundation supports many endeavors, including public education.

- **Federal grants** and contracts are not granted directly to organizations for lobbying purposes, but they may be given to support a project the organization supports. For example, Jesse Jackson's community-development organization called PUSH was heavily supported by federal grants from various agencies. The Reagan administration reduced grants to interest groups, at least partly because much of the money was going to liberal causes. More recent controls on the use of federal funds generally only apply to the funds themselves, so their use to promote their cause is limited. Groups retain their right to promote issues with private funding.

- **Direct solicitation** – Most groups heavily rely on direct mail to solicit funds. By using computers, groups can mail directly to selected individuals identified from lists developed by staff or purchased from other groups. Many groups maintain websites that encourage visitors to contribute to their causes.

EFFECTIVE INTEREST GROUPS

Many factors contribute to the success of an interest group, including its size, intensity and financial resources.

- **Size** – It seems logical that large interest groups would be more effective than small ones, but almost the opposite is true. If a group has a large membership, it tends to have a **free rider** problem. Since there are so many members, individuals tend to think someone else will do the work. It is inherently easier to organize a small, rather than a large, group for action, and interest groups are no exception. The problem is particularly acute for public interest groups who seek benefits for all, not just for themselves. In contrast, smaller business-oriented lobbies often provide tangible, specific advantages for their members.

- **Intensity** – Groups that are intensely committed to their goals are quite logically more successful than those that are not. A single-issue group, devoted to such causes as pro-life, anti-nuclear energy, or gun control, often is most intense. Their members often are willing to actively protest or push for legislation. For example, the proponents of gun control gathered their forces more intensely after the presidential advisor Jim Brady was shot and almost killed during the assassination attempt on Ronald Reagan in 1982. They gathered support from Brady's wife and launched a campaign to regulate guns that culminated in the passage of the Brady Bill in 1993.

- **Financial resources** – An interest group has only a limited influence if it does not have financial resources adequate to carry on its work. Most of their activities – such as lobbying, electioneering, and writing amicus curaie briefs – cost money, so successful fund-raising is crucial to the success of any type of interest group.

THE "REVOLVING DOOR"

Interest groups are often criticized for a type of interaction with government known as the **"revolving door."** Through this practice, government officials – both in Congress and executive agencies – quit their jobs to take positions as lobbyists or consultants to businesses. Many people fear that the "revolving door" may give private interests unfair influence over government decisions. For example, if a government official does a favor for a corporation because he or she is promised a job after leaving government, then the official is not acting for the good of the public.

How widespread is this practice? Does it compromise the government's ability to act only for the public good? The evidence is uncertain. There are high-profile cases, such as that of Michael Deaver, Ronald Reagan's deputy chief of staff who was convicted of perjury after he left his position to work in the private sector. An investigation found that he used government contacts to help the clients of his public-relations firm. On the other hand, businesses argue that former government officials seldom abuse their jobs while in office, and that there is nothing wrong with seeking advice from those who have been in government. According to this point of view, former government employees should be able to use their expertise to gain employment in the private sector.

The federal government has made several attempts to limit the influence of lobbies on policy-making. Congress passed the **Lobbying Disclosure Act of 1995** to provide disclosure of lobbying activities intended to influence the federal government. The law set the terms for registering lobbyists working in both the House and Senate. It also set fines and prison terms for those found in violation of the law.

The Jack Abramoff scandal encouraged reform to provide more disclosure on lobbyists' activities. In 2006 Abramoff was sentenced to prison for issues relating to defrauding Indian tribes by secretly lobbying against them while also representing them as a lobbyist. The Honest Leadership and Open Government Act was passed in September, 2007, partly in response to the "K-Street Project," an effort to pressure lobby groups – often located on K Street in Washington – to hire Republican lobbyists who would have better access to the Republican controlled government. The law amended the Lobbying Disclosure Act of 1995 to make the relationship between lobbyists and Congress more transparent through improved disclosure of funds spent by lobbyists. The Federal Elections Commission also proposed new regulations to implement campaign contribution bundling disclosure by lobby groups.

Presidents have also demonstrated concern regarding connections between executive branch employees and lobbyists. President Clinton restricted all senior appointed officials from lobbying an agency up to five years after leaving the federal government. However, he revoked the order on December 28, 2000, just before a Republican government was set to take office. Barack Obama campaigned for the presidency for lobbyist reform, and when he took office in 2009, he too issued restrictions on executive appointees. Obama restricted executive agency appointees from accepting gifts from lobbyists, and required that they not work for lobbyists for two years after leaving government service before being appointed. However, he allowed the restriction on previous employment by a lobbyist to be waived through the Office of Management and Budget if the appointee was important to national security and the economy.

So, are interest groups contributors or distracters from the democratic process? Do they help or hinder the government in making good decisions that benefit citizens of the country? Does our system of checks and balances work well in keeping the influence of particular groups in proportion to that of others? Whatever your point of view, it is clear that interest groups have had a long-lasting influence on the American political system, and they show no signs of weakening now or in the near future.

IMPORTANT DEFINITIONS AND IDENTIFICATIONS:

- 527s
- *amicus curiae*
- Bipartisan Campaign Reform Act
- bundling
- class action lawsuits
- electioneering
- elitist theory
- Emily's List
- foundation grants
- free rider problem
- Honest Leadership and Open Government Act, 2007
- hyperpluralist theory
- individual interests
- institutional interests
- interest groups
- labor unions
- lobbying
- Lobbying Disclosure Act of 1995
- McCain-Feingold Act, 2002
- *McConnell v Federal Election Commission,* 2003
- pluralist theory
- political action committees
- public interest groups
- the "ratings game"
- revolving door
- *Shays v Federal Election Commission,* 2004
- union shop

CHAPTER NINE
MASS MEDIA

Any study of linkage institutions would be incomplete without a consideration of the role that mass media plays in the American political system. Political parties and interest groups serve as important links between citizens and government, but an increasingly important component is mass media that provides information, and also shapes, fosters, or censures it. Mass media has become such an integral part of the political system that it is sometimes called **"the fourth branch"** of government, and it both reflects and influences public opinion. The media link public opinion and the government, and the influence of the mass media on politics is enormous.

THE FUNCTIONS AND STRUCTURE OF THE MEDIA

Mass media may be broken down into three major components: print media, electronic media, and the internet. Print media has played a role in American politics almost from the beginning, when the early political parties published their own, very partisan newspapers. Electronic media became a force during the 20th century, first with the invention of radio, and later with the invention and widespread access to television. The internet first came to be used in the early 1970s by the government, and developed into a major medium of communication by the century's end.

FUNCTIONS OF THE MEDIA

The mass media perform a number of functions in American society, and all have an impact on the political system.

- **Entertainment** – Radio and television both emphasize entertainment, with prime-time ratings for television often making or breaking the overall success of the networks and individual stations. Particularly in recent years politics has been a topic for entertainment, with numerous movies focused on the president as the star of fictional political sagas. A popular TV series, *The West Wing*, began as an obvious take-off on the real White House Office of President Bill Clinton, but it survived the transition to the very different style and personnel of George W. Bush's staff. Popular late-night shows, such as *Saturday Night Live, The Daily Show with Jon Stewart* and the *Colbert Report* also entertain people with their humorous and satirical treatment of political figures and events. This type of entertainment may play an important role in political socialization, shaping opinions of political institutions and practices at the same time they are entertaining us. In 2008 *Saturday Night Live* regained some of the impact of its early years with the emergence of

115

Republican vice-presidential candidate Sarah Palin. Actress Tina Fey had an uncanny resemblance to her, and many viewers tuned in to see her parodies. The contribution of the *Daily Show with Jon Stewart* has been important since the 2000 election when its reference to the election as "Indecision 2000" turned out to be prophetic. By 2007 the Pew Research Center reported that Jon Stewart, who insists he is a fake news anchor, was 4th on the list of most trusted journalists, tied with real news broadcasters Brian Williams, Tom Brokaw, Dan Rather and Anderson Cooper. Newsweek calls it "the coolest pit stop on television" with Stewart regularly interviewing authors of political books and politicians, including presidential candidates. Despite the criticism that these shows have little real political impact, many may see the programs as a continuation of American political comedy and satire in the tradition of Will Rogers, the *Smothers Brothers Comedy Hour,* and the long-running *Saturday Night Live.*

- **News Reports** – Reporting the news has been a major function of print media since the early 19th century, and newspapers and magazines remain an important source for people interested in simply finding out what is happening in the country and the world outside. Today more people rely on television than on newspapers and magazines to provide news. In the early days of television, news was generally reported early every evening in a fifteen-minute segment before the night's entertainment began. Today network news has expanded to thirty and sixty minute segments, but cable television has made round-the-clock news reporting possible, with CNN, Fox News, and MSNBC focusing on news stories and commentaries virtually 24 hours a day. While TV remains the most important medium for news information, the internet increasingly is becoming a viable alternative. In December, 2008 the Pew Research Center reported that, for the first time, the internet surpassed newspapers as a major source for both national and international news by Americans. The largest one year jump occurred in 2008 when the use of the internet as a news source increased from 24% in 2007 to 40% in 2008.

- **Agenda Setting** – One important source of political, social, and economic power is the ability of the media to draw public attention to particular issues. Equally important are the issues that the media *doesn't* focus on. For example, the media may promote terrorism as a major issue in American society by airing the latest tape by Osama bin Laden, but Americans may remain unconcerned about the AIDS epidemic in Africa because the media is silent about that issue. The media may promote a president's agenda by focusing on his proposals, or they may distract from a president's agenda by focusing on a "sideshow," such as they did with Bill Clinton's personal and financial life. Conservative radio hosts, such as Rush Limbaugh, have developed large audiences that are influenced not just by the opinions expressed, but are also encouraged to focus on some issues but not on others.

- **Creation of Political Forums** – Politicians have learned to use the mass media to make important announcements or to encourage citizens to focus on their issues. The media wants to make politics interesting so that viewer ratings remain high, so politicians often respond by "making news" that will draw attention from the media. A presidential candidate may dress up in hunting gear, or pose in a "photo op" with a respected former president, as John Kerry did in 2004. The use of the media by a candidate was taken to a new level in the 2008 presidential campaign when Barack Obama purchased a half-hour of prime-time television to promote his candidacy to the American public shortly before the election. Members of Congress may call attention to their causes through filibusters or public announcements of popular legislation passed. The individual that has the most direct access to the media is the president, who may command prime time for important announcements and speeches. Presidential press conferences usually get extensive coverage, and the president's daily activities are followed carefully.

THE STRUCTURE OF THE MEDIA

In the past 50 years, the broadcast, or electronic, media have gradually replaced the print media as the main source of political information. Today, the internet is the most rapidly growing type of mass media.

- **Print Media** – Most newspapers today are still locally based, although many of them are part of massive media conglomerates, such as Gannett, Knight, Ridder, and Newhouse. However, papers such as *The New York Times* and *The Washington Post* have a national readership that makes them an important force in policymaking. Most magazines do not focus on politics, but news magazines, such as *Time, Newsweek, U.S. News* and *World Report, Nation,* and *New Republic*, have considerable influence on American government and politics. In recent years, newspapers have had difficulty competing with free, online news sources. As a result, their circulation numbers have declined, and some fear that investigative reporting may suffer as well. Since newspapers have traditionally monitored political officials and their policies, critics argue that their demise could upset the very foundations of our democratic society.

- **Electronic Media** – Radio was first invented in 1903, but made its big debut in politics when a Pittsburgh station broadcast the 1920 election returns. President Franklin Roosevelt used radio successfully in his "fireside chats" to the nation. Despite the advent of television in the mid-20th century, radio remains an important linkage institution, especially since many Americans spend time in their cars for work commutes and travel. Conservative talk shows provide commentary on national politics, and National Public Radio puts a great deal of focus on political events and personalities. Television's influence on the American public is tremendous, especially with the advent of cable television. Americans not only get information from television, but they also listen to commentaries and analysis of the news.

- **The Interne**t – Internet technology and access has transformed communications in a very short period of time, particularly during the late 1990s and early 21st century. The internet has become a tool for researching almost any topic under the planet, and also serves as a major entertainment outlet for millions. People across the globe may instantaneously contact one another by e-mail, and written letters have almost become a thing of the past. Today **"blogs"** and list serves devote much time to political topics, and provide an interactive forum for people to express and react to political opinions. Internet communications played an integral role in the election campaign of 2004, when candidates raised unprecedented amounts of money on campaign websites. In addition, 527s established internet sites that not only raised money, but spread their influence through interactive "chats." On election day in 2004, electronic news media pledged to not make public reports from exit polls until everyone had voted. However, internet sources made no such commitment, and strong rumors passed around the websites that predicted victory for Democratic candidate John Kerry. The predictions were wrong, and President George W. Bush was reelected, but the election affirmed the growing political influence of the internet. One online news source – only available in hard-copy in Washington, D.C. – is *Politico*, which provides a non-partisan approach to national politics on its website, Politico.com. **YouTube** has also become an important source of communication for politicians. Early in his administration President Obama began posting public addresses on YouTube. The 111th Congress (2009-2011), both the House and the Senate, began to experiment with postings on YouTube to remain connected to voters. While many believe this activity may increase the government's transparency, it is unclear as to whether or not the new forum will provide an opportunity for citizen input into the policymaking process.

GOVERNMENT REGULATION OF THE MEDIA

As a general rule, print media has much fewer government restrictions than does electronic media. The First Amendment to the Constitution has been interpreted to mean that no governmet, federal or state, can place **"prior restraint"** on the press before stories are published. Once something is published, a newspaper or magazine may be sued or prosecuted for libel or obscenity, but these charges are very difficult to prove. Most journalists value **confidentiality of sources**, or the right to keep the sources for their information private. However, the Supreme Court has upheld the right of the government to compel reporters to divulge information as party of a criminal investigation, so the conflict between reporters and the government is still an issue.

In contrast, broadcasting is carefully regulated by the government. No one may operate a radio or television station without a license from the **Federal Communications Commission**. The government must renew licenses, and until recently the FCC used its power of renewal to influence what the station put on the air. For example, they sometimes required networks to change their depictions of racial or ethnic groups, restrict the number of commercials aired, or decrease the number of shows that emphasize violence. In recent years a movement to deregulate both television and radio has taken hold. With the increasing choice of television and radio shows available to the American public, supporters of deregulation argue that competition should be allowed to determine how each station defines and serves community needs. Now many of the old rules are less vigorously enforced. Radio broadcasting has been deregulated more than televisions, and in 1996 the **Telecommunications Act** allowed one radio company to own as many as eight stations in large markets and as many as it wished nationally. In February, 2008 a report was issued by the FCC regarding media ownership rules and their impact on competition, localism and diversity. It confirmed most of its major rulings including radio/television cross ownership rules. The commission continued to permit one company in a single market, regardless of its size, to own one TV station and one radio station.

Despite these recent trends, the content of radio and television is still regulated in ways that newspapers and magazines are not. One example is the equal time rule that requires a station selling time to one candidate for office to make the same amount of time available to another. Also in force is the right-of-reply rule that allows a person who is attacked on a broadcast the right to reply over that same station. A candidate may also reply if a broadcaster endorses an opponent. For many years a fairness doctrine was in place, which required broadcasters to give time to opposing views if they broadcast a program giving one side of a controversial issue. The FCC abolished the doctrine in 1987, arguing that it inhibited the free discussion of issues. However, most broadcasters still follow the rule voluntarily. In March, 2008 Congress attempted to reinstate the fairness doctrine but President George W. Bush vetoed the law.

THE IMPACT OF MEDIA ON POLITICS

The media influences the political system in many ways, as reflected in the functions of the media summarized earlier in this chapter. Electronic media has been criticized for forcing political figures and events to conform to "**sound bites**," or comments compressed into several-second segments. Although newspapers and magazines have longer formats, most Americans today are much more reliant on television and radio for their news. As a result, stories are boiled down to their basics, and those that don't fit are not covered. The impact of the internet is yet to be seen, but the interactive nature of the medium allows the user to spend as much or little time with an issue as he or she likes.

THE MEDIA AND POLITICAL CAMPAIGNS

Media influence is probably most obvious during political campaigns for office, especially during presidential years. Because television is the primary news source for Americans, candidates and their consultants spend much of their time strategizing as to how to use it to their benefit. Television is widely used by presidential and senatorial candidates, and increasingly by candidates for the House of Representatives.

- **Advertising** – Television advertising is very expensive, and as a result, the cost of campaigns has skyrocketed. Most campaign ads are negative, making them even more controversial. The typical pattern is for one candidate to "attack" the other, who in turn "counterattacks." Even though most people claim to dislike these ads, political consultants believe that they work, so it appears as if negative ads have become the norm. Critics worry that this type of advertising reduces political participation and encourages citizens to be cynical about politics.

- **News Coverage** – Television ads cost money, but news coverage – as long as you can get it – is free. So candidates and consultants spend a great deal of time planning "news events" that will be covered on the evening news and by cable news shows. They may also arrange to be invited to appear on news shows to comment on particular issues or events. As a result, an invitation to appear on CNN's *Larry King* show can be worth thousands of dollars in campaign ads. Some campaign staff specialize in media techniques, such as camera angles, necessary equipment, timing, and deadlines, so that even if the news coverage is free the advice is not. An important position on any campaign staff is that of **spin doctor**, or one who tries to influence journalists with interpretations of events that are favorable to a particular candidate.

- **Presidential Debates** – The most famous series of television events in American politics are the presidential debates. The television precedent was set in 1960, when the Democratic candidate, John Kennedy, was generally perceived to "defeat" the sitting Vice President Richard Nixon. Challengers generally benefit more than incumbents from the debates because they are not as well known. However, the results are often unpredictable, since usually the differences come down to style. Both candidates are prepared extensively for the debates, and usually don't make any serious mistakes. An exception occurred in 1976 when President Gerald Ford argued that eastern European countries were not communist. In 2004 President George W. Bush was criticized for inconsistent performances over the course of the debates, but challenger John Kerry was widely criticized by the media (and the Republican Party) for bringing up the sexual orientation of Vice President Cheney's daughter. The 2008 debates did not provide any serious problem for either John McCain or Barack Obama but rather emphasized the style of each candidate. Candidates have had to adjust to different debate styles. The format of a moderator with timed responses has been used along with the "town hall" forum which allows questions from the audience. As a result, candidates must prepare for different formats and be prepared for a variety of questions. The debates give the public an opportunity to see both candidates together, and even though the ability of debates to change votes has been questioned, they are now a part of political campaigning tradition.

- **Accountability of Candidate Claims** – In the 2008 election news services provided ways for voters to evaluate the claims of candidates. Although newspapers have done this before, these sites provided a regular examination of political campaign claims. Some examples were:

  - **PolitiFact.com** – During the 2008 campaign the *St. Petersburg Times* (Fl) and the Congressional Quarterly teamed up to provide a non-partisan examination of claims made by the candidates in speeches, commercials, and interviews. Statements were rated with the "truth-o-meter". For 15 months during the election approximately 750 rulings were made ranging from " the truth" to "pants on fire". Although PolitiFact shut down after the election, the *St. Petersburg Times* brought it back after the 2009 inauguration in order to provide a check on claims made by the Obama administration, Congress, interest groups, and lobbyists regarding issues. In addition, the "Obamameter" tracks the progress of campaign promises made by President Obama's administration.

  - **FactChecker.org** – The Annenberg Political Fact Check website is dedicated to "holding politicians accountable" and provided the same service as PolitiFact.com during the 2008 election. It continued as a post-election service to check claims made by politicians and interest groups specifically focusing on the "spin" that can result from political claims.

  - **Fact-Checker** – Similar to PolitiFact.com, and the Annenberg site, the *Washington Post* Fact-Checker used Pinocchio's nose as a measure of truth. It was shut down after the election as a continuing source of accountability.

THE MEDIA AND GOVERNMENT OFFICIALS

The media impacts all officials in government on local, state, and national levels. Town newspapers often cover local school board candidates, and town meetings often appear in full broadcasts on local television stations. Governors – particularly those in large states – often have staff members that help them with news coverage. On the national level, members of Congress must share the stage with 534 others. However, party leaders and committee chairmen often play to media events. The importance of the presidency is reflected in the existence of the **White House press corps** that is assigned full-time to cover the activities of the president. Once or twice a day they are briefed by the president's **press secretary**, who is responsible for handling the press corps. Because the reporters are in close proximity to the president, they tend to report almost every visible action he takes. Presidents, then, live their lives in public view, a situation that they may use to their benefit since they have a built-in audience. However, the need to get a story may lead reporters to emphasize the trivial and leave a president frustrated by a focus on matters he considers to be unimportant.

The media do not make direct policy decisions, but their influence on American government and politics is tremendous. Whether they manipulate the policymakers or are manipulated by the politicians is a matter of some dispute, but their presence is an integral part of American society. They link the public to government and often set the public agenda, two very important components of the political system.

THE FUTURE OF MEDIA – USE OF THE INTERNET

Major media technological changes are expected for the immediate future. According to internet analysts more Americans will continue using more advanced technology for information and news. It is anticipated that they will not just continue to use the internet but will use mobile devices such as cell phones. It is yet to be seen if this technology will increase transparency in government and permit more interaction between individuals to aid the continued development of democratic institutions. Whatever the outcome, the number of Americans who use the internet more than one hour a day almost doubled between 2003 and 2008, from 26% to 48%. As expected, those under 30 years old and those more affluent with higher levels of education use it more frequently, with 6 out of 10 using the internet over one hour a day.

While television is still used by 70% of Americans as the main source of information, that number is falling among young people. In September, 2007 it was reported that 68% of young people used the TV as their main news source but that number fell to 58% in 2008. Television will remain an important media source for Americans; however, it is clear that the internet will continue to be an increasing method of accessing information.

IMPORTANT DEFINITIONS AND IDENTIFICATIONS:

- agenda setting
- "blogs"
- confidentiality of sources
- equal time rule
- fairness doctrine
- Federal Communications Commission
- "fourth branch"
- press secretary
- prior restraint
- right of reply
- sound bites
- spin doctor
- Telecommunications Act of 1996
- White House press corps
- YouTube

UNIT THREE QUESTIONS

The Rise of the Thin Cats

1. Which of the following best illustrates the point being made in the cartoon above?

   (A) Candidates rely too much on elites for campaign funds.
   (B) Democrats are using traditional ways to raise money for campaigns.
   (C) Both political parties are taking more control of campaign funding.
   (D) Political candidates are funding campaigns from a variety of sources.
   (E) The Federal Election Commission has increased control of campaign funding.

2. Which of the following is the best single reason why the United States has a two-party system?

   (A) an election system characterized by proportional representation
   (B) a winner-take-all plurality election system
   (C) a consensual political culture
   (D) long standing culture wars
   (E) the system is modeled after the British two-party design

3. What comment is the cartoon above making about the election of 2008?

   (A) Barack Obama was a stronger presidential candidate than John McCain because
        of his vice-presidential choice.
   (B) John McCain was a weaker presidential candidate than Barack Obama because
        he is too old.
   (C) John McCain challenged the historic nature of Barack Obama's candidacy
        through his vice presidential choice.
   (D) John McCain's candidacy was historic because he was the first candidate over 70
        to run for the presidency.
   (E) Both vice-presidential candidates were unexpected choices.

4. Which of the following is the most accurate description of the 2008 presidential
    primaries?

   (A) The Democratic Party had more control over the scheduling of state primaries
        than did the Republican Party.
   (B) The Republican Party was more successful than the Democratic Party in
        controlling the number of presidential candidates.
   (C) The Democratic Party was unsuccessful in attempting to change most states to a
        caucus system.
   (D) Both parties were able to control the presidential primary system schedule, but
        local races were directed by state and local party organizations.
   (E) The Democratic Party primaries took longer to determine the preferred
        presidential candidate than did the Republicans.

5. Which of the following has been most characteristic of party politics throughout American history?

   (A) Most often the legislature has been controlled by Democrats and the presidency by Republicans.
   (B) Most often the legislature has been controlled by Republicans, and the presidency by Democrats.
   (C) Republicans have generally controlled both branches.
   (D) Divided government was the norm until the 1960s.
   (E) Most of U.S. history may be divided into eras in which one party or the other controlled both branches.

6. Political parties officially name their presidential nominee through

   (A) a series of party caucuses
   (B) the national conventions of the political parties
   (C) a national meeting of party governors
   (D) a series of state presidential primary elections
   (E) the selection of "super delegates" at the party conventions

7. Which of the following is specifically prohibited by the Constitution with regard to voting?

   (A) Poll taxes
   (B) Butterfly ballot design
   (C) Gerrymandered districts
   (D) Closed primaries
   (E) Absentee voting

8. Which of the following was president during an era of divided government?

   (A) Andrew Jackson
   (B) Abraham Lincoln
   (C) Theodore Roosevelt
   (D) Franklin Roosevelt
   (E) George H. Bush

9. The original Constitution dealt with the issue of voting by

   (A) granting the right to vote to all U.S. citizens
   (B) granting all male adults the right to vote
   (C) setting property requirements for all voters
   (D) permitting states to determine voter qualifications
   (E) setting voter requirements for national elections but not state and local ones

10. Which of the following is the best description of changes in elections and campaigns during the late 20th century?

    (A) Candidates took more and more control of their campaigns from the political parties.
    (B) Primary elections became less and less important in selecting candidates.
    (C) Party bosses gained more power in determining candidates for office.
    (D) Party conventions gained more power in determining presidential candidates for office.
    (E) Races for congressional seats became more competitive than they had been in previous years.

11. Which of the following is used by the state of Iowa as a way to select delegates to the party conventions?

    (A) the electoral college
    (B) open primaries
    (C) closed primaries
    (D) blanket primaries
    (E) caucuses

12. The Supreme Court decision in *Buckley vs. Valeo* (1976) was significant because it

    (A) ruled that federal funding for campaigns must apply to Congressional candidates
    (B) ruled that advocacy groups could not make political contributions without the approval of their membership
    (C) put severe limits on individual contributions to political parties
    (D) ruled that limits on candidates campaign spending was the same as limits on speech
    (E) approved restrictions on campaign contributions from foreigners

13. Straight-ticket voting occurs when

    (A) the candidate for office is running unopposed
    (B) a voter chooses candidates from different parties
    (C) states combine national and state candidates on the same ballot
    (D) a person votes for candidates from the same party
    (E) a person votes for the same party candidates in two or more election cycles

14. America Coming Together, the Media Fund, Swift Vets and POWs for Truth, and Progress for America Voter Fund are examples of

(A) PACs
(B) Interest groups that supported the Republicans in the election of 2004
(C) Interest groups that supported the Democrats in the election of 2004
(D) 527s
(E) Public interest groups that do not take sides in an election

15. States wanting more influence in the selection of party presidential candidates during the 2008 primaries

(A) restricted their ballots to only Republican and Democratic candidates
(B) began frontloading the time of their primaries
(C) rejected the caucus form developing primary election systems
(D) permitted the use of same-day registration
(E) began using an open primary system

16. Critical realigning elections are said to occur when

(A) one party has dominated the presidency for four straight elections
(B) one party has controlled both the legislative and executive branches of government for at least twenty years
(C) voters start supporting one party or the other by voting a straight ticket
(D) voters begin to vote for third parties
(E) voting blocks rearrange themselves in a different alignment of support for the major parties

17. Frontloading occurs in a political campaign when

(A) one candidate gets more money than the others
(B) party bosses make the decisions regarding candidates to run for office
(C) early primaries tend to be more important than later ones
(D) one party gets way ahead of the other one in raising campaign money
(E) a candidate convinces convention delegates to ignore the results of primary elections in their states

18. Which of the following statements is most likely to be made by a political scientist that supports hyperpluralist theory?

   (A) The political system is out of control because the government tries to please every interest and allows each to dictate policy in their area.
   (B) Groups usually follow the rules, and those that don't get bad publicity that helps to keep them in line.
   (C) Groups provide linkage between people and government. They allow people's voices to be heard in ways that otherwise would be lost.
   (D) The government is run by a few big groups trying to preserve their own interests.
   (E) Although many groups exist, most of them have no real power.

19. Which of the following interest groups is composed primarily of institutional memberships?

   (A) AFL-CIO
   (B) National Association for the Advancement of Colored People
   (C) National Association of Counties
   (D) American Association of Retired Persons
   (E) The Sierra Club

20. An area of concern that was addressed in the Bipartisan Campaign Reform Act of 2002 was the use of

   (A) campaign ads from advocacy groups
   (B) newspaper editorials in endorsing candidates
   (C) hard money for campaigns
   (D) state regulations for primary elections
   (E) the internet by political candidates

21. An important difference between interest groups and political parties is that interest groups

   (A) have a broad base of support
   (B) focus their efforts in several areas of interest
   (C) change their positions frequently
   (D) also have non-political agendas
   (E) prefer to work primarily through the courts

22. In which of the following activities is a lobbyist most likely to participate?

    (A) selecting candidates for interest groups to support for office
    (B) contacting government officials by phone, e-mail, or letter
    (C) raising money from members for election campaigns
    (D) organizing recruitment efforts for new members to support the interest group
    (E) planning efforts to influence decisions make by federal judges

23. Which of the following was an important new feature that many states added to their voting procedures after the 2000 election?

    (A) Election-day registration
    (B) Voter fees
    (C) On-line voting
    (D) Early voting systems
    (E) Smaller voting districts

24. *Amicus curiae* briefs are used by interest groups to influence decisions made by

    (A) bureaucrats in the executive branch
    (B) candidates for public office
    (C) the president
    (D) court judges
    (E) members of Congress

25. "Ratings games" are played by interest groups to

    (A) identify members of Congress favorable to their causes
    (B) successfully compete with other groups for federal dollars
    (C) rank order legislation that they support
    (D) influence discretionary decisions made by bureaucrats
    (E) identify people who would be successful lobbyists

26. An election that results in a dramatic shift in party allegiance in a particular region is known as a

    (A) gerrymandered election
    (B) primary election
    (C) realigning election
    (D) divided election
    (E) dealigning election

27. Which of the following is the best example of agenda setting by the media?

(A) agreeing to run negative ads for election campaigns
(B) competing with other media outlets by doing almost anything to be the first to get a story
(C) deliberately ignoring an issue important to the president and focusing on one less important to him
(D) opposing a policy supported by one political party in order to receive a favor from another party
(E) reporting the news in very brief summaries so that no stories receive in-depth coverage

28. Which type of media outlet is subject to the most controls and regulations by government?

(A) internet
(B) local newspapers
(C) magazines
(D) television stations
(E) national newspapers

29. Which of the following rights for the media is most likely to be protected from government intervention?

(A) confidentiality of sources
(B) libel
(C) pornography
(D) freedom from prior restraint
(E) suspension of the equal time rule

30. The major responsibility of the "spin doctor" is to

(A) be sure that candidates create big news events
(B) prepare presidential candidates for debates
(C) craft effective ads for television
(D) write effective speeches for candidates
(E) influence how journalists and the public interpret news events

FREE RESPONSE QUESTION

Political parties use primary systems as a way to select candidates for public office.

a) Explain one reason why primary election systems are often seen as a democratizing feature of the U.S. electoral process.

b) Evaluate the democratic features of two of the following types of primaries.

Blanket Primary

Open Primary

Closed Primary

UNIT FOUR

INSTITUTIONS AND POLICY PROCESSES OF GOVERNMENT

CHAPTER TEN
CONGRESS

The founding fathers intended for Congress to be the central policy-making body in the federal government. Although the power of Congress has fluctuated over the years, today it shares with the presidency and the judiciary the responsibility of making key policy decisions that shape the course of the nation.

THE PEOPLE'S INFLUENCE

Although the founders saw Congress as the body most directly in touch with the people, most people today have negative overall views of both houses. Approval ratings have hovered for years at about 30%, although in recent years those ratings have climbed somewhat higher. However, during 2006 Congressional approval ratings dipped into the 20s. The Democratic Party took a slight majority in both the House and Senate in the 2006 mid-term election which brought a change of approval ratings up to about 40%. But, by mid-2008 Congressional approval had fallen again to about 30%. In spite of this, the majority of voters express higher approval ratings (60%) for the members of Congress from their districts. Individual members of Congress are seen as working for their constituents, but Congress as a whole supposedly represents the nation as a whole. These seemingly contradictory expectations create different pressures on members of Congress.

Americans elect their senators and representatives. This direct link between the legislature and the people is a very important part of our democracy. Should Congress, then, reflect the will of the people? Or should they pay attention to their own points of view, even if they disagree with their constituents? Many considerations influence the voting patterns of members of Congress, including the following:

- **Constituents' Views.** Members of Congress often visit their home districts and states to keep in touch with their constituents' views. They also read their mail, keep in touch with local and state political leaders, and meet with their constituents in Washington. Some pay more attention than others, but they all have to consider the views of the folks back home.

- **Party Views.** Congress is organized primarily along party lines, so party membership is an important determinant of a member's vote. Each party develops its own versions of many important bills, and party leaders actively pressure members to vote according to party views. It is not surprising that representatives and senators vote along party lines about three-fourths of the time.

- **Personal Views.** What if a representative or senator seriously disagrees with the views of his constituents on a particular issue? How should he or she vote? Those who believe that personal views are most important argue that the people vote for candidates who they think have good judgment. Representatives should feel free to exercise their own personal views. After all, if the people are unhappy, they can always vote them out of office.

CONGRESS IN THE CONSTITUTION

At its creation in 1789 the legislative branch was a unique invention. Rule by kings and emperors was an old style of government, and the legislature in many ways represented the new. Almost certainly, the founders intended that Congress have more important powers than they granted to the president and the judiciary. However, they placed many checks and balances on the legislature that have shaped what we have today. They controlled power not only by checks from the other branches, but also by creating a **bicameral (two-house) Congress** – the Senate and the House of Representatives. The powers of Congress are both constitutional and evolutionary.

THE STRUCTURE OF CONGRESS

Originally, the Constitution provided for members of the House of Representatives to be elected directly by the people and the Senate to be chosen by the legislatures of each state. The membership of the House was based on population with larger states having more representatives, and the Senate was to have equal representation, two senators per state. In 1913 the 17th amendment provided for direct election of senators.

A representative was required to be 25 years old, seven years a citizen of the United States, and a citizen of the state represented. A representative's term was set at two years. A senator served a six-year term and was to be at least 30 years old, nine years a citizen, and a citizen of the state represented. The number of terms either representatives or senators could serve was not limited. The original number of representatives was 65; in 1911, the size was limited to 435. These 435 representatives are reapportioned among the states every ten years after the census is taken.

CONSTITUTIONAL POWERS

The powers of Congress are defined in Article I, section 8 of the Constitution:

- To lay and collect taxes, duties, imports, and excises
- To borrow money
- To regulate commerce with foreign nations and among the states
- To establish rules for naturalization and bankruptcy
- To coin money
- To fix the standard of weights and measures
- To establish a post office and post roads
- To issue patents and copyrights

- To create courts (other than the Supreme Court)
- To define and punish piracies
- To declare war
- To raise and support an army and navy
- To provide for a militia
- To exercise exclusive legislative powers over the District of Columbia and other federal facilities

In addition, the **"elastic" clause** (also called the "necessary and proper" clause) allowed the government to "make all laws which shall be necessary and proper for carrying into execution the foregoing powers, and all other powers vested by this Constitution in the government of the United States."

The Constitution also gives each house of Congress some special, exclusive powers. Such powers given to the House of Representatives are:

- **Revenue bills** must originate in the House of Representatives. Although this power is still honored today, it tends to have blurred over the years. Often tax bills are considered simultaneously in both houses, and tax policy has also become a major initiative of the president.

- **Impeachment power,** the authority to charge the president, vice president, and other "civil officers" with "high crimes and misdemeanors" is given to the House. The Senate conducts trials for impeachment, but only the House may make the charge.

Special, exclusive powers given to the Senate are:

- **Major presidential appointments** must be confirmed by the Senate. The Senate offers "advice and consent" to the president by a majority vote regarding the appointments of federal judges, ambassadors, and Cabinet positions.

- **Treaties with other nations** entered into by the president must be approved by a two-thirds vote of the Senate. This provision is an illustration of checks and balances, and it has served as a very important restriction to foreign policy powers of the American president.

Important Constitutional Differences between the House and the Senate	
House	**Senate**
Initiates all revenue bills	Must confirm many major presidential appointments
Initiates impeachment procedures and passes articles of impeachment	Tries impeachment charges against officials
Two-year terms	Six-year terms (One-third up for reelection every two years)
435 members (apportioned by population)	100 members (two from each state)
Members at least 25 years of age, 7 years a citizen	Senators at least 30 years of age, 9 years a citizen
Chooses the president if no candidate reaches a majority of Electoral College votes.	Chooses the vice president if no candidate reaches a majority of the Electoral College votes.
	Approves treaties

EVOLUTIONARY POWERS

The "elastic" (or "necessary and proper" clause) gives Congress the authority to pass laws it deems "necessary and proper" to carry out its enumerated functions. Many congressional powers that have evolved over the years are based on this important clause.

Two important evolutionary powers are:

- **Oversight of the budget.** Congress reviews and restricts the annual budget prepared by the executive branch. When a law is passed setting up a government program, Congress must pass an **authorization** bill that states the maximum amount of money available. When the nation's budget is set, only Congress can set the **appropriations** – the actual amount available in a fiscal year – for each program that it has authorized.

- **Investigation.** Congress may investigate both issues that warrant study and wrong doings by public officials. Through committee hearings, Congress has examined issues such as crime, consumer safety, health care, and foreign trade. Although Congress must abide by protected individual rights, their committees have examined many allegations against elected officials. Famous recent investigations include the Watergate and the Clinton-Lewinsky hearings.

LEADERSHIP

Political parties are very important in both the House of Representatives and the Senate today. Even though political parties don't play as big a role in elections as they once did, they still provide the basic organization of leadership in Congress.

After each legislative election the party that wins the most representatives is designated the "**majority**" in each house, and the other party is called the "**minority**." Usually, the same party holds both houses, but occasionally they are split. For example, from 1983 to 1985, the House majority was Democratic and the Senate majority was Republican. The split happened again in 2001, when an evenly-divided Senate became Democratic when Senator Jim Jeffords dropped his affiliation with the Republican Party to become an independent. The Republicans regained control of both houses in 2002 and retained it in 2004. However, in 2006 the Democrats took control of both the House and Senate for the first time since the 103rd Congress ended in 1995. These designations are important because the majority party holds the most significant leadership positions.

LEADERSHIP IN THE HOUSE OF REPRESENTATIVES

The **Speaker of the House** is the most important leadership position in the House. This office is provided for in the Constitution, and even though it says, "The House of Representatives shall choose their Speaker and other Officers," in truth the majority party does the choosing. Before each Congress convenes the majority party selects its candidate, who almost always is the person selected. The Speaker typically has held other leadership positions and is a senior member of the party. Around the turn of the century, the Speaker was all-powerful, especially under the leadership of Joe Cannon and Thomas Reed. A revolt by the membership in 1910 gave some of the Speaker's powers to committees, but the Speaker still has some important powers:

- recognizing members who wish to speak
- ruling on questions of parliamentary procedure
- appointing members to select and conference committees
- directing business on the floor
- exercising political and behind-the-scenes influence
- appointing members of the committees who appoint members to standing committees
- exercising substantial control over which bills get assigned to which committees
- appointing the party's legislative leaders

The Speaker's most important colleague is the **majority leader**, whose position is often a stepping-stone to the Speaker's position. The majority leader is responsible for scheduling bills and for rounding up votes for bills the party favors. The 110th (2007-2009) Congress is notable for choosing Nancy Pelosi, a Democrat from California, as the first woman Speaker of the House. Ms. Pelosi is the first woman to serve in a leadership position in either chamber of Congress.

The **minority leader** is the spokesperson for the minority party, and usually steps into the position of Speaker when and if his or her party gains a majority in the House. Assisting each floor leader are the **party whips**, who serve as go-betweens for the members and the leadership. They inform members when important bills will come up for a vote, do nose-counts for the leadership, and pressure members to support the leadership.

LEADERSHIP IN THE SENATE

The Senate is characterized by its highest positions actually having very little power. By Constitutional provision, the **president of the Senate** is the vice-president of the United States. A vice-president can vote only in case of a tie and seldom attends Senate sessions. The Senate selects from among the majority party a largely ceremonial *president pro tempore*, usually the most senior member in the party. The *president pro tempore* is the official chair, but since the job has no real powers, the job of presiding over the Senate is usually given to a junior senator.

The real leaders of the Senate are the **majority leader** and the **minority leader**. The Senate majority leader is often the most influential person in the Senate, and has the right to be the first senator heard on the floor. The majority leader determines the Senate's agenda and usually has much to say about committee assignments. The majority leader may consult with the minority leader in setting the agenda, but the minority leader generally only has as much say as the majority leader is willing to allow. The Senate also has **party whips** that serve much the same functions as they serve in the House.

COMMITTEES AND SUBCOMMITTEES: CONGRESS AT WORK

Most of the real work of Congress goes on in committees and subcommittees. Bills are worked out or killed in committees, and committees investigate problems and oversee the executive branch.

TYPES OF COMMITTEES

There are four types of committees:

- **Standing committees** are the most important type because they handle bills in different policy areas, thus shaping legislation at a very critical point. The Senate and the House have separate standing committees: the Senate currently has 20 and the House has 22. The numbers may fluctuate slightly, but they tend to "stand" for a long time.
- **Select committees** are formed for specific purposes and are usually temporary. A famous example is the select committee that investigated the Watergate scandal. Other select committees, like the Select Committee on Aging and the Select Committee on Indian Affairs, have existed for a number of years and actually produce legislation. Sometimes long-standing select committees eventually become standing committees.

- **Joint committees** are similar in purpose to select committees, but they consist of members from both the House and Senate. They are set up to conduct business between the houses and to help focus public attention on major issues. They investigate issues like the Iran-Contra affair in the 1980s, and they oversee institutions such as the Library of Congress.

Examples of Joint Committees

Printing – oversee the government printing office.
Economic – review economic conditions and make recommendations.
Taxation – review the operation and effects of internal taxes, study
taxation simplification, review proposed refunds or credit of taxes.

- **Conference committees** also consist of members from both the House and Senate, but they are formed exclusively to hammer out differences between House and Senate versions of similar bills. A bill goes to a conference committee after it has been approved in separate processes in the two houses, and a compromise bill is sent back to each house for final approval.

STANDING COMMITTEES	
House Committees	**Senate Committees**
Agriculture	Aging
Appropriations	Agriculture, Nutrition and Forestry
Armed Services	Appropriations
Budget	Armed Services
Education and Labor	Banking, Housing and Urban Affairs
Energy and Commerce	Budget
Energy Independence and Global Warming	Commerce, Science and Transportation
Financial Service	Energy and Natural Resources
Foreign Affairs	Environment and Public Works
Oversight and Government Reform	Ethics
Homeland Security	Finance
House Administration	Foreign Relations
Intelligence	Health, Education, Labor and Pensions
Judiciary	Homeland Security and Governmental Affairs
Natural Resources	Indian Affairs
Rules	Intelligence
Science and Technology	Judiciary
Small Business	Rules and Administration
Standards of Official Conduct	Small Business and Entrepreneurship
Transportation and Infrastructure	Veterans Affairs
Veterans Affairs	
Ways and Means	

THE WORK OF COMMITTEES

More than 11,000 bills are introduced in the House and Senate over the two-year life span of a Congress, and all of them cannot possibly be considered by the full memberships. Each bill is submitted to a committee that has life or death control over its future. The majority of bills are **pigeonholed,** or forgotten for weeks or forever, and never make it out of committee. They are submitted to a subcommittee that will discuss them and possibly hold hearings for them. About 3000 **staff members assists** the various committees and subcommittees, conducting research and administrative and clerical work. Supporters and critics of the bill appear at the hearings and are questioned by subcommittee members.

The bills that survive this far into the process are then **marked up** (changed or rewritten) and returned to the full committee where they may be altered further. If the committee approves a bill, it will then be sent first to the Rules Committee in the House, and then to the floor. The bill is sent directly to the floor in the Senate.

COMMITTEE MEMBERSHIP

Committee membership is controlled by the parties, primarily by the majority party. The chairman and a majority of each standing committee come from the majority party. The remaining committee members are from the minority party, but they are always a minority on the committee. In the House of Representatives, a Committee on Committees places Republicans on committees, and the Steering and Policy Committee selects the Democrats. In the Senate, each party has a small Steering Committee that makes committee assignments. Assignments are based on the personal and political qualities of the member, his or her region, and whether the assignment will help reelect the member.

Getting on the right committee is very important to most members of Congress. A member from a "safe" district whose reelection is secure may want to serve on an important committee that promotes a power base in Washington. On the other hand, a member who has few ambitions beyond his or her current position and whose reelection is less secure may want to serve on a committee that suits the needs of constituents. For example, a less secure representative from rural Kansas may prefer to serve on the Agriculture Committee.

COMMITTEE CHAIRMEN

Committee chairmen are the most important shapers of the committee agenda. Their positions were made more powerful in the House by the 1910 revolt, which transferred power from the Speaker to the chairmen. From 1910 until the early 1970s, chairmen were strictly chosen by the **seniority system**, in which the member with the longest continuous service on the committee was placed automatically in the chairmanship. In the early 1970s, the House decided to elect committee chairmen by secret ballots from all the majority members. As a result, several committee chairmen were removed, and although most chairmen still get their positions through seniority, it is possible to be removed or overlooked.

THE RULES COMMITTEE IN THE HOUSE

The Rules Committee in the House of Representatives plays a key role in shaping legislation because it sets very important rules for debate when the bill is presented to the House after it leaves the committee.

- A **closed rule** (sometimes called a "gag rule) sets strict time limits on debates and forbids amendments from the floor, except those from the presenting committee. Under closed rule, members not on the committee have little choice but to vote for or against the bill as it is.

- An **open rule** permits amendments and often has less strict time limits, allowing for input from other members. The Rules Committee is controlled by the Speaker, and in recent years, it has put more and more restrictions on bills, giving Rules even more power.

CAUCUSES

Although Congress is organized formally through its party leadership and committee system, equally important is the informal network of **caucuses**, groupings of members of Congress sharing the same interests or points of view. There are currently more than one hundred of these groups, and their goal is to shape the agenda of Congress, which they do by elevating their issues or interests to a prominent place in the daily workings of Congress. Caucus members keep track of legislation important to the caucus, gain information on the issues, and leadership experience by participating in caucuses. Members are also better able to explain their positions on bills that affect their constituents.

Some caucuses are regionally based, such as the Conservative Democratic Forum (also known as the Boll Weevils because they are mostly from the South), the Sunbelt Caucus, and the Northeast-Midwest Congressional Coalition. Others share racial, ethnic, or gender characteristics, such as the Congressional Black Caucus, Native American Caucus or the Women's Caucus. One of the oldest is an intra-party caucus called the Democratic Study Group which encourages unity among liberal Democrats. However, the "Blue Dog Democrats" formed in 1995 (formal name is the Coalition) is made up of moderate-to-conservative Democrats who prefer more moderate policies on issues such as welfare and the budget. Other caucuses share specialized interests, such as the Steel Caucus, Textile Caucus and the Mushroom Caucus.

Within Congress caucuses press for committees to hold hearings, and they organize votes on bills they favor. Caucuses also pressure agencies within the bureaucracy to act according to their interests of the caucus. As such, caucuses will continue as congressional institutions due to the help they provide for members to achieve policy goals and serve their constituents.

STAFF

More than 30,000 people work in paid bureaucratic positions for Congress. About half of them serve as personal staff for members of Congress or as committee staff members. The personal staff includes professionals that manage the member's time, draft legislation, and deal with media and constituents. Staffers also must maintain local offices in the member's home district or state. The average Senate office employs about thirty staff members, but senators from the most populous states commonly employ more. House office staffs are usually about half as large as those of the Senate. Overall, the number of staff members has increased dramatically since 1960.

STAFF AGENCIES

In addition to personal and committee staffers Congress has three important staff agencies that help in its work. They are:

Congressional Research Service (CRS) – Administered by the Library of Congress since 1914, the CRS responds to requests for information and supplies nonpartisan studies. It develops summaries of bills, tracks the progress of major bills and makes this information available to members of Congress. As a politically neutral body, it does not pursue policy recommendations but instead researches facts and provides arguments both for and against proposed policies.

General Accounting Office (GAO) – Created in 1921 the GAO's original purpose was to complete financial audits of money spent by the executive branch departments. The role of the GAO has expanded today to include investigations of agencies and policies to be sure that the legislative intent of laws is being followed. It is also to investigate policy effectiveness.

Congressional Budget Office (CBO) – Since 1974 the CBO advises Congress on the possible economic effects of various spending programs and policies. It also analyzes the president's budget and makes economic projections about the performance of the economy. Congress is aided with information to use in debates over the budget and other financial issues.

WHO IS IN CONGRESS?

Members of Congress are far from typical Americans, but they have a number of characteristics in common:

- 90% are male.
- Most are well educated.
- Most are from upper-middle or upper income backgrounds.
- Most are Protestants, although in recent years, a more proportional number have been Roman Catholic and Jewish. A Muslim and two Buddhists were elected in 2006.
- Most are white, with only a handful of African Americans, Asian Americans, Hispanics, and Native Americans
- The average age of senators is about 60; representative average about 55.
- 40% are lawyers; others are business owners or officers, professors and teachers, clergy, and farmers.

The fact that members of Congress represent privileged Americans is controversial. Some argue that the composition of Congress does not provide adequate representation for ordinary Americans. Others believe that a group of demographically average Americans would have difficulty making major policy decisions and that elites can represent people who have different personal characteristics from themselves.

It is important to note that Congress has gradually become less male and less white. Between 1950 and 2005 the number of women senators rose from 2 to 14, and female representatives have increased from 10 to 68. In 2006 a record number of 90 women were elected to the 110th Congress (74 in the House and 16 in the Senate). There were 40 black representatives in the 109th Congress (2005-2007), as compared to 2 in the 82nd (1951-53). Although there was only one black senator in the 109th and 110th Congress there were none in the 82nd Congress. The number of Hispanics increased slightly from the 109th to the 110th Congress. The House went from 23 to 26 Hispanics, while the Senate went from 2 to 3 Hispanic members.

The 110th Congress demonstrated characteristics of elitism while also representing average Americans. Higher education was evident with almost 400 members holding bachelor degrees, 124 with master's degrees and 22 with doctoral degrees. 236 members had law degrees. Four members were graduates of the U.S. Military Academies while two senators were Rhodes Scholars. However, in the same Congress were carpenters, bank tellers, a furniture salesman, a waitress, a paper mill worker, a taxicab driver and a river boat captain among others.

Just as a record number of women were a part of the 110th Congress, 2007- 2009, religious ground was also broken as two Buddhists and one Muslim were elected. They joined various Protestant denominations, Roman Catholic (the largest single religious group), Jewish, Quaker, Greek Orthodox, and Christian Scientist religious groups.

While the 110th Congress demonstrates that members of Congress are still likely to have law degrees, it does indicate some change. Acceptance of minorities and those with different theological views is evident. It also demonstrates that people from different backgrounds are attracted to public service by serving in Congress.

The 111th Congress (2009-2011) results indicate continued acceptance of minorities as women, blacks, and Hispanics either made slight gains or remained stable in the number serving in Congress. Women increased to 95 members (78 in the House and 17 in the Senate), and Hispanics increased to 31 members (28 in the House and 3 in the Senate). The number of African American members remained stable with 40 members (39 in the House and 1 in the Senate). Religious diversity continued in the 111th Congress much as it was in the 110th Congress with one slight change; 2 Muslims were elected, increasing the number of Muslim members by one. Higher education was again evident in the 111th Congress with 95% of the members holding a university degree or higher. Only 27 representatives and 1 senator had degrees no higher than a high school diploma.

CONGRESSIONAL DIVERSITY

Diversity is seen by many scholars as helping Congress represent the different issues important to all Americans. Health issues, economic and educational opportunities along with cultural diversity are some of the areas that diversity in Congress would help to address. Federal help in combating sickle cell anemia, breast cancer and fetal alcohol syndrome are some health areas that were promoted by members of Congress representing minorities. Senator Ben Nighthorse Campbell, Colorado, has been instrumental in promoting cultural issues of Native Americans. He served in the U. S. House of Representatives from 1987 – 1993 and in the Senate from 1993 – 2005. For some of that time he was the only Native American serving in the U.S. Congress. He sponsored legislation renaming Custer Battlefield National Monument to Little Bighorn Battlefield National Monument to honor all those who fought there, including Native Americans. He also was instrumental in establishing the National Museum of American Indians within the Smithsonian.

While it is evident that members of Congress who are not members of a minority or a particular religious group must relate to these concerns in order to be elected, the presence of minorities has provided a forum for ideas and debate. By forming caucuses and promoting legislation, minority groups have demonstrated an important presence in Congress.

INCUMBENTS

During the 1800s most members of Congress served only one term, returning home to their careers when they completed their service. During the 20th century, serving in Congress has become a lifetime career for most members, and the number of incumbents, or those who already hold the office, with secure seats has increased dramatically.

Scholars do not agree on all the reasons for the incumbency trend. Some believe that with fewer voters strongly attached to parties, people are voting for individuals, not for candidates because they are Democrats or Republicans. Incumbents have more name recognition than challengers; therefore they are more likely to be elected. Incumbents enjoy free mailings (called the **franking privilege**), more experience with campaigning, and greater access to the media. They also raise campaign money more easily than challengers because lobbyists and political action committees seek their favors. Today $8 of every $10 of PAC money is given to incumbents.

In spite of their advantages incumbents can be vulnerable in elections. Some may be naïve about their campaigns and take re-election for granted. Scandal or corruption may also take its toll on a long-time member of Congress as angry voters may take out their frustration during elections. The check-cashing scandal where many members of Congress were bouncing checks at the House bank caused a number of incumbents to lose their seats in 1992. Negative publicity indicating a sense of entitlement may cause members to lose their job.

Incumbents may also be redistricted out of their districts. Another party or rival faction of a party may take control of the state and want to remove the member from Congress. This forces incumbents out of familiar territory and constituents causing them to be vulnerable in the next election. This problem may be overcome with a good reputation and attention to constituent service, but it is also an effective way to challenge an incumbent.

National political changes may also make an incumbent vulnerable at election time. In 1994 public mood turned against Democratic incumbents. It caused 34 in the House and 2 in the Senate to lose their seats. As a result, Republicans took control of both houses and Newt Gingrich became Speaker of the House. This happened again in 2006 but against the Republican majority. Once again, enough seats changed so that Democrats were able to take a slight majority in both houses.

One way to control the incumbency advantage is the idea of Congressional **term limits.** Reformers in the 1980s grew concerned about the incumbency problem but the idea finally caught on with the Republican **Contract with America,** which made Congressional term limits one of its goals. However, since a Constitutional amendment is necessary it was difficult to accomplish. Although some states imposed term limitations on state legislatures, the Supreme Court ruled in *U.S. Term Limits, Inc. et al. v Thornton et al.* (1995) that state-imposed limits on members of Congress were unconstitutional.

REPRESENTATION

For many years, any state with more than one representative has elected their representatives from single-member districts. Two problems emerge from single-member districting:

- **malapportionment** – For many years states often drew districts of unequal sizes and populations. As a result, some citizens had better access to their representatives than others did. After the Supreme Court ruling in *Baker v Carr* in 1962 which permitted voters to challenge the constitutionality of voting districts in the courts, the problem was addressed by the Supreme Court in the 1964 case, *Wesberry v. Sanders*. In *Wesberry* the Court ordered that districts be drawn so that one person's vote would be as equal as possible to another (the "one man one vote" decision).

- **gerrymandering** – This common practice was originally meant to give one political party an advantage over the other. District boundaries are drawn in strange ways in order to make it easy for the candidate of one party to win election in that district). The term "gerrymandering" is derived from the original gerrymanderer, Eldrige Gerry, who had a Massachusetts district drawn in the shape of a salamander, to ensure the election of a Republican. Over the years both parties have been accused of manipulating districts in order to gain an advantage in membership in the House.

MINORITY/MAJORITY DISTRICTING

Gerrymandering continues to be an issue today. A more recent form that appeared shortly after the 1990 census is **minority/majority districting**, or rearranging districts to allow a minority representative to be elected, is just as controversial as the old style party gerrymandering. The Justice Department ordered North Carolina's 12th district to redraw their proposed boundaries in order to allow for the election of one more black representative. This action resulted in a Supreme Court case, *Shaw v. Reno* (1993), with the plaintiffs charging the Justice Department with reverse discrimination based on the equal protection clause of the 14th Amendment. The Court ruled narrowly, but allowed the district lines to be redrawn according to Justice Department standards.

During the 1990s several cases were brought to the Supreme Court regarding racial gerrymandering. The Court ruled in ***Easley v. Cromartie*** (2001) that race may be a factor in redistricting, but not the "dominant and controlling" one. An important result of the various decisions has been a substantial increase in the number of black and Latino representatives in the House.

After the census every 10 years, states redraw lines which often become controversial, particularly those that gained or lost seats due to the population adjustment. After the 2000 census, Texas, having gained two seats, was one of those states. But in 2003 the Texas legislature drew new district lines again resulting in **mid-decade redistricting**. The reason was to better reflect the increase of Republican voters indicated by the voting results in 2000 and 2002. This second redistricting was challenged and reviewed by the Supreme Court in *League of United Latin American Citizens et al. v Perry, Governor of Texas* (2007). The Court ruled that the mid-decade redistricting plan did not violate the Constitution. It stated that nothing in the Constitution prevented the state from redrawing its electoral boundaries as many times as it wanted so long as it did so at least once every ten years. However, the Court ruled that the districts were drawn in a way to deny Latino voters as a group the opportunity to elect a candidate of their choosing. As such it was a violation of the Voting Rights Act.

HOW A BILL BECOMES A LAW

Creating legislation is what the business of Congress is all about. Ideas for laws come from many places – ordinary citizens, the president, offices of the executive branch, state legislatures and governors, congressional staff, and of course the members of Congress themselves. Constitutional provisions, whose primary purposes are to create obstacles, govern the process that a bill goes through before it becomes law. The founders believed that efficiency was the hallmark of oppressive government, and they wanted to be sure that laws that actually passed all the hurdles were the well-considered result of inspection by many eyes.

Similar versions of bills often are introduced in the House and the Senate at approximately the same time, especially if the issues they address are considered to be important. The vast majority of bills never make it out of committee, and those that survive have a complex obstacle course to run before they become laws.

INTRODUCTION OF A BILL

Every bill must be introduced in the House and Senate by a member of that body. Any member of the House simply may hand a bill to a clerk or drop it in a "hopper". In the Senate the presiding officer must recognize the member and announce the bill's introduction. House bills bear the prefix "H.R.", and Senate bills begin with the prefix "S." If a bill is not passed by both houses and signed by the president within the life of one Congress, it is dead and must be presented again during the next Congress.

In addition to bills Congress can pass **resolutions**, which come in several types:

- A **simple resolution** is passed by either the House or the Senate, and usually establishes rules, regulations, or practices that do not have the force of law. For example, a resolution may be passed congratulating a staff member for doing a good job or having an anniversary. Sometimes simple resolutions set the rules under which each body operates.
- A **concurrent resolution** comes from both houses, and often settles housekeeping and procedural matters that affect both houses. Simple and concurrent resolutions are not signed by the president and do not have the force of law.
- A **joint resolution** requires the approval of both houses and the signature of the president, and is essentially the same as a law. Joint resolutions are sometimes passed when the houses of Congress react to an important issue that needs immediate attention. For example, after the terrorist attacks on New York and Washington on September 11, 2001, Congress passed a joint resolution condemning the attacks and authorizing President George. W. Bush to take preliminary military actions.

BILLS IN COMMITTEE

After introduction, a bill is referred to committee, whether in the House or the Senate. The Constitution requires that "all bills for raising revenue shall originate in the House of Representative," but the Senate can amend bills almost beyond recognition. However, because of this special power, the committee in the House that handles revenue legislation – the Ways and Means – is particularly powerful.

In the past if a bill needed to be considered by several groups it would be submitted to several committees at once in a process known as **multiple referral**. However, this proved to slow down the bill process even more. It was difficult for committees to meet and iron out problems and also provided many ways for opponents to stop the bill. Since 1995 this has been replaced in the House with a **sequential referral**. As a result the Speaker may send the bill to another committee once one has completed its work. Parts of the bill may also be referred to separate committees. So far this process has not delayed the progress of bills.

An important role of subcommittees is conducting public hearings. Through witnesses' testimony and evidence obtained, members of Congress gain important expertise while interested groups are able to speak out on issues.

Most bills die in committee, especially if they are only introduced to satisfy constituents or get publicity for the member of Congress that introduces it. In the House a **discharge petition** may be signed by 218 members to bring it to the floor, but the vast majority of bills are referred to the floor only after committee recommendation.

CALENDARS

For a bill to come before either house, it must first be placed on a calendar: five in the House, and two in the Senate.

The Congressional Calendars are as follows:

House

- **Union Calendar** – Bills to raise revenue or spend money
- **House Calendar** – Nonmoney bills of major importance
- **Private Calendar** – Private bills that do not affect the general welfare
- **Consent Calendar** – Noncontroversial bills
- **Discharge Calendar** – Discharge petitions

Senate

- **Executive calendar** – Presidential nominations, proposed treaties
- **Calendar of Business** – All legislation

Before a bill can go to the floor in the House of Representatives, it must first go to the Rules Committee that sets time limits and amendment regulations for the debate. Bills in the Senate go straight from committee to the floor.

FLOOR DEBATE

Important bills in the House, including all bills of revenue, must first be referred to a **Committee of the Whole** that sits on the floor, but is directed by the chairman of the sponsoring committee. The quorum is not the usual 218 members, but 100 members, and the debate is conducted by the committee chairman. Sometimes bills are significantly altered, but usually the bill goes to the full floor, where the Speaker presides, and debate is guided by more formal rules. The bills are not changed drastically, largely because many are debated under closed rules. If amendments are allowed, they must be **germane,** or relevant to the topic of the bill.

Bills in the Senate go directly to the floor where they are debated much less formally than in the House. Senators may speak for as long as they wish, which leads more and more frequently to a **filibuster**, the practice of talking a bill to death. Although one-man filibusters are dramatic, usually several senators who oppose a bill will agree together to block legislation through delay tactics, such as having the roll called over and over again. A filibuster may be stopped by a **cloture**, in which three-fifths of the entire Senate membership must vote to stop debate. For example, Democratic senators have filibustered several of Republican President George W. Bush's nominees to the judiciary, resulting in those judgeships going unfilled. No limit exists on amendments, so riders, or non-germane provisions, are often added to bills from the floor. A bill with many riders is known as a **Christmas-tree bill**, and usually occurs because individual senators are trying to attach their favorite ideas or benefits to their states.

VOTING

Voting is also more formal in the House than in the Senate. House members may vote according to several procedures:

- **teller vote**, in which members file past the clerk, first the "yeas" and then the "nays."
- **voice vote,** in which they simply shout "yea" or "nay".
- **division vote**, in which members stand to be counted.
- **roll call vote** which consists of people answering "yea" or "nay" to their names. A roll call vote can be called for by one-fifth of the House membership.
- **electronic voting**, that permits each members to insert a plastic card in a slot to record his or her vote. This form is the most commonly one today.

The Senate basically votes in the same ways, but it does not have an electronic voting system.

CONFERENCE COMMITTEE ACTION

If a bill is passed by one house and not the other, it dies. If a bill is not approved by both houses before the end of a congressional session, it must begin all over again in the next session if it is to be passed at all. When the House and the Senate cannot resolve similar bills through informal agreements, the two versions of the bill must go to **conference committee**, whose members are selected from both the House and the Senate. Compromise versions are sent back to each chamber for final approval.

PRESIDENTIAL ACTION

A bill approved by both houses is sent to the president who can either sign or **veto** it. If the president vetoes it, the veto may be overridden by two-thirds of both houses. The president has ten days to act on a proposed piece of legislation. If he receives a bill within ten days of the adjournment of the congressional session, he may simply not respond and the bill will die. This practice is called a **pocket veto**.

The **line-item veto** permits executives to veto sections of a bill that are objectionable to them. Congress gave this authority to President Clinton, but the law was ruled unconstitutional by the *Supreme Court in Clinton v City of New York* (1998). The court ruled that this power was only permissible through a constitutional amendment. However, the use of **signing statements** has been a way for presidents to qualify approval of a law. The president's signing statements can be used for positive or negative comments concerning the law. Presidents have also used this method to state that a part or parts of the bill are unconstitutional and, therefore, will not be enforced. Signing statements are not new since they have been used by presidents dating back to James Monroe. The use of them has, however, increased in recent administrations with President Clinton using them in over 300 instances and President Bush over 150 times. President Bush's use of signing statements became a point of controversy over the extent of executive power under the

Patriot Act. In reauthorizing the Patriot Act, Congress included more oversight of executive action with regard to expanded police powers. President Bush included a signing statement indicating that this oversight would intrude on his constitutional executive power.

CRITICISMS OF CONGRESS

Congress is criticized for many things, but these practices are particularly controversial:

PORK-BARREL LEGISLATION/LOGROLLING/EARMARKS

By the 1870s members of Congress were using the term **"pork"** to refer to benefits for their districts, and bills that give those benefits to constituents in hope of gaining their votes were called pork barrel legislation. The term comes from the pre-Civil War days when it was the custom in the South to take salt pork from barrels and distribute it among the slaves, who would often rush on the barrels. Critics point out that such actions do not insure that federal money goes to the places where it is most needed, but to districts whose representatives are most aggressive or most in need of votes. A particularly controversial example was the mammoth **2005 Consolidated Appropriations Act**, which funded about 11,000 projects, from building a Civil War Theme Park, renovating and building museums and health care facilities, constructing several different halls of fame, and funding community swimming pools and parking garages. The act was criticized largely because so much of the money went to constituencies well represented on the Appropriations Committees in Congress.

In 2005 Congress also passed the Transportation Equity Act that resulted in a controversial project known as the **"Bridge to Nowhere"**. It was a project to provide a bridge for a small city in Alaska (about 9000 residents) to an island (about 50 residents) where the airport was located. Criticisms ranged from the cost of the project (approximately $200 million), the small number of people immediately impacted, to the fact that a ferry service already existed. The timing of the project also proved problematic as damage costs to aid the city of New Orleans after Hurricane Katrina became evident. Although the governor of Alaska eventually refused federal funding for the bridge, the term, "Bridge to Nowhere" has since become symbolic of the financial irresponsibility of pork projects.

Logrolling occurs when a member of Congress supports another member's pet project in return for support for his or her own project. The term comes from pioneer days when neighbors would get together to roll logs from recently cleared property to make way for building houses. This "cooperation" occurs in Congress in the form of "you scratch my back, I'll scratch yours." As with **pork barrel legislation**, bills may be passed for frivolous reasons.

An **earmark** is any part of a spending bill that provides money for a specific project, location or institution. For instance, an appropriations bill may provide funding for the National Park Service. It becomes an earmark when a portion of that spending is set aside (or earmarked) for a particular project such as increasing or improving campsites in a particular park. Once approved the money earmarked must be used for the project specified in the law. Earmarks become controversial when they are **hidden earmarks**. which are inserted in committee reports sent back to Congress with the final bill. Since they are not in the official language of the bill, hidden earmarks are not voted on by Congress. Members of Congress can insert specific projects for their own district as hidden earmarks making them similar to pork. Once the bill becomes law, bureaucracies feel obligated to enforce the hidden earmarks, or they may suffer a reduction in funding during the next budget cycle.

Legislative earmarks are not new. Whenever appropriations bills are passed, both general and specific spending is usually included. For instance, Department of Defense appropriations include spending for new materials but also may include the amount of money to be spent on a specific jet fighter and where the jet fighter parts will be made. These are similar to pork projects since members of Congress ensure that specific projects are sent to their districts. Executive earmarks may also be included by the president for his special projects.

Although pork legislation has been around for a long time, public profile of earmarks has increased in the past decade in a negative way. President Bush ordered all federal agencies to ignore earmarks that were not voted on by Congress or not specified in the law. He also threatened to veto appropriations bills if earmarks overall were not seriously reduced. The Supreme Court also ruled that "language contained in committee reports is not legally binding." (*Cherokee Nation v Leavitt*, 2005) The reason for all of this attention is probably due to the increase in the number of earmarks. In 1995 there were approximately 1,400 earmarks but by 2005 there were close to 14,000. However, in spite of their negative features, many earmarks have been used for positive programs such as crime prevention, substance abuse, mental health and child abuse programs. Those promoting earmark reform are more focused on the hidden element of the process, with reformers demanding more transparency.

THE TERM-LIMITS DEBATE

The Constitution imposes no limits on the number of terms members of Congress can serve. Just as an amendment was passed during the 1950s to limit the term numbers of presidents, many argue that terms of members of Congress should be limited as well.

With the growing prevalence of incumbency, supporters of term limits believe that popular control of Congress has weakened and that members may become dictatorial or unresponsive to their constituents. They point out that the framers envisioned that elected representatives would fulfill their civic duty and then retreat to private life. Others believe that the most experienced members would be forced to leave when their terms expire, leaving Congress without their expertise. The seniority system and methods of selecting party leaders would be seriously altered with questionable results. The demand for term limits grew during the 1990s under House Speaker Newt Gingrich's leadership, but Congress did not vote to impose them. While many Americans support a constitutional amendment to impose term limits on Congress, they appear conflicted on the issue since they continue to re-elect their own representative or senator.

INEFFICIENCY

Particularly in this age when gridlock often slows the legislative process, many people criticize Congress for inefficiency. Some believe that the long process that bills must go through in order to become laws does not work well in modern America. However, the process affirms the Constitutional design put in place by the founders. Their vision was that only well-reasoned bills become law and that many voices should contribute to the process. From that viewpoint, then, the nature of democratic discourse does not insure a smoothly running, efficient Congress, but rather one that resolves differences through discussion, argument, and the eventual shaping of legislation.

One reason for more recent Congressional inefficiency is **party polarization,** a growing distance between policy views of the average members of each party. This has made the legislative process more cumbersome since it is more difficult to reach a consensus. The extent of polarization between the two parties is most evident when debating the role of government and health issues.

IMPORTANT DEFINITIONS AND IDENTIFICATIONS:

- 2005 Consolidated Appropriations Act
- appropriation
- authorization
- bicameral
- *Baker v Carr*
- "Bridge to Nowhere"
- caucuses
- "Christmas-tree bill"
- closed rules, open rules
- cloture
- Committee of the Whole
- conference committees
- congressional calendars
- contract with America
- discharge petition
- earmarks
- *Easley v. Cromartie*
- "elastic clause"
- filibuster
- franking privilege
- germane amendments
- gerrymandering
- hidden earmarks
- incumbency
- joint committees
- *League of United Latin American Citizens et al. v Perry, Governor of Texas*
- line-item veto
- logrolling
- majority leader of the House
- majority leader of the Senate
- malapportionment
- marking up
- mid-decade redistricting
- minority leader of the House
- minority leader of the Senate
- minority/majority districting
- multiple referral
- oversight
- party polarization
- party whips
- pigeonholing
- pocket veto
- pork barrel legislation
- *president pro tempore*
- resolutions: simple, concurrent, joint
- revenue bills
- select committees
- seniority system
- sequential referral
- *Shaw v. Reno*
- signing statements
- Speaker of the House
- standing committees
- term limits
- veto
- votes: teller, voice, division, roll call, electronic
- *Wesberry v. Sanders*

CHAPTER ELEVEN
THE PRESIDENCY

When the founders created the three branches of the government, they disagreed about the amount of power to be vested in the executive. Many feared more than anything a strong president whose powers could be compared to those of the king of England. Others believed, in the words of Alexander Hamilton, that "energy in the executive is a leading characteristic of good government." As the modern presidency has evolved, Hamilton's point of view seems to prevail today, as the president is the single most powerful individual in the American political system. Although the checks and balances set in motion in 1787 still operate, the presidency described in the Constitution is much different from the one that we have today.

THE EVOLUTION OF THE PRESIDENCY

Constitutional provisions limited the early presidency, although the personalities of the first three presidents – George Washington, John Adams, and Thomas Jefferson – shaped it into an influential position by the early 1800s. However, all through the 1800s up until the 1930s, Congress was the dominant branch of the national government. Then, in the past seventy years or so, the balance of power has shifted dramatically, so that the executive branch currently has at least equal power to the legislative branch. How did this shift happen?

THE PRESIDENCY IN THE CONSTITUTION

Article II of the Constitution defines the qualifications, powers, and duties of the president and carefully notes some important checks of the executive branch by the legislature.

Qualifications

- The president must be a "natural-born citizen." Only individuals born as citizens may seek the presidency; all others are excluded from consideration. This provision has become controversial in recent years, with a movement backing California Governor Arnold Schwartznegger, a naturalized citizen, for president. Recent Secretaries of State Madeline Albright and Henry Kissinger were also unqualified for the presidency under this constitutional provision.
- The president must have lived in the United States for at least 14 years before his election, although the years don't have to be consecutive.
- The president must be at least 35 years old (in contrast to a minimum age of 30 for a senator and 25 for a representative). This provision has never been seriously challenged, since presidents tend to be considerably older than 35. The youngest presidents were Theodore Roosevelt and John F. Kennedy, who both took office at the age of 43.

Powers and Duties

The Constitutional powers and duties of the president are very limited. Those specifically granted are as follows:

According to Article II, Section One, the president holds "the executive power" of the United States. The "executive" was meant to "execute", or administer the decisions made by the legislature. This phrase at least implies an executive check on the legislature, and in fact, has been the source of presidential power over the years.

Military power

The president is **commander-in-chief** of the armed services. The intention of the founders was to keep control of the military in the hands of a civilian, avoiding a military tyranny. In Madison's words (Federalist No. 51), "Ambition must be made to counteract ambition." As commander-in-chief, the president has probably exercised more authority than in any other role. Although Congress has the sole power to declare war, the president can send the armed forces into a country in situations that are the equivalent of war. Congress has not officially declared war since December 8, 1941 (one day after the attack on Pearl Harbor), yet the country has fought in Korea, Vietnam, and the Middle East. Congress attempted to control such military activities when it passed the **War Powers Resolution** in 1973, requiring the president to consult with Congress when activating military troops. The president must report to Congress within forty-eight hours of deploying troops, and unless Congress approves the use of troops within sixty days or extends the sixty-day time limit, the forces must be withdrawn. Even so, the president's powers as commander-in-chief are more extensive today than they have ever been before. There is reason to believe that the Supreme Court would consider the law's use of the **legislative veto** (the ability of Congress to pass a resolution to override a presidential decision) to be a violation of the doctrine of separation of powers.

The advent of the nuclear age put more foreign policy decisions in the president's hands as he has staff, such as the Central Intelligence Agency and National Security Council, along with the ability to respond quickly to an emergency. From the Cuban Missile Crisis to the attack on the World Trade Center, Congress has deferred to the president in order to handle emergencies. However, Congress exerts itself periodically with its "power of the purse". By refusing or limiting funds Congress has the power to shorten or end military action, but Congress has been leery of using this power since it would cut funds to American soldiers, especially those in Iraq. Another power that Congress has to limit the president's military power is impeachment, but this has been used only twice in U.S. history. Although there have been threats to impeach President George W. Bush over the country's involvement in Iraq they have not gone far.

Since September 11, 2001 and the attack on the World Trade Center and the Pentagon, the increased military powers of the president have focused on national security. While not new (the Cuban Missile Crisis for one), the idea that another attack may be possible has enabled the president to assume more unilateral powers over the military as commander-in-chief. President George W. Bush issued the "Bush Doctrine" declaring that the United

States must be ready for "preemptive action" to defend itself. Statements such as these do not require Congressional approval as they are an expression of the executive's intentions.

Diplomatic power

The president makes treaties with foreign nations, but only with the **"advice and consent"** of the Senate. Two-thirds of the Senate must approve a treaty; a president's signature is not enough to make it binding. This provision is a check of the executive by the legislature. However, presidents have gotten around this provision by using **executive agreements** made between the president and other heads of state. Such agreements do not require Senate approval, although Congress may withhold funding to implement them. Whereas treaties are binding on future presidents, executive agreements are not. The Constitution also gives the president the power of **diplomatic recognition**, or the power to recognize foreign governments. When twentieth century presidents have withheld this recognition, it has often served as a powerful comment on the legitimacy of governments. For example, the U.S. did not recognize the Soviet government created in 1917 until the 1930s, nor did the president recognize the People's Republic of China (created in 1949) until the early 1970s.

Appointment power

The president appoints ambassadors, other public officers, and judges of the Supreme Court, but again, only with the **"advice and consent"** of the Senate. Two-thirds must confirm the appointments. The president may appoint many lower positions without Senate approval, but those positions are created and defined by Congress. The appointment power is generally limited to cabinet and subcabinet jobs, federal judgeships, agency heads, and about two thousand lesser jobs. Most government positions are filled by civil service employees, who compete for jobs through a merit system, so presidents have little say over them. Presidents generally have the power to remove executives from power, with a 1926 Supreme Court decision (***Myers v. United States***) affirming the president's ability to fire those executive-branch officials whom he appointed with Senate approval. Judges may be removed only through the impeachment process, so presidents have little power over them once they have been appointed.

Veto power

A president can veto a legislative bill by returning it, along with a veto message or explanation, within ten days to the house in which it originated. Congress in turn may override the veto by a two-thirds vote. The president may also exercise the **pocket veto**. If the president does not sign the bill within ten days and Congress has adjourned within that time, the bill will not become law. Of course, the pocket veto can only be used just before the term of a given Congress ends.

STRENGTHENING THE PRESIDENCY

From the very beginning, informal influences have shaped the presidency. The framers almost certainly fashioned the president in the image of George Washington, the man unanimously selected to first occupy the office. Washington's qualities of wisdom, moderation, and dignity defined the more formal duties and powers, and his nonpartisan attitudes created expectations for behavior in presidents that followed. Other strong presidents have contributed to the presidency as it exists today, such as Andrew Jackson, who first used the veto power extensively; Abraham Lincoln, who carried the meaning of "commander in chief" to new heights during the Civil War; and Franklin Roosevelt, who formulated sweeping New Deal policies that were finally checked by the Supreme Court. Many informal qualifications, powers, and duties of the president have evolved that are not mentioned in Article II of the Constitution.

Executive Privilege

The Constitution says nothing about presidential rights to keep private communications between himself and his principal advisers, but presidents have traditionally claimed the privilege of confidentiality – **executive privilege**. Their claim is based on two grounds:

- Separation of powers keeps one branch from inquiring into the internal workings of another branch.
- Presidents and advisers need the assurance of private discussions to be candid with one another without fear of immediate press and public reaction. This need for privacy is especially important with matters of national security.

Even though Congress has never liked executive privilege, the right was not questioned seriously until 1973 when the Supreme Court addressed the issue directly. As a part of the Watergate investigations, a federal prosecutor sought tape recordings of conversations between Richard Nixon and his advisers. Nixon refused to give the tapes over, claiming executive privilege. In *United States v. Nixon* the Court held that there is no "absolute unqualified presidential privilege of immunity from judicial process under all circumstances." In this case, executive privilege would have blocked the constitutionally defined function of federal courts to decide criminal cases.

Executive privilege has been further defined by *Nixon v. Fitzgerald* (1982), which states that presidents cannot be sued for damages related to official decisions made while in office. In 1997 President Clinton tried to extend this protection to cover all civil suits, but in *Clinton v. Jones* the Court ruled against his argument that civil suits against a chief executive distract him from presidential duties. These decisions have restricted and helped define executive privilege, but they have not eliminated it. In all cases the Court has assumed that the president has the right of executive privilege.

Impoundment of Funds

Impoundment is the presidential practice of refusing to spend money appropriated by Congress. Although many previous presidents impounded funds, the test case came with Richard Nixon. A major goal of his administration was to reduce federal spending, and when the Democratic Congress passed spending bills, he responded by pocket-vetoing twelve bills and then impounding funds appropriated under other laws that he had not vetoed. Congress in turn passed the **Budget Reform and Impoundment Act of 1974** that required the president to spend all appropriated funds, unless Congress approved the impoundment. Federal courts have upheld the rule that presidents must spend money that Congress appropriates.

The President as Morale Builder

The founders had no way of knowing the evolutionary importance of the symbolic and morale-building functions a president must perform. People turn to their presidents for meaning, healing, assurance, and a sense of purpose. This function is particularly important during times of crisis, such as the period following the attacks on the World Trade Towers and the Pentagon on September 11, 2001. The president is expected to help unify the nation, represent our common heritage, and create a climate that encourages diverse elements to work together.

Agenda Setting

The Constitution provides the basis for the important power of **agenda setting** – or determining policy priorities – for the nation. According to Article Two, Section Three:

"He shall from time to time give to the Congress Information of the State of the Union, and recommend to their Consideration such Measures as he shall judge necessary and expedient."

Even though Congress is charged with passing legislation, the president is expected to make policy proposals in many areas. Presidents often initiate foreign policy, economic goals and plans, and programs that improve the quality of life of citizens. Franklin Roosevelt set a precedent when he shepherded his New Deal policies through the legislature, taking responsibility for programs to get the country out of the Great Depression.

Sometimes initiatives are outlined as campaign issues and are refined by the executive office staff, special task forces, and by Congress. For example, President George W. Bush introduced Social Security reform in the 2000 presidential campaign, an issue that he promoted as president, especially after his reelection in 2004. At the start of his second term, President Bush created the President's Commission to Strengthen Social Security which recommended that younger workers be able to invest part of their payroll taxes in personal retirement accounts as part of the reform. However, Social Security reform failed. Presidents generally have more leeway in foreign policy and military affairs than they have in domestic matters, largely because the founders anticipated a special need for speed and unity in our relations with other nations.

The Power of Persuasion

An effective president is a good politician, a mobilizer of influence in the American political system. Because his formal powers are limited, he must spend much time persuading people to support his agenda.

The president's persuasive powers are aimed at three audiences: fellow politicians and leaders in Washington, party activists and officeholders outside Washington, and the public, with its many different views and sets of interests. All three audiences influence the decision-making process, and the president has the visibility and power to persuade them to listen to his priorities. A powerful president is often at the center of the give-and-take negotiations among these groups, and an effective persuader can be the catalyst that makes it all work.

Executive Orders

Congress allows the president to issue **executive orders** that have the force of law. These executive orders may enforce the Constitution, treaties, or legislative statutes, or they may establish or modify rules and practices of executive administrative agencies. The only restriction on executive orders is that they must be published in the *Federal Register*, a daily publication of the U.S. Government.

The Changing Veto Power

In recent years many critics have suggested a **line-item veto** reform that would allow presidents to veto sections of bills without rejecting the whole thing. Congress passed the Line-Item Veto Act in 1996, which allowed the president to veto sections of appropriations bills only. When President Clinton exercised this new provision, the law and the president's action were challenged in *Clinton v. City of New York* (1997). The Supreme Court ruled both the law and the action unconstitutional, criticizing them for permitting the president to construct legislation – an abuse of the principle of separation of powers.

PRESIDENTIAL CHARACTER

Just as early presidents were held to the standards of Washington's personal qualities, modern presidents are judged in terms of the public perception of their personality and character. In his book ***The Presidential Character***, Professor James Barber assessed presidents by two character-based criteria:

- active vs. passive inclinations
- positive vs. negative points of view

He concluded that these basic personality characteristics shape a president's approach to his job and largely determine important decisions. For example, Franklin Roosevelt's positive, activist character forged the New Deal programs and U.S. foreign policy during World War II. Likewise, Richard Nixon's negative, activist character made it difficult for him to mobilize support from Congress, the media, and the public, even though he actively pursued his ambitious foreign policy goals. A passive, positive president, such as Gerald Ford, may be genial and well liked, but the lack of aggressive goals and administration of policy made his presidency an undistinguished one. Scholars disagree over whether Barber's theories work, but few deny the importance of personality and character in presidential decisions.

THE ISSUE OF GRIDLOCK

Over the past fifty years, a significant trend has developed: **divided government**, or a government in which one party controls the White House and a different party controls one or both houses of Congress. Until 2003, only two exceptions occurred. Between 1993 and 1995, the Democrats controlled both branches, and for a few months in early 2001, when the Republicans briefly dominated. However, with the midterm election of 2002, Republicans gained control of both houses, putting both branches under Republican control. Although the election of 2004 affirmed this arrangement, in 2006 the Democrats took control of both the House (233 – 202 in favor of the Democrats) and Senate (49 Democrats with 2 Independents declaring for the Democrats and 49 Republicans). Despite the slim majority, the election recreated the problems of a divided government.

Many people criticize divided government because it produces "**gridlock**," or the inability to get anything done because the branches bicker with one another and make decisions difficult. A unique illustration of gridlock occurred in 1995 and 1996 when Congress and the president could not agree on the federal budget, thus shutting down many government operations, including national parks and federal offices, until an agreement could be reached. Even though gridlock may slow the process of decision-making, some supporters of divided government believe that it is not necessarily bad because better balanced policies result. Others believe that a unified government is a myth, with struggles between the branches a natural part of the give and take of checks and balances. In this scenario, gridlock is just as likely to occur when one party controls both branches as it is when a "divided government" exists. Democratic filibusters in 2003 and 2004 against judicial nominees put forward by President George W. Bush support the notion that gridlock between the branches is an ongoing process.

PRESIDENT OR PRIME MINISTER?

While the United States prefers a presidential form of government as created by the founders, most democracies have chosen a parliamentary form. As such they have a prime minister rather than a president. Significant differences are evident in each executive as demonstrated by the table below:

PRESIDENT	PRIME MINISTER
Elected by the people	Selected by the legislature
Separate branch from the legislature	Elected member of the legislature – represents a district or constituency
Head of Party but does not hold a leadership position in the legislature. Can have a large impact on party policy but is limited by leadership in the legislature.	Party leader – chosen by the majority party in the legislature to serve as prime minister. Directs the party policy.
Usually limited to time in office by term limits as in the US form. Result can be a lame duck or weaken power period.	Holds power as long as the party or coalition wants the person in the executive position
Power can be limited with divided government	Represents the majority party so does not face divided government
Weaker party discipline – members of legislature re-election depend on loyalty of constituents more than support of president. No vote of confidence is possible on the executive but does suffer from a lame duck period.	Strong party discipline. Party majority held in legislature translates into support of party programs. Loss of support for prime minister may result in a loss of control in the legislature. Vote of Confidence may result.
Experience can be varied – governor, Senate, member of the House, Cabinet, party leader. May not always have national level experience. (Of the last 6 presidents 4 were governors between1980 and 2009).	National experience more likely due to role of shadow government. Service in a cabinet or shadow cabinet necessary for training providing national exposure and experience.

Why the presidential form for the U.S.? The framers of the U.S. Constitution were concerned about concentration of power in one person or a small group. As such there was a strong focus on fragmented power with the separation of powers design. Not only are the branches separate, they are also chosen differently. (The framers even divided the legislature into two houses to prevent this concentration of power.) In order to further curb power further, a system of checks and balances was built to have the branches watch over each other. The framers believed that centralized power made control of the government or corruption easier if in the hands of a person or group which reduces the people's ability to control the government.

OTHER IMPORTANT MEMBERS OF THE EXECUTIVE BRANCH

Just as the power of the presidency has grown tremendously in recent years, so have the numbers of people that surround him in high-level jobs in the executive branch. George Washington began his first term with only his nephew to help him with office work. Washington paid even that salary out of his own pocket. Today many advisors in the White House Office, the cabinet, and the Executive Office assist the president in his work. The vice president and the "first lady" also have large staffs that complement all the president's aides.

THE VICE-PRESIDENT

"I do not choose to be buried until I am already dead."

A nineteenth century presidential hopeful, Daniel Webster, declined the vice presidency with the above words, expressing a sentiment repeated by many vice presidents over time. The founders paid little attention to the office and assigned it only two formal duties:

- to preside over the Senate, but without a vote except to break a tie. This power is seldom claimed by the vice president who defers to the president *pro tempore* who in turn usually hands the responsibility to a junior senator.
- to help decide the question of presidential disability, as provided in the 25th Amendment in 1967. To date, the vice president has never had to decide a question of presidential disability.

The most important function of the vice president is to take over the presidency if the president is unable to fill his term. That has only happened nine times in history, but of course, the vice president must be qualified to take over the presidency.

A vice president's role in any administration is almost entirely up to the president. Although the original constitution designated the runner-up for the presidency as the vice president, the **12th Amendment** was passed in 1804, which provided for electors to vote for a president/vice-president slate. Traditionally, a presidential candidate chooses a vice presidential partner, usually based on a "balance" to the ticket (region, age, popular base, party subgroup).

In recent years, presidents have given more and more important duties to vice presidents. They often represent the president for important ceremonies, sit on boards or lead/participate in projects, and advise him on major, sometimes specialized, issues. For example, Vice President Al Gore advised President Bill Clinton on environmental issues and headed a national review of the federal bureaucracy. President George W. Bush has involved Vice President Dick Cheney in many policy areas, including those shaped in reaction to the terrorist acts of September 11, 2001.

The vice president is often considered as a presidential candidate when the president's term expires, although George H. Bush was the first vice president to succeed immediately to the presidency since Martin Van Buren succeeded Andrew Jackson in 1837.   Even though a vice president may receive his party's nomination, he doesn't always win the general election. Examples include Richard Nixon in 1960, Hubert Humphrey in 1968, Walter Mondale in 1984, and Al Gore in 2000.

THE WHITE HOUSE OFFICE

Some of the most influential people in government are in the president's White House Office. The organization of the staff is entirely up to the president, and their titles include "chief of staff," "counsel," "counselor," "assistant to the president," "special consultant," or "press secretary." These aides are appointed by the president without Senate confirmation, and they may be fired at will. Often they do not serve an entire presidential term.

The organization of the White House Office has been analyzed according to two models:

- **the "pyramid" model** – In this organizational model, most assistants report through a hierarchy to a chief of staff and/or a chief aide. This model is relatively efficient and it frees the president's calendar for only the most important issue. On the other hand, the president may become isolated or his top advisers may gain a great deal of power, as happened to president Richard Nixon in the early 1970s.

- **the "circular" model** – Presidents that use this model have more direct contact with their staff members, with many cabinet secretaries and assistants reporting directly to the president. Bill Clinton employed this structure, especially in the early years of his presidency, when many task forces, committees, and informal groups of friends and advisers dealt directly with the president. This model allows better access to the president, and ideas are not filtered through one or two top aides. Critics say that the model promotes chaos and that the president's time is not well used.

THE EXECUTIVE OFFICE OF THE PRESIDENT

The Executive Office consists of agencies that report directly to the president and perform staff services for him. Some agencies are large bureaucracies. The president appoints the top positions, but unlike the White House Staff members, these Executive Office appointees must be confirmed by the Senate. The Executive Office agencies include the following:

- **The National Security Council** advises the president on American military affairs and foreign policy. The NSC consists of the president, the vice president, and the secretaries of state and defense. The president's national security adviser runs the staff of the NSC and also advises the president.

- **The Office of Management and Budget** (OMB) is the largest office in the EOP, and it has the job of preparing the national budget that the president proposes to Congress every year. The OMB also monitors the spending of funds approved by Congress and checks the budgets and records of executive agencies.

- **The National Economic Council** helps the president with economic planning. The council consists of three leading economists and is assisted by about 60 other economists, attorneys, and political scientists. The NEC is the president's major source of advice and information about the nation's economy.

THE CABINET

The cabinet is the oldest traditional body of the executive branch. The first cabinet members were appointed by Washington to serve as secretary of state, secretary of the treasury, secretary of war, and attorney general. From the earliest feuds between Thomas Jefferson and Alexander Hamilton, the cabinet almost never has served as a deliberative body of presidential advisers. In truth, the cabinet does not have much influence over presidential decisions, nor does it help the president to gain control over the bureaucracy.

Cabinet officers are the heads of fifteen major departments. The order of their creation is important for protocol. When the cabinet meets, the secretary of state sits on one side and secretary of the treasury on the other, and so forth down the table so that the newest departments are the farthest away from the president. They are appointed by the president and must be confirmed by the Senate. The original four positions of secretary of state, treasury, attorney general, and war (secretary of war is now called "secretary of defense"), are known as the "**inner cabinet**," and still generally have the most power and influence.

The president has very little power over cabinet departments partly because he cannot appoint more than a small number of all a department's employees. The most important reason that the departments operate independently from the president is that cabinet members spend the large majority of their time on departmental business, and seek to defend and promote their own organizations in cabinet meetings. What results is that they often compete with one another for precious resources and attention, and represent the departments to the president rather than function as the president's representative to the departments.

INDEPENDENT AGENCIES AND COMMISSIONS

The president also appoints people to agencies and commissions that by law often have an independent status. In contrast to the heads of "executive" agencies, the heads of independent agencies serve by law for fixed terms of office and can be removed only "for cause." The agencies are created by Congress, and include such well-known bodies as the Federal Reserve Board, the Federal Communications Commission, the Federal Deposit Insurance Corporation, the Interstate Commerce Commission, and the Securities and Exchange Commission.

SELECTION OF THE PRESIDENT

One very important characteristic of the American political system is that no one seriously questions the process of selecting a president. Nor have we ever had anything other than a peaceful transition between presidents. Of course, people criticize the men that we choose, not to even mention the fact that we have never chosen a women. What people accept almost completely is *how* a president is chosen or *that* he should leave office when his time is up.

THE ELECTORAL COLLEGE

The method of selection of the president was one of the most controversial topics at the Constitutional Convention. Most of the framers did not trust the public to directly elect the president, but under the checks and balances system, neither could Congress be allowed to select the head of the executive branch. The solution to the dilemma was to create an electoral college, a group of electors chosen by each state who would meet in their respective state capitals to vote for president and vice president. Many framers believed that states would vote for favorite sons and that often the election would be decided by the House of Representatives. It did not work out as they expected, largely because they did not foresee the important role that political parties would play in presidential selection.

Today, all major presidential candidates are selected by their political parties, even though Ross Perot tried to capture the presidency in 1992 without the backing of a party. In 1996, he proved the importance of political parties in the selection process when he tried to run again, but as head of a third party. Presidential candidates are chosen through presidential primaries, and are nominated at a party convention in the summer before a general election in November. The **electoral college** members in each state vote – either by law or tradition – for the same candidate that the majority of voters in the state chose.

RECENT CONTROVERSY

Until the election of 2000, the electoral college was regarded primarily as a formality that didn't affect the outcomes of presidential election. However, in 2000 Democratic candidate Al Gore won the popular vote, but George W. Bush became president because he won the electoral vote. The situation opened a debate, with electoral college supporters arguing that the system protects regional and local balance, and its critics claiming that the electoral college voting system is undemocratic. In the election of 2004 a few thousand changes of votes from George W. Bush to John Kerry would have created the situation again, but in reverse. However, President Bush's narrow victory in Ohio meant that he gained both a popular and electoral majority.

PRESIDENTIAL DISABILITY AND SUCCESSION

According to the original Constitution, the president's elected term of office is four years, but no mention is made of the number of terms a president may serve. By a precedent set by George Washington, who retired after two terms, no president before Franklin Roosevelt served longer than two terms. However, in the midst of economic depression and a world war, Roosevelt ran for and won a third and fourth term of office, although he died before he completed the last one. Because the tradition was seen as a safeguard against tyranny, Congress added the **22nd Amendment** to the Constitution, limiting a president to election to two terms and/or serving no more than ten years. A vice president who becomes president with less than two years remaining in the previous president's term may run for the office two times on his own.

Presidential Disability

Among twentieth century presidents, Woodrow Wilson became incapable of carrying out his job after he suffered a stroke, and his wife apparently made many presidential decisions. Likewise, Dwight Eisenhower was unable to function as president for several weeks after a debilitating heart attack. The **25th Amendment** (1967) to the Constitution covers these important problems concerning the presidential term: disability and succession. It permits the vice president to become acting president if the vice president and the cabinet determine that the president is disabled. If the president challenges the executive decision, Congress decides the issue. The amendment also outlines how a recovering president can reclaim the Oval Office.

Presidential Succession

The 25th Amendment also created a method for selecting a vice president when the office is vacated. The president nominates a new vice president, who assumes office when both houses of Congress approve the nomination by a majority vote. A vice president who assumes the presidency then nominates a new vice president who is also confirmed by Congress. If there is no vice president, then a 1947 succession law governs: next in line are the speaker of the house, the Senate *pro tempore*, and the thirteen cabinet officers, beginning with the secretary of state.

The disability provision has never been used, but the vice presidential succession policy has. In 1973, Vice President Spiro Agnew resigned amidst charges of bribery, and President Nixon appointed Gerald Ford in his place. The next year, Nixon resigned as a result of the Watergate scandal, Ford became president, and he appointed Nelson Rockefeller as vice president. For the first time in history, both the presidency and vice presidency were held by appointed, not elected, officials.

THE IMPEACHMENT PROCESS

The Constitution provides a way to remove a president before his term is over, but it is not an easy process. The House of Representatives may, by majority vote, impeach the president for "Treason, Bribery, or other high Crimes and Misdemeanors." Once the House impeaches the president, the case goes to the Senate, which tries the president, with the chief justice of the Supreme Court presiding. By a two-third vote, the Senate may convict and remove the president from office. Only two presidents have been impeached:

- Andrew Johnson was impeached by the House in 1868 in the wake of post-Civil War politics, but the Senate failed to convict him (by a one vote margin), and he remained in office.
- Bill Clinton was impeached by the House in 2000 on two counts: committing perjury and obstructing justice in the investigation of sex scandals surrounding the president's relationships with Paula Jones and Monica Lewinsky.

Richard Nixon came close to impeachment when on July 31, 1974, the House Judiciary Committee voted to recommend his impeachment to the House as a result of the Watergate scandal. Nixon avoided impeachment by resigning from the presidency a few days later.

Other civil officers besides the president may be impeached, but the provision has had the most meaning for federal judges, who serve for life and are constitutionally independent of the president and Congress. Fifteen judges in U.S. history have been impeached by the House, and seven of these have been convicted by the Senate.

Despite gridlock, the recent impeachment proceedings, and the disputed election of 2000, the institution of the presidency has survived. The responsibilities and privileges have changed over time so that the office is much more powerful than the one created by the Constitution. Even though events of recent years have checked presidential power, most people would argue that the president is still the most influential and respected single political leader in the country.

IMPORTANT DEFINITIONS AND IDENTIFICATIONS:

- "advice and consent"
- agenda setting
- Budget Reform and Impoundment Act of 1974
- circular model
- *Clinton v. City of New York*
- *Clinton v. Jones*
- commander-in-chief
- diplomatic recognition
- divided government
- electoral college
- executive agreements
- Executive Office of the President
- executive orders
- executive privilege
- gridlock
- impeachment process
- impoundment

- inner cabinet
- legislative veto
- line-item veto
- *Myers v United States*
- National Economic Council
- National Security Council
- *Nixon v. Fitzgerald*
- Office of Management and the Budget
- presidential succession
- pyramid model
- *The Presidential Character*
- *United States v. Nixon*
- War Powers Resolution
- White House Office
- 12th Amendment
- 22nd Amendment
- 25th Amendment

CHAPTER TWELVE
THE BUREAUCRACY

Many Americans have a negative view of the federal bureaucracy. The very mention of the world "bureaucracy" often conjures up a memory of an important document lost, or a scolding for some alleged misconduct of personal business. Political scientists acknowledge the influence of the bureaucracy by referring to it as the "fourth branch of government," a power that is felt in almost all areas of American life. However, bureaucracies are barely mentioned in the Constitution. Bureaucratic agencies are created and funded by Congress, but most of them report to the president, who supervises them as he takes "care that the laws shall be faithfully executed" (Article II, Section 3 of the Constitution). This dual responsibility to Congress and to the president is an indication of the complex nature of the organization and functioning of federal government bureaucracies.

BUREAUCRACY IN MODERN GOVERNMENTS

A **bureaucracy** is a large, complex organization of appointed, not elected, officials. Bureaucracies exist in many countries in many areas of life, including corporations, universities, and local and state governments. The term actually comes from the French word "bureau," a reference to the small desks that the king's representatives set up in towns as they traveled across the country doing the king's business. So "bureaucracy" literally means something like "government with small desks."

MAX WEBER'S BUREAUCRACY

Max Weber was one of the first people in modern times to think seriously about the importance of bureaucracy. He wrote in Germany during the early 20th century, when developing capitalism was spawning more and more large businesses. The changing economic scene had important implications for government. He created the classic conception of bureaucracy as a well-organized, complex machine that is a "rational" way for a modern society to organize its business. He did not see them as necessary evils, but as the best organizational response to a changing society.

According to Weber, a bureaucracy has several basic characteristics:

- **hierarchical authority structure** – A chain of command that is hierarchical; the top bureaucrat has ultimate control, and authority flows from the top down.
- **task specialization** – A clear division of labor in which every individual has a specialized job.
- **extensive rules** – Clearly-written, well-established formal rules that all people in the organization follow.
- **clear goals** – A clearly-defined set of goals that all people in the organization strive toward.

- **the merit principle** – Merit-based hiring and promotion; no granting of jobs to friends or family unless they are the best qualified.
- **impersonality** – Job performance that is judged by productivity, or how much work the individual gets done.

Weber emphasized the importance of the bureaucracy in getting things done and believed that a well-organized, rational bureaucracy is key to the successful operation of modern societies.

THE AMERICAN FEDERAL B UREAUCRACY

The American federal bureaucracy shares common characteristics with other bureaucracies, but it has its own characteristics that distinguish it from others.

1. **Divided supervision** – Congress has the power to create, organize, and disband all federal agencies. Most of them are under the control of the president, although few of them actually have direct contact with him. So the bureaucracy has two masters: Congress and the president. Political authority over the bureaucracy is shared, then, according to the principles of separation of powers and federalism. On the national level, both Congress and officials in the executive branch have authority over the bureaucracy. This divided authority encourages bureaucrats to play one branch of government against the other. Also, to complicate things even more, many agencies have counterparts at the state and local level. Many federal agencies work with other organizations at state and local levels of government.

2. **Close public scrutiny** – Government agencies in this country operate under closer public scrutiny than they do in most other countries. The emphasis in American political culture on individual rights and their defense against abuse by government makes court challenges to agency actions more likely. About half of the cases that come to federal court involve the United States government as either defendant or plaintiff.

3. **Regulation rather than public ownership** – United States government agencies regulate privately owned enterprises, rather than operate publicly owned ones. In most Western European nations the government owns and operates large parts of the economy; the U.S. government prefers regulation to ownership.

THE GROWTH OF THE FEDERAL BUREAUCRACY

The Constitution made little mention of a bureaucracy other than to make the president responsible for appointing (with the "advice and consent of the Senate") public officials, including ambassadors, judges, and "all other officers of the United States whose appointments are not herein otherwise provided for, and which shall be established by law" (Article II, Section 3). No provisions mentioned departments or bureaus, but Congress created the first bureaucracy during George Washington's presidency.

PATRONAGE

The bureaucracy began in 1789 when Congress created a Department of State to assist the new Secretary of State, Thomas Jefferson. From 1789 to about 1829, the bureaucracy was drawn from an upper-class, white male elite. In 1829, the new President Andrew Jackson employed a **spoils system** to reward party loyalists with key federal posts. Jackson believed that such rewards would not only provide greater participation by the middle and lower classes, but would insure effectiveness and responsiveness from those who owed their jobs to the president. The spoils system ensured that with each new president came a full turnover in the federal service.

THE PENDLETON ACT

Late in the nineteenth century the **spoils system** was severely criticized because it allowed people with little knowledge and background to be appointed to important government positions. Some accused presidents of "selling" the positions or using them as bribes to muster support for their election campaigns. After President James Garfield was assassinated in 1881 by a disappointed office seeker, Congress passed the **Pendleton Act**, which set up a limited merit system for appointing federal offices. Federal service was placed under the **Civil Service Commission**, which supervised a testing program to evaluate candidates. Federal employees were to be selected and retained according to merit, not party loyalty, but in the beginning the merit system only covered about 10 percent of all federal employees.

THE MODERN BUREAUCRACY

By the 1950s the merit system had grown to cover about 90 percent of all federal employees, and in 1978, the functions of the Civil Service Commission were split between two new agencies:

- **The Office of Personnel Management** administers civil service laws, rules, and regulations. The OPM administers written examinations for the competitive service, which includes about two-thirds of all appointed officials. The OPM is in charge of hiring for most agencies. When a position opens, the OPM sends three eligible names to the agency, and the agency must hire one of them, except under unusual circumstances. Once hired, a person is assigned a **GS (General Schedule) Rating**, ranging from GS 1 to GS 18, which determines salaries. At the top of the civil service system is the Senior Executive Service, executives with high salaries who may be moved from one agency to another.

- **The Merit Systems Protection Board** protects the integrity of the federal merit system and the rights of federal employees. The board hears charges of wrongdoing and employee appeals against agency actions and orders disciplinary actions against agency executives or employees.

The federal bureaucracy grew tremendously as a result of Roosevelt's New Deal programs and World War II, but the number of federal bureaucrats has leveled off in the years since then. Whereas the number of employees of state and local governments has grown tremendously in the past fifty years, the number of federal employees has remained a relatively constant three percent of all civilian jobs. One reason for the growth on the state and local levels is that many recently created federal programs are administered at the lower levels of government, not by federal employees.

WHAT TO REDUCE?

It is popular for politicians to talk about how the "bloated bureaucracy" needs to be reduced in size in order to save money. The problem is determining which bureaus must be reduced or removed in order to be more fiscally responsible. Bureaus have ties with interest groups that support their programs to guarantee they are not affected by the proposed budget cuts. In spite of the apparent unpopularity of the bureaucracy in general, it does provide services that citizens need and enjoy such as national park rangers, prison guards, air traffic controllers, various inspectors, and postal workers. Natural disasters such as Hurricane Katrina that affected New Orleans and the Gulf Coast in August, 2005, also provide evidence of the importance of bureaucracies for providing aid during emergencies. Although the performance of the Federal Emergency Management Agency (FEMA) was found lacking, the national discussion focused on FEMA improvements, not its demise.

Two ways the federal government may reduce bureaucracies are:

- **Devolution** – This does not remove the service or program but sends it to the states to implement, resulting in uneven services from state to state. Since the 1996 welfare reform gave states more control over their programs, some states, such as Wisconsin, designed innovative approaches while other states, such as Idaho, almost dismantled welfare. Devolution also accounts for the growth in state employees to administer these state-run programs.
- **Privatization** – Just as with devolution, the program is not removed but is provided by a private contractor usually through a competitive bidding system. The programs are still government-funded and supervised, but the workers are not considered part of the bureaucracy. Private companies can sometimes provide the service cheaper and more efficiently, particularly in areas requiring a high level of technology. Weapons systems and equipment for the Pentagon are examples of the benefits of privatization.

According to the Constitution, any reduction or reform of the bureaucracy must come from Congress. As a result, Congress also has the power of **oversight** and must hold hearings to investigate complaints or suggested reforms to be sure that the bureaucracies are adequately fulfilling the intent of the laws they were created to carry out.

WHO ARE THE BUREAUCRATS?

Bureaucrats work in the executive branch in the fifteen cabinet-level departments and in the more than fifty independent agencies, including about 2,000 bureaus, offices, services, and other subdivisions of the federal government. The five biggest employers are the Departments of Army, Navy, and Air Force, the Department of Veterans Affairs, and the U.S. Postal Service. A total of about 3.2 million civilians and 1.8 million military are employed by the executive branch of the federal government.

Most people still think of a bureaucrat as being a white, middle-aged man, but the permanent bureaucracy today is more representative of the American people than are members of Congress, judges, or presidential appointees in the executive branch.

Consider the following statistics for federal civilian employees:

- About 56% are male, 44% are female.
- About 68.6% are white, 31.4% are minority (includes blacks, Asians, Native Americans, and Hispanics).
- About 35 % are hired by the Defense Department, 13% by the Department of Homeland Security, 9% by the Department of Veterans Affairs, and 43% in other agencies.
- Only about 10% work in the Washington area; 90% work in other parts of the United States.
- The average age is about 46.9.
- The number of federal employees per 1,000 people in the U.S. population has decreased from over 14 in the early 1970s to a little over 10 by the late 1990s.
- Bureaucrats hold a huge variety of jobs, but most federal employees are white-collar workers, such as secretaries, clerks, lawyers, inspectors, and engineers.
- Nearly 20,000 federal civilian employees work in U.S. territories, and another 100,000 work in foreign nations.

Reference: Office of Personnel Management, "Federal Civilian Workforce Statistics," The Fact Book, 2005 Edition, http://www.opm.gov/feddata/factbook/2005/factbook2005.pdf

THE ORGANIZATION OF THE BUREAUCRACY

Agencies of the executive branch may be organized into four basic types:

THE CABINET DEPARTMENTS

Each of the fifteen cabinet departments is headed by a secretary, except for the Department of Justice, which is headed by the attorney general. All of the heads are chosen by the president and approved by the Senate, and each manages a specific policy area. Responsibility is further divided among undersecretaries and assistant secretaries, who manage various agencies. The fifteen cabinet departments, in order of creation, are:

- The Department of State (founded in 1789)
- The Department of Treasury (founded in 1789)
- The Department of Defense (created in 1947, but replaced the Department of War, founded in 1789)
- The Department of Justice (created in 1870 to serve the attorney general, a position created by George Washington in 1789)
- The Department of the Interior (created in 1849)
- The Department of Agriculture (created in 1862)
- The Department of Commerce (created in 1903 as the Department of Commerce and Labor)
- The Department of Labor (separated from the Department of Commerce in 1913)
- The Department of Health and Human Services (created as the Department of Health, Education, and Welfare in 1953)
- The Department of Housing and Urban Development (created in 1966)
- The Department of Transportation (created in 1966)
- The Department of Energy (created in 1977)
- The Department of Education (separated from the Department of Health, Education, and Welfare in 1979)
- The Department of Veterans Affairs (created in 1988)
- The Department of Homeland Security (created in 2002)

Each department is organized somewhat differently, but the real work of a department usually is done in the bureaus (sometimes called services, offices, or administrations). Until the 1970s, the largest department was the Department of Defense, but today the Department of Health and Human Services spends more money, although the Department of Defense still has more employees.

THE 2004 INTELLIGENCE BILL

In late 2004 President George W. Bush signed the **Intelligence Reform and Terrorism Prevention Act** that called for the most sweeping overhaul of the nation's intelligence-gathering apparatus in a half-century. The legislation created a position for a Director of National Intelligence, a move recommended by a special commission that spent 20 months investigating the pre-September 11, 2002 intelligence failures. The legislation put 15 intelligence agencies under the control of the director, including the CIA and the FBI, and it created a National Counterterrorism Center to serve as the primary organization that processes all terrorism-related intelligence. The reorganization will impact many of the cabinet departments, as well as the operation of several independent agencies. One implication of the law (in addition to the increased time at airports for security screening) is the increased need for passports for U.S. citizens. Previously, Americans could travel to certain places such as the Caribbean Islands, Mexico or Canada and return without documentation; however, U.S. citizens now need a passport when traveling outside the United States. The law states that it is, "unlawful for any citizen of the United States to depart from or enter the United States unless he bears a valid United States passport." This caused some problems for Americans as the demand for passports increased and took longer than expected to receive.

THE INDEPENDENT REGULATORY AGENCIES

These agencies regulate important parts of the economy, making rules for large industries and businesses that affect the interests of the public. Because regulatory commissions are "watchdogs" that by their very nature need to operate independently, they are not part of a department, and most are not directly controlled by the president. Some examples are:

The Interstate Commerce Commission (ICC) – Founded in 1887, the ICC is the oldest of the regulatory agencies. It first regulated railroads, but now oversees trucking as well.

The Federal Trade Commission (FTC) – The FTC regulates business practices and controls monopolies.

The National Labor Relations Board (NLRB) – The NLRB regulates labor-management relations.

The Federal Reserve Board (FRB) – The FRB governs banks and regulates the supply of money.

The Securities and Exchange Commission (SEC) – The SEC polices the stock market.

The regulatory agencies are governed by small commissions – five to ten members appointed by the president and confirmed by the Senate. These commissioners are somewhat more "independent" than are the cabinet secretaries because they cannot be removed by the president during their terms of office.

THE GOVERNMENT CORPORATIONS

Government corporations are a blend of private corporation and government agency. They were created to allow more freedom and flexibility than exists in regular government agencies. They have more control over their budgets, and often have the right to decide how to use their own earnings. Since they still ultimately are controlled by the government, they do not operate like true private corporations.

Some examples are:

- **The Corporation for Public Broadcasting** – This controversial government corporation still operates public radio and television stations. Although largely funded by private donations, the government still provides policies and money to support its programs.
- **The Tennessee Valley Authority** – This corporation was created as one of Franklin Roosevelt's New Deal programs. Its mission is to harness the power of the Tennessee River to protect farmlands and provide cheap electricity.
- **The U.S. Postal Service** – The P.O. is a corporation that competes with private services.

- **Amtrak** – Congress created Amtrak to provide railroad passenger service that is heavily subsidized by the federal government. Part of the motivation for its creation was the lack of private companies providing the service, and Amtrak has suffered some huge financial losses. Recently, in an attempt to make the corporation more profitable, Congress has allowed Amtrak to drop some of its less popular routes.

INDEPENDENT EXECUTIVE AGENCIES

Other agencies that do not fall into the first three categories are called independent executive agencies. Independent agencies closely resemble cabinet departments, but they are smaller and less complex. Generally, they have narrower areas of responsibility than do cabinet departments. Most of these agencies are subject to presidential control and are independent only in the sense that they are not part of a department. Their main function is not to regulate, but to fulfill a myriad of other administrative responsibilities.

Some well-known examples are

- **The General Services Administration** (GSA) – The GSA operates and maintains federal properties, handling buildings, supplies, and purchasing.
- **The National Science Foundation** (NSF) – The NSF supports scientific research.
- **The National Aeronautics and Space Administration** (NASA) – NASA administers the United States space program, financing ventures into space since 1958.

WHAT DO BUREAUCRATS DO?

Most people think that bureaucrats only follow orders. Of course, anyone who works in the executive branch is there to implement decisions, but in reality their work is more complicated. The power of bureaucrats depends on how much **discretionary authority** they have. Congress passes laws, but they cannot follow through on all the little decisions that have to be made as laws are translated into action. Bureaucrats, then, may make policies and choose actions that are not spelled out in advance by laws. Their main function is to do the nuts and bolts of "executing" policies that are made by Congress, the president, and the Supreme Court.

IMPLEMENTATION

Most policies do not implement themselves. After the president signs a bill into law, the bureaucracy must implement it. Bureaucrats develop procedures and rules for implementing policy goals, and they manage the routines of government, such as delivering mail and collecting taxes.

Usually Congress announces the goals of a policy, sets up a broad administrative apparatus, and leaves the task of working out details to the bureaucracy. The implementers take a policy handed down to them from Congress, the president, or the Court, and actually put it into effect, with real consequences for real people.

Implementation involves more power in the policymaking process than is readily apparent. During this stage, many key decisions are made. Congress often passes ambiguous legislation, or the supporters of a bill that is passed into law get involved with other bills and lose contact with laws passed on to the executive branch. By the very nature of the compromise that passed the bill into law in Congress, it often sets general goals and passes the responsibility for interpretation on to the bureaucrats. As a result, the bureaucracy is given latitude in translating general guidelines into specific directives.

REGULATION

The function of regulation of private sector activities has developed over the course of the twentieth century. The earlier function of service (the Post Office, benefits to veterans, agriculture) dominated the bureaucracy until the early twentieth century Progressive Movement, when the government began to regulate businesses.

As early as 1877 the Supreme Court upheld the right of government to regulate business in *Munn v. Illinois*, a case that upheld the rights of the state of Illinois to regulate the charges and services of a Chicago warehouse. The New Deal legislation of the 1930s created more regulatory agencies, and World War II allowed government a great deal more regulation than ever before.

Today all sorts of activities are subject to federal regulation from automobile production to buying and selling stock to the production and distribution of meat and poultry. Hundreds of agencies supervise and enforce a vast array of regulations.

As regulators, agencies first receive a grant of power from Congress to sketch out the means of executing broad policy decisions. Next, the agency develops a set of guidelines to govern an industry, usually in consultation with people who work in those industries. Next, the agency must apply and enforce its rules and guidelines, often through its own administrative procedures, but sometimes in court. Sometimes it reacts to complaints, and other times it sends inspectors out to the field. Regulation may be executed by requiring applicants to acquire a permit or license to operate under their guidelines and congressional policies.

ACCOUNTABILITY

The biggest difference between a government agency and a private organization is the number of constraints placed on agencies from other parts of government and by law. A government bureau cannot hire, fire, build, or sell without going through procedures set by Congress, often through law. Presidents also exert considerable power over the bureaucracies.

CONGRESS

Congress often acts as the problem-solving branch of government, setting the agenda and then letting the agencies decide how to implement them. On the other hand, Congress serves as a check on the activities of the bureaucracy. Congress oversees the bureaucracy in a number of ways.

1) **Duplication** – Congress rarely gives any one job to a single agency. For example, drug trafficking is the task of the Customs Services, the FBI, the Drug Enforcement Administration, the Border Patrol, and the Defense Department. Although this spreading out of the responsibility often leads to contradictions among agencies and sometimes inhibits the responsiveness of government, it also keeps any one agency from becoming all powerful.

2) **Authorization** – No agency may spend money unless it has first been authorized by Congress. Authorization legislation originates in a legislative committee, and states the maximum amount of money that an agency may spend on a given program. Furthermore, even if funds have been authorized, Congress must also appropriate the money. An **appropriation** is money formally set aside for a specific use, and it usually is less than the amount authorized. The Appropriations Committees in both houses of Congress must divide all available money among the agencies, and almost always they cut agency budgets from the levels authorized.

3) **Hearings** – Congressional committees may hold hearings as part of their oversight responsibilities. Agency abuses may be questioned publicly, although the committee holding the hearings typically has the oversight responsibility, so a weak agency may reflect weak oversight.

4) **Rewriting legislation** – If they wish to restrict the power of an agency, members of Congress may rewrite legislation or make it more detailed. Every statute is filled with instructions to its administrators, and the more detailed the instructions, the better able Congress is to restrict the agency's power. Still, an agency usually finds a way to influence the policy, no matter how detailed the orders of Congress.

THE PRESIDENT

Agencies are also accountable to the chief administrator of the U.S. government: the president. Presidents use a number of methods to impress their policy preferences on the bureaucracy.

- **Appointments** – The most obvious control the president has over the executive branch is his power to appoint the senior bureaucrats, including agency heads and subheads. If a president disagrees with the policies of an agency, he can appoint a head that agrees with him. This strategy may lead to problems because the agency can work against the new head, possibly seeking support in Congress. Also, because agencies tend to have strong points of view, a new head may sometimes be swayed to their beliefs.

- **Executive Orders** – A president may issue executive orders to agencies that they must obey. More typically, aides may pass the word informally to agencies as to the president's wishes. Even though agencies may resist, they usually pay attention to the president's preferences.

- **Economic powers** – The president may exercise authority through the Office of Management and the Budget, which is the president's own final authority on any agency's budget. The OMB may cut or add to an agency's budget, although Congress ultimately does the appropriating.

- **Reorganization** – The president may reorganize or combine agencies to reward or punish them. This power is limited, however, because entrenched bureaucracies, Congress, and supporting interest groups may keep a president from acting as he might like.

THE COURT

What if an agency is not perceived as upholding its responsibility? Since the judiciary is responsible for the interpretation of laws and must settle disputes, it has a role in determining bureaucratic responsibilities. In the case *Massachusetts v Environmental Protection Agency* (2008), the Supreme Court examined the role of the EPA with regard to regulating greenhouse gases and global warming. Ten states (including Massachusetts), some cities, and environmental groups, petitioned the EPA to regulate carbon dioxide emissions and other gases contributing to global warming. The Bush administration and the EPA consistently rejected putting caps on greenhouse gas emissions, preferring incentives for voluntary emissions cuts by industries.

The Supreme Court ruled that the EPA was responsible to issue emissions standards for motor vehicles under the Clean Air Act because greenhouse gases are "air pollutant agents". The EPA had delayed regulation until studies on the matter were concluded, but the Court stated that it was improper to delay its action. The Court also stated that Massachusetts had standing to sue in this instance because a state has a "stake in protecting its quasi-sovereign interests". Although a close decision, 5 – 4, this case clarified that courts have a role in the bureaucratic process.

THE BUREAUCRACY AND INTEREST GROUPS

Although interest groups have no formal control over agencies, the informal ties between them may greatly influence the implementation of policy. Interest groups may provide agencies with valuable information they need to execute a policy. Interest groups may pressure agency bureaucrats to interpret policy in ways that are favorable to the interests they represent. Bureau chiefs may also recruit interest groups as allies in pursuing common goals. They often share with them a common view that more money should be spent on federal programs run by the bureau in question.

IRON TRIANGLES

Alliances among bureaucrats, interest groups, and congressional subcommittee members and staff sometimes form to promote their common causes. Such an alliance is sometimes described as an **iron triangle**. These triangles are sometimes so strong that they are referred to as subgovernments – the place where the real decisions are made. For example, an important issue that government has recently addressed is the effect of tobacco on health and the government's role in regulating it. The tobacco farmers and industry have numerous interest groups, which form a "tobacco lobby" that provide information to the tobacco division of the Department of Agriculture and to subcommittees of the House and Senate agricultural committees. They support the agency's budget requests and make contributions to the election campaigns of the subcommittee members. The subcommittees pass legislation affecting tobacco farmers and other members of the industry and approve higher budget requests from the agency. The agencies give the subcommittees information, help with constituents' complaints, and develop rules on tobacco production and prices. They all have a common interest – the promotion of tobacco farming and industry – and they can help one another achieve their goals. As a result, the president and Congress beyond the subcommittee have little decision-making power.

ISSUE NETWORKS

The iron triangle may be criticized because interest groups today are so prolific that they are bound to create cross-demands on subcommittees and the bureaucracy. In the tobacco issue discussed above, interest groups have formed demanding that tobacco products be banned or heavily restricted by the federal government. With these competing demands, the policymaking process would not run so smoothly and would broaden the number of people involved in the system. The issue is discussed on many levels, both inside and outside government. An agency, then, may be described as being embedded, not in an iron triangle, but in an **issue network**. These issue networks consist of people in interest groups, on congressional staffs, in universities, and in the mass media who regularly debate an issue. The networks are contentious, with arguments and disagreements occurring along partisan, ideological, and economic lines. When a president appoints a new agency head, he will often choose someone from the issue network who agrees with his views.

REFORMING THE BUREAUCRACY

Throughout American history, presidents and Congress have attempted to reform the bureaucracy to make it work better and cost less. The Intelligence Reform and Terrorism Prevention Act of 2004 is a recent example. Many other reforms have been suggested for the future.

THE MERIT SYSTEM AND THE HATCH ACT

The merit system tries to ensure that the best-qualified people get government jobs and that party politics (patronage) has nothing to do with the hiring process. In 1939 Congress passed the **Hatch Act**, which required employees, once they were hired, to have as little to do with political parties as possible. The Hatch Act forbid employees from engaging in many party activities. For example, they could not run for public office or raise funds for a party or candidate, nor could they become officers in a political organization or a delegate to a party convention.

In the early 1970s some bureaucrats complained that their 1st amendment rights were being violated by this law. The issue made its way to the Supreme Court, where the justices ruled that the Hatch Act did not put unreasonable restrictions on employees' rights. However, in 1993 Congress softened the Hatch Act by making many forms of participation in politics permissible. Federal bureaucrats still cannot run as candidates in elections, but they may be active in party politics.

CRITICISMS OF THE BUREAUCRACY

Americans criticize their political bureaucracies in many ways, but some frequently mentioned ones (sometimes know as **"pathologies"**) are:

- **"red tape"** – the maze of government rules, regulations, and paperwork – makes government so overwhelming to citizens that many people try to avoid any contact.
- **conflict** – agencies often work at cross purposes with one another.
- **duplication** – a situation in which two agencies appear to be doing the same thing.
- **unchecked growth** – the tendency of agencies to grow unnecessarily and for costs to escalate proportionately.
- **waste** – spending more on products and/or services than is necessary.
- **lack of accountability** – the difficulty in firing or demoting an incompetent bureaucrat.

SUGGESTIONS FOR REFORM

Some suggestions for reforming the bureaucracy are:

- **Limiting appointments to 6-12 years.** After the appointment expires, the bureaucrat would then have to go through reexamination and his or her performance would be reviewed for possible rehire.
- **Making it easier to fire a bureaucrat.** Civil service rules that are meant to protect workers from partisan politics have made it difficult to fire anyone for poor performance. Reformers want to remove those rules.
- **Rotating professionals between agencies and from outside.** Reformers believe that this practice would bring new blood to agencies and encourage workers to get a broader view of government service.
- **Rewarding employee initiatives and fewer rules.** The bureaucracy is criticized for having rigid rules that restrict new ideas and individual initiatives. Reformers suggests that rules be streamlined and modernized, and that suggestions from employees should be encouraged and rewarded.
- **Emphasizing customer satisfaction.** Government bureaucrats are often criticized for not caring about their customers. Unlike private businesses, government agencies do not have to compete for customers, so their clients are not given the attention they deserve.

Finding the practical solutions that everyone can agree on is a difficult process in our government, largely because our system of checks and balances is not particularly efficient. But that doesn't stop presidents and many others from suggesting and implementing reform of the bureaucracy.

IMPORTANT DEFINITIONS AND IDENTIFICATIONS:

- 2004 Intelligence Reform and Terrorism Prevention Act
- accountability
- appropriations
- authorizations
- bureaucratic pathologies
- bureaucracy
- Civil Service Commission
- devolution
- discretionary authority
- duplication
- government corporations
- GS Rating
- Hatch Act
- independent executive agencies
- independent regulatory agencies
- iron triangle
- issue network
- *Massachusetts v Environmental Protection Agency*
- Max Weber
- merit principle
- Merit Systems Protection Board
- *Munn v. Ohio*
- Office of Personnel Management
- oversight
- patronage
- Pendleton Act
- privatization
- "red tape"
- spoils system

CHAPTER THIRTEEN
THE JUDICIARY

In most modern democracies the executive and legislative branches hold considerable power, but most grant little policymaking power to the judicial branch. An important exception to this general rule is the United States, whose judiciary is truly a coequal branch with as much power as the other two. And yet our government did not begin with this almost equal balance of power; the founders almost certainly saw the judiciary as an important check on the legislative and executive branches, but not as a policymaking body.

The court system is a cornerstone of our democracy. According to our ideals, judges make impartial and wise decisions that elected officials find difficult to make. Members of Congress, state governors, and the president must always worry about elections and popular opinion. As a result, they may lose sight of the need to preserve our values, and they sometimes set hasty or unjust policies. Under the guidance of Constitutional principles, the courts serve as watchdogs of the other branches of government.

THE COMMON LAW TRADITION

Although the U.S. judiciary differs in many ways from the British system, the tradition of English common law is still very important to both. **Common law** is a collection of judge-made laws that developed over centuries and is based on decisions made by previous judges. The practice of deciding new cases with reference to former decisions is called **precedence**. The doctrine of *stare decisis* ("let the decision stand") is based on precedent, and is a cornerstone of English and American judicial systems. So, when a court overturns a previous court's decision, it is a major event, because to do so breaks the strong tradition of *stare decisis*.

THE JUDICIARY IN THE CONSTITUTION

The Constitution painstakingly defines the structure and functions of the legislative branch of the government. It clearly, although less thoroughly, addresses the responsibilities and powers of the president. However, it treats the judicial branch almost as an afterthought. Article III specifically creates only one court (the Supreme Court), allows judges to serve for life and to receive a compensation, broadly outlines original and appellate jurisdiction, and outlines the procedure and limitations for those accused of treason. Article III consists of three section:

- **Section 1:** The only court mentioned in the Constitution is the Supreme Court, and Congress is given the right to create all other federal courts. Judgeships are to be held "during good behavior" (in other words, there are no terms of office), and judges' compensations are not allowed to be diminished while they hold office.

- **Section 2:** The jurisdiction of the federal courts is defined, with all cases affecting ambassadors, ministers, and consuls and those in which a state is a party going automatically to the Supreme Court (original jurisdiction). Also, federal jurisdiction is held in cases of admiralty and maritime jurisdiction, cases involving the U.S. as a party, controversies between two or more states or between citizens of different states, and cases of states or their citizens against foreign countries. **Appellate jurisdiction** is given to the Supreme Court in these cases. In other words, they can only be appealed to the Supreme Court after first being heard in a lower court. Section 2 also provides for trial by jury for all criminal (not civil) cases.

- **Section 3:** Treason is defined as not only waging war against the United States, but as "adhering to their enemies" and "giving them aid and comfort." A person may be convicted for treason only if he or she confesses in court or on the testimony of two witnesses. Punishment for treason is declared by Congress, but "corruption of blood" (paying for the treason of a relative) and forfeiture of property after the individual is dead are forbidden.

Surprisingly, nothing else is said. Article III clearly reflects the traditional 18th century view of courts: they judge disputes between people and decide which of the two parties is right, usually awarding the wronged party "damages," or money. The role of judges, then, is simply to find and apply existing law. Under this scenario, judges cannot make laws, but they are required to interpret them in order to apply them. This power of interpretation implies a limited judiciary role in "checking and balancing" the other two branches: laws passed by Congress and actions by the president and other executives.

JUDICIAL REVIEW

The early Supreme Court gave few indications that the judicial branch would someday be coequal to the legislative and executive branches. Their first session began in 1790, and lasted only ten days. No cases were heard, and their time was spent admitting lawyers to practice before the Court. Not until the early 1800s did the fourth Chief Justice, John Marshall, claim power for the court in the famous *Marbury v. Madison* case. The power he claimed was judicial review, a concept considered by the framers and implied by but not mentioned in Article III of the Constitution. Judicial review allows the courts to rule on the constitutionality of laws and actions, giving them the power to strike down or reinforce policy, not just to apply and interpret it. **Judicial review** is the key to understanding the unusual power of the United States judiciary.

MARBURY V. MADISON (1803)

When President John Adams failed to win reelection in 1800, he was forced to cede the office to his political rival Thomas Jefferson. For the first time in U.S. history, a president from one political party (the Federalists) had to step down for one from the opposite party (the Democratic Republicans). Fearing that Jefferson would undo Federalist policies, Adams worked hard to "pack the courts" with 57 Federalist judges before he had to leave office. All but seventeen letters of appointment were delivered before the change of office, but these letters were left for the incoming secretary of state – James Madison – to send out. Madison never delivered the letters. Four of the seventeen men (one was named Marbury) who never received their letters sued Jefferson and Madison, calling on the Supreme Court to issue a **writ of mandamus** ordering Madison to make the appointments.

The Chief Justice of the Court, Federalist John Marshall, was put in a bind by the lawsuit. The Court had been given the power to issue writs of mandamus (from the Latin "I command") by the Judiciary Act of 1789, but this influence was largely untested. What if the Court issued the order to Madison and he refused to comply, what could the Court do? It had no troops to enforce its orders. Even if Madison cooperated, the Democratic Republican Congress almost certainly would impeach him. On the other hand, if he allowed Madison to get away with it, the power of the Supreme Court would be seriously compromised.

Marshall's solution not only avoided a constitutional crisis, a standoff among the three branches, but it changed the nature of judicial power completely. The court refused to issue the writ of mandamus, but in his majority opinion, Marshall claimed that the Judiciary Act of 1789 was unconstitutional. According to Article III, original jurisdiction is given to the Supreme Court only in certain cases; the Judiciary Act gave original jurisdiction for the Court to issue writs not mentioned in the Constitution; therefore, the law was unconstitutional. As a result, a showdown was avoided, Jefferson and Madison were happy, and Marshall awarded the Court an unprecedented power: judicial review. From then on, no one seriously questioned the Court's right to declare laws unconstitutional, and Marshall's 34 years as Chief Justice were spent building on that power.

THE STRUCTURE OF THE FEDERAL COURT SYSTEM

The only federal court required by the Constitution is the Supreme Court. Article III left it up to Congress to establish lower federal courts, which they began to do in the Judiciary Act of 1789. The Constitution also does not specify how many justices shall be on the Supreme Court (originally there were six; now there are nine). Congress created two general types of lower federal courts: constitutional and legislative.

Constitutional Courts

Constitutional courts exercise the judicial powers found in Article III, so their judges are given the constitutional protection of lifetime terms. There are 94 district courts, with at least one in each state, the District of Columbia, and Puerto Rico; and 13 courts of appeals, one of which is assigned to each of 12 judicial circuits, or region. A special appeals court called the U.S. Court of Appeals for the Federal Circuit hears cases regarding patents, copyrights, and trademarks, claims against the United States, and international trade.

- **District courts** are trial courts of original jurisdiction, the starting point for most litigation in the federal courts. They hear no appeals, and they are the only federal courts in which trials are held and juries may sit. Each district court has between two and twenty-seven judges, depending on its caseload. The courts' jurisdiction includes federal crimes, civil suits under federal law, and civil suits between citizens of different states where the amount exceeds fifty thousand dollars.

- **Courts of appeal** have appellate jurisdiction only; no cases go to them first. They review any final decisions of district courts, and they may review and enforce orders of many federal regulatory agencies, such as the Securities and Exchange Commission. Most cases come from the district courts. Each Court of Appeals normally hears cases in panels of three judges, but important cases may include more. Decisions are made by majority vote of the participating judges.

Legislative Courts

Congress also has set up legislative courts for specialized purposes. These courts include the Court of Claims, the Court of International Trade, the Tax Court, and the Court of Military Appeals. Legislative courts are sometimes called Article I courts because they help carry out the legislative powers the Constitution has granted to Congress. Because they do not carry out Article III judicial powers, their judges are not protected for life; they serve fixed terms of office, may be removed without impeachment, and may have their salaries reduced.

PARTICIPANTS IN THE JUDICIAL SYSTEM

The major participants in the courtroom are the judge, the litigants, the lawyers, sometimes a jury, and the audience, such as the press, interest groups, and the general public.

LITIGANTS

The litigants include the **plaintiff**, or the person bringing the charges, and the **defendant**, or the person charged. In **criminal law** cases an individual is charged with violating a specific law and the government prosecutes; in **civil law** cases no charge of criminality is made, but one person accuses another of violating his or her rights. Civil law defines the relations between individuals and defines their legal rights. Litigants wind up in court for many reasons. Plaintiffs may be seeking justice and/or compensation; defendants may be brought to court reluctantly, particularly if they are accused of a crime, or they may see themselves as defending their rights against a lawsuit.

The United States government is involved in about two-thirds of the cases brought to federal court, either as a plaintiff or defendant. In criminal cases the government is the prosecutor, but in civil cases, the government can either initiate a lawsuit as the plaintiff or can defend itself against lawsuits.

Litigants must always have **standing to sue**, or a serious interest in the case, usually determined by whether or not they have personally suffered injury or are in danger of being injured directly. Just being opposed to a law does not generally provide standing; the individual must be directly affected by it. The concept of standing to sue has been broadened in recent years by class action suits, which permit a small number of people to represent all other people similarly situated. For example, *Brown v. Board of Education* of *Topeka* was a **class action suit** in 1954, when Linda Brown of Topeka, Kansas, represented black students from several school districts around the country suing for discrimination in public education.

LAWYERS

Lawyers have become virtually indispensable in the judicial system. In criminal cases federal lawyers are the prosecutors, or those who formally charge an individual with a crime. Prosecution falls to the Department of Justice. The attorney general, the **solicitor general** (who represents the government to the Supreme Court), other attorneys, and assistant attorneys must also serve as defense lawyers if the government is being sued.

The federal government also provides public defenders for people who cannot afford defense attorneys in criminal cases. The 1964 case ***Gideon v. Wainwright*** determined that all accused persons in state criminal trials should be supplied with a lawyer, free if necessary, if the crime charged was a felony. Prosecutors negotiate with the defense lawyers and often work out a plea bargain, in which a defendant agrees to plead guilty to avoid having to stand trial.

THE JURY

The right to a trial by jury is fundamental to our justice system, but most trials do not involve them. In many cases, but not all, a jury, a group of citizens (usually twelve), is responsible for determining the innocence or guilt of the accused. Trial by jury is used less often today than in the past. Defendants and their lawyers either make plea bargains or elect to have their cases decided by a judge alone. Even in criminal cases, only a small number are actually tried before a jury. Trials by jury take more time and money than do bench trials, which are heard before judges only.

THE AUDIENCE

Interest groups sometimes seek out litigants to represent a cause they support. One of the most successful groups is the National Association for the Advancement of Colored People, which has defended numerous civil rights cases, including ***Brown v. Board of Education of Topeka***. The American Civil Liberties Union is another interest group that actively seeks litigants to protect principles of individual liberties. The press actively influences sensational cases, particularly if a celebrity or a highly publicized case is involved. The press corps is often instrumental in getting the public interested in a case.

THE JUDGES

The central figure in the court room is of course the judge, who must draw upon his or her background and beliefs to guide decision making. If a jury is present, it decides the facts of the case and the judge makes determinations as to the law. In criminal trials, except in capital cases, the jury renders a verdict of guilt or innocence and the judge sentences.

THE JURISDICTION OF THE FEDERAL COURTS

The United States has a **dual court system** – one federal, as outlined above, and one state. The Constitution gives certain kinds of cases to federal courts, and by implication leaves all the rest to state courts. Federal courts hear cases "arising under the Constitution, the law of the United States, and treaties" (**federal-question cases**) and cases involving citizens of different states (**diversity cases**).

Some kinds of cases may be heard in either federal or state courts. For example, if citizens of different states sue one another in a civil case where more than $50,000 is involved, their case may go to either federal or state court. If a state bank with federal insurance is robbed, the case may be tried in either type of court. Sometimes defendants may be tried in both state and federal courts for the same offense. Under the doctrine of **dual sovereignty**, state and federal authorities may prosecute the same person for the same conduct under both state and federal law. Also, some cases that go to state courts may be appealed to the U.S. Supreme Court if they involve a significant **constitutional question**. For example, if the highest court in a state has held a law to be in violation of the Constitution or has upheld a state law that a plaintiff has claimed to be in violation of the Constitution, the matter may be appealed to the Supreme Court.

Most cases considered in federal courts begin in the district courts, where the volume of cases is huge and growing larger. Most cases involve straightforward application of law; very few are important in policymaking. Likewise, the vast majority of cases heard in state courts do not reach federal courts, with each state having its own Supreme Court that serves as the final judge for questions of state law.

THE SELECTION OF JUDGES

Legendary Justice Oliver Wendell Holmes once said that a Supreme Court justice should be a "combination of Justinian, Jesus Christ, and John Marshall." Why do we look to venerable former justices for guidance in understanding necessary qualities for federal judges and justices? The main reason is that the Constitution is silent on their qualifications. The Constitution meticulously outlines qualifications for the House of Representatives, the Senate, and the presidency, but it does not give us any help with judicial appointments, other than the fact that justices should exhibit "good behavior." As a result, the question of who is chosen is governed primarily by tradition.

THE NOMINATION PROCESS

The Constitution provides broad parameters for the nomination process. It gives the responsibility for nominating federal judges and justices to the president. It also requires nominations to be confirmed by the Senate. But let's do the numbers. Hundreds of federal judges sit on district courts and courts or appeals, and nine justices make up the Supreme Court. Since they all have life terms, no single president will make all of these appointments, but certainly many vacancies will occur during a president's term of office.

Appointing judges, then, could be a president's full time job. Logically, a president relies on many sources to recommend appropriate nominees for judicial posts. Recommendations often come from the Department of Justice, the Federal Bureau of Investigations, members of Congress, sitting judges and justices, and the American Bar Association. Some judicial hopefuls even nominate themselves.

The Lower Courts

The selection of federal judges for district courts is heavily influenced by a tradition that began under George Washington: **senatorial courtesy**. Usually the Senate will not confirm a district court judge if the senior senator from the state where the court is located objects, nor will it confirm a court of appeals judge not approved by the senators from the judge's home state. As a result, presidents usually check carefully with senators ahead of time, so the Senate holds a great deal of power in the appointment of federal judges.

The Supreme Court

The president is usually very interested in opportunities to appoint justices to the Supreme Court, and a great deal of time and effort go into the nominations. Because justices retire at their own discretion, some presidents are able to appoint more than others. For example, Richard Nixon was able to nominate four justices in his first three years in office, but Jimmy Carter wasn't able to appoint any. Both President Clinton and President Bush appointed two members each to the court. Bill Clinton appointed Ruth Bader Ginsberg and Stephen Breyer while George W. Bush appointed Chief Justice John Roberts and Samuel Alito. In both cases they successfully appointed members to the court that better reflected their political philosophies.

SENATE CONFIRMATION

Because senators suggest more nominees for federal district courts, the Senate confirmation required by the Constitution is only a formality for most. However, for appointments to appeals courts and especially to the Supreme Court, the confirmation process may be less routine. The Senate Judiciary Committee interviews the nominee and holds hearings before he or she goes before the entire Senate. If the Judiciary Committee does not recommend the candidate, the Senate usually rejects the nomination. Through 2008, 28 of the 148 individuals nominated to be Supreme Court justices have not been confirmed by the Senate. Harriet Miers, nominated by George W. Bush, withdrew her name from consideration due to questions about her judicial qualifications but also due to weak support from conservatives.

SELECTION CRITERIA

Presidents use a number of criteria in selecting their nominations:

- **Political ideology** – Presidents usually appoint judges that seem to have a similar political ideology to their own. In other words, a president with a liberal ideology will usually appoint liberals to the courts. The same goes for conservative presidents. However, presidents have no real way of predicting how justices will rule on particular issues. Behavior doesn't always reflect ideology, and political views also change. For example, President Dwight Eisenhower – a Republican – appointed Earl Warren and William Brennan, who surprised him by becoming two of the most liberal justices in recent history.

- **Party and personal loyalties** – A remarkably high percentage of a president's appointees belong to his political party. Overall, about 90 percent of judicial appointments since the time of Franklin Roosevelt have gone to members of the president's party. Although it isn't as common today as it once was, presidents still appoint friends and loyal supporters to federal judgeships.

- **Acceptability to the Senate** – Because the Senate must confirm judicial nominations, the president must consider candidates that are acceptable to the Senate. Even if he does informally consult with the Senate, he may still run into problems with the Senate Judiciary Committee, who first interrogates nominees and recommends them to the full Senate. If a nominees runs into trouble in the confirmation process, they often withdraw their names from consideration. If this happens, the president must start all over again, as happened to Ronald Reagan in 1988 when he nominated Douglas Ginsburg, who was criticized for using marijuana while a law professor at Harvard.

- **Judicial experience** – Typically justices have held important judicial positions before being nominated to the Supreme Court. Many have served on courts of appeals, and others have worked for the Department of Justice. Some have held elective office, and a few have had no government service but have been distinguished attorneys. The work of the Supreme Court is so unique that direct judicial experience is often less important than it is for the other courts of appeals.

- **Race and gender** – The first black American, Thurgood Marshall, was appointed to the Supreme Court by Lyndon Johnson in 1967, and the first woman, Sandra Day O'Connor, was appointed in 1981 by Ronald Reagan. Since then one other black, Clarence Thomas, and two woman, Ruth Ginsburg and Sonia Sotomayor have been appointed as well. Before 1967 all justices were white and male. The percentage of women and minority federal judges appointed has increased significantly in recent years.

- **The "Litmus Test"** – Although most senators and presidents deny it, some observers believe that candidates must pass a "litmus test," or a test of ideological purity, before they may be nominated and/or confirmed to the Supreme Court. One recent litmus test supposedly has been the individual's attitude toward abortion rights. Nominees David Souter and Clarence Thomas both were grilled by the Senate Judiciary Committee about their opinions on prominent abortion cases. Abortion was still a concern during the confirmation hearings (2005) for John Roberts who was being considered for the Chief Justice position. While many were skeptical, Roberts responded that abortion rights are "a precedent of the court" and that he would rule on the issue as such. After the terrorist attacks on September 11, 2001, another form of litmus test has been for civil rights and civil liberties, such as the right of habeus corpus and unwarranted monitoring of phone calls and emails.

HOW THE SUPREME COURT WORKS

The power of the Supreme Court is reflected in the work that they do, and their decisions often shape policy as profoundly as any law passed by Congress or any action taken by the president. The Court does much more than decide specific cases. It resolves conflicts among the states and maintains national supremacy. It also ensures uniformity in the interpretation of national laws, and many of the most important cases that determine the constitutionality of laws and government actions are decided in the Supreme Court.

There are nine justices on the Supreme Court: eight associates and one chief justice. The number is set by law and has varied from six to ten over the course of history, but it has remained at nine since the 1870s. All the justices sit together to hear cases and make decisions.

Supreme Court justices are in session from the first Monday in October through the end of June. They listen to oral arguments for two weeks and then adjourn for two weeks to consider the cases and write their opinions. In the event of a tie (if one or more justices has not participated in the case), the decision of the lower court remains, although on rare occasions a case may be reargued.

SELECTION OF CASES

Most cases come to the Supreme Court by means of a **writ of certiorari**, a Latin phrase that means "made more certain." The court considers all petitions it receives to review lower court decisions. If four justices agree to hear a case, cert (a shortened reference) is issued and the case is scheduled for a hearing. This practice is known as the **rule of four**. Only a tiny fraction of cases appealed to the Supreme Court are actually accepted. The Court also hears the few cases in which it has original jurisdiction according to Article III of the Constitution, but for the vast number of cases, the Court has control of its agenda and decides which cases it wants to consider.

BRIEFS AND ORAL ARGUMENTS

Before a case is heard in court, the justices receive printed briefs in which each side presents legal arguments and relevant precedents (previous court decisions). Additionally, the Supreme Court may receive briefs from *amicus curiae* ("friends of the court") individuals, organizations, or government agencies that have an interest in the case and a point of view to express. When oral arguments are presented to the court counsel for each side generally is limited to 30 minutes, a policy that often aggravates the lawyers, since justices often interrupt them to ask questions.

THE CONFERENCE

Wednesday afternoons and all day Friday the justices meet in conference. Before every conference, each justice receives a list of the cases to be discussed, and the discussions are informal and often spirited, with the chief justice presiding. No formal vote is taken, but at the end of discussion, each justice is asked to give his or her views and conclusions.

OPINIONS

Once decisions have been made in conference an opinion, or statement of the legal reasoning behind the decision, must be formally stated. The most senior justice in the majority assigns the task of writing the **majority opinion**, the official opinion of the court. Unless the decision is unanimous, the most senior justice on the losing side decides who will write the **dissenting opinion** of those justices who do not agree with the Court's majority decision. A justice may write a **concurring opinion** if he or agrees with the majority decision but does so for different reasons than stated in the majority opinion.

The content of an opinion may be as important as the decision itself. For example, John Marshall established judicial review in his majority opinion in the *Marbury v. Madison* case. Opinions also instruct the judges of all other state and federal courts on how to decide similar cases in the future.

IMPLEMENTING COURT DECISIONS

Court decisions carry legal authority, but courts have no police officers to enforce them. They must rely on the other branches, or state officials, to enforce their decisions. **Judicial implementation**, then, refers to the translation of court decisions into actual policy that affects the behavior of others.

Although Congress or a president may ignore or side-step a Supreme Court ruling, decisions in which enforcement requires only the action of a central governmental agency usually become effective immediately. Implementation is more difficult if a decision requires the cooperation of a large number of officials. For example, when the Court ruled required prayers in public schools unconstitutional, some school boards continued their previous practices. Also, despite the fact that the Court ruled segregated schools unconstitutional in 1954, public schools remained largely segregated for more than ten years after the first ruling.

THE COURTS AND DEMOCRACY

Of the three branches of government, the courts are the least democratic. Federal judges are not elected (except for some positions on the local level), they may not be removed from office except by the drastic means of impeachment, and the decisions of the courts may only be reversed by higher courts.

POPULAR INFLUENCE

The courts are not entirely independent of popular influence for two reasons.

1) The justices are appointed by the president, at least partly because they agree with his political points of view and ideologies. Therefore, even though they do not have the pressure to seek reelection, they are chosen at least partly because of their political biases.
2) Justices follow election returns, read newspapers, get mail supporting both sides of the issues they must decide, and understand that their decisions either support or refute popular opinion. Justices are aware that court orders that flagrantly go against public opinion are likely to be ignored. Such a case was the Dred Scott decision, which infuriated the North because it supported slaveholders outside the South.

CONSERVATISM AND LIBERALISM

Although justices are theoretically "above politics," they do have personal ideologies, and their points of view often influence their decisions. For example, the Supreme Court under Earl Warren (1953-1969) and Warren Burger (1969-1986) made decisions that were notably liberal, most famously in *Brown v. Board of Education of Topeka* (1954) and *Roe v. Wade* (1973). When William Rehnquist became Chief Justice in 1989, the court took a rightward shift. In September, 2005 Rehnquist died and in January 2006, Sandra Day O'Connor retired from the court. When President George W. Bush's nominees, John Roberts as chief justice and Samuel Alito as associate justice, were confirmed by the Senate the court continued its move to the right. In 2009 Sonia Sotomayor was confirmed replacing David Souter who had resigned. This did not change the move of the court to the right as both Souter and Sotomayor are more liberal to moderate. Currently, four justices are consistently conservative (John Roberts, Antonin Scalia, Clarence Thomas and Samuel Alito); four are liberal to moderate (Ruth Ginsberg, Steven Breyer, David Souter, and John Paul Stevens); and one is moderate to conservative (Anthony Kennedy). As a result, Justice Kennedy often serves as the "swing" vote, with decisions resting on his point of view (before O'Connor's resignation she was also a "swing" vote.) In the two years of the Roberts Court there have been many decisions with only a 5 – 4 majority. Two recent examples are *Boumendiene v Bush*, 2008 and *District of Columbia v Heller*, 2008. The *Boumendiene* decision guaranteed the right of habeas corpus to the Guantanamo detainees and the *Heller* case ensured the right of individuals to own a gun for private use (not just for service in the militia). In both of these cases Justice Kennedy provided the swing vote, one for the liberal side in *Boumendiene* and one for the conservative view in the *Heller* case.

CONSTRAINTS ON THE POWER OF THE FEDERAL COURTS

Judicial review gives the federal courts a power unmatched in any other modern democracy, but the courts operate under a number of constraints.

1) Policy must be made within the setting of an **adversarial system**, a neutral arena in which two parties present opposing points of view before an impartial arbiter (a judge.) The system is based on the assumption that justice will emerge from the struggle. Judicial power, then, is passive – the case must come to the court, and not vice versa.

2) The case must represent a **justiciable dispute** – an actual situation rather than a hypothetical one, and one that may be settled by legal methods.

3) Courts have developed a doctrine of **political questions**, which provides grounds to avoid settling disputes more appropriately resolved by Congress and the president, or that require knowledge of a non-legal character. A political question is a matter that the Constitution leaves to another branch of government, like deciding which group of officials of a foreign nation should be recognized as the legitimate government.

The other two branches of government provide some important checks on the power of the courts.

- The president controls the nature of the courts with his power to appoint all federal judges.
- Congress must confirm presidential appointments.
- Congress may alter the very structure of the court system, determining the numbers of courts and justices that serve on them.
- Congress has the power to impeach justices, with two federal justices being removed from office most recently in 1989.
- Congress may also amend the Constitution if the Courts find a law unconstitutional, though this happens only rarely. For example, after the Supreme Court declared a federal income tax law unconstitutional, the Sixteenth Amendment was added to make it constitutional for Congress to pass an income tax.

THE POLICYMAKING POWER

Although the vast majority of cases decided by the federal courts only apply existing law to specific cases, courts do make policy on both large and small issues. Opinions differ widely on the question of how strong the policymaking role of the judicial branch should be.

Many favor a policy of **judicial restraint**, in which judges play minimal policy-making roles, leaving policy decisions to the other two branches. Supporters of judicial restraint believe that because the judicial branch is the least democratic, judges are not qualified to make policy decisions and courts should not function as "super-legislatures." According to judicial restraint, the other branches should take the lead because they are more closely connected to the people. According to Justice Antonin Scalia, "The Constitution is not an empty bottle…it is like a statute, and the meaning doesn't change."

On the other side are supporters of **judicial activism**, in which judges make policy decisions and interpret the Constitution in new ways. Judicial activists believe that the federal courts must correct injustices that the other branches do not. For example, minority rights have often been ignored, partly because majorities impose their will on legislators. Prayers in public schools support the beliefs of the majority, but ignore the rights of the minority. The Constitution, then must be loosely interpreted to meet the issues of the present. In the words of former Justice Charles Evans Hughes: "We are under a Constitution, but the Constitution is what the judges say it is." Although judges with both viewpoints are committed to determining the original intent of the founders, activists are more inclined to interpret their intentions more loosely.

Despite the debate over what constitutes the appropriate amount of judicial power, the United States federal courts remain the most powerful judicial system in world history. Their power is enhanced by life terms for judges and justices, and they play a major role in promoting the core American values of freedom, equality, and justice.

IMPORTANT DEFINITIONS AND IDENTIFICATIONS:

- adversarial system
- amicus curiae
- appellate jurisdiction
- *Boumediene v Bush*
- civil law
- class action suits
- common law
- concurring opinion
- constitutional question
- criminal law
- defendant
- District Courts
- dissenting opinion
- *District of Columbia v Heller*
- diversity cases
- dual court system
- dual sovereignty
- federal-question cases
- *Gideon v. Wainwright*
- justiciable dispute
- judicial activism vs. judicial restraint
- judicial implementation

- judicial review
- justiciable dispute
- legislative courts
- litigants
- "litmus test"
- majority
- *Marbury v. Madison*
- opinions: majority, dissenting, concurring
- original jurisdiction
- plaintiff
- political question
- precedence
- public defenders
- rule of four
- senatorial courtesy
- solicitor general
- standing to sue
- stare decisis
- writ of certiorari
- writ of mandamus

UNIT FOUR QUESTIONS

1. Which of the following BEST describes the influence of a political party holding a majority in either house of Congress?

   (A) All standing committees are chaired by senior members of the majority party.
   (B) Strong party discipline ensures that the majority party controls the policymaking process.
   (C) The majority party greatly restricts the president's control of foreign policy.
   (D) The majority party in the House is controlled more by formal rules than in the Senate .
   (E) Judicial appointment confirmations are not controlled by the majority party.

2. Which of the following is NOT a correct comparison of the House of Representatives and the Senate?

   (A) Representatives must be at least 25 years old; senators must be at least 30.
   (B) The House of Representatives has 435 members; the Senate has 100.
   (C) Both representatives and senators must live in the area that they represent.
   (D) Senators must be native-born citizens, but representatives may be naturalized citizens.
   (E) Representatives have two year terms; senators have six year terms

3. Which of the following powers does the Constitution prevent Congress from exercising?

   (A) to lay and collect taxes
   (B) to borrow money
   (C) to regulate interstate commerce
   (D) to pass laws known as Bills of Attainder
   (E) to determine the number of justices serving on the Supreme Court

4. Which of the following powers does the Constitution grant to the House of Representatives?

   (A) to ratify treaties signed by the president
   (B) to try the president and other civil officers after the Senate has impeached them
   (C) to confirm major presidential appointments
   (D) to originate all bills of revenue
   (E) to vote on laws declared unconstitutional by the courts

5. Congress determines the actual amount available for government agencies to spend in a fiscal year when it sets

   (A) appropriations
   (B) authorizations
   (C) schedules for marking up bills
   (D) pigeonholes
   (E) rules for debate

6. In the Senate a vote of cloture is sought in which of the following circumstances?

   (A) to declare war
   (B) to approve appropriations bills
   (C) to prevent a filibuster
   (D) to overturn a presidential veto
   (E) to ratify a treaty

7. Which of the following powers is NOT given to the Speaker of the House of Representatives?

   (A) appointing chairmen of standing committees
   (B) exercising control over which bills get assigned to which committees
   (C) appointing the party's legislative leaders
   (D) directing business on the floor
   (E) recognizing members who wish to speak on the floor

8. Which of the following most accurately compares the majority leader in the House of Representatives to the majority leader in the Senate?

   (A) The majority leader is usually not the most powerful leader in the House; the Senate majority leader has the top leadership post.
   (B) Both majority leaders have the top positions in their respective houses, but the majority leader in the House has more concentrated power.
   (C) The majority leader in the Senate is likely to cooperate with the minority leader; the House majority leader has little choice but to cooperate with the minority leader.
   (D) The majority leader in the House is usually more dependent on the good will of the president than the Senate majority leader is.
   (E) Both majority leaders have comparative powers within their respective houses.

9. Which of the following usually has little power in determining Congressional proceedings?

   (A) the Speaker of the House
   (B) the majority leader in the Senate
   (C) the president of the Senate
   (D) the majority leader in the House
   (E) the minority leader in the Senate

10. Which of the following types of committees is permanently set up to consider legislation within a particular area?

    (A) conference committees
    (B) joint committees
    (C) party committees
    (D) select committees
    (E) standing committees

11. In which of the following settings is a bill the most likely to be changed/rewritten?

    (A) in full committee
    (B) in sub-committee
    (C) by the Rules Committee
    (D) by the Committee of the Whole
    (E) on the House or Senate floor

12. A representative who wants to ensure that projects for his district are properly funded would seek membership on the

    (A) Armed Services Committee
    (B) Appropriations Committee
    (C) Judiciary Committee
    (D) Veterans Affairs Committee
    (E) Agriculture Committee

13. A closed rule for debate on the floor of the House of Representatives would mean that

    (A) only the bill's supporters will be recognized to speak
    (B) a discharge petition has resulted in a bill's appearance for floor debate
    (C) amendments from the floor are permitted
    (D) the bill has strict time limits for debate
    (E) the speaker of the house does not lead the debate

14. The informal networks of members of Congress who share the same interests are called

    (A) caucuses
    (B) select committees
    (C) bureaucracies
    (D) subcommittees
    (E) linkage groups

(Questions 15 & 16 are based on the following chart):

Characteristics of Congress

Characteristic	108th Congress(2003-05)		109th Congress (2005-07)		110th Congress (2007-09)	
	House of Representatives	Senate	House of Representatives	Senate	House of Representatives	Senate
Women	63	14	68	14	71	16
African American	39	0	40	1	40	1
Hispanic	25	0	26	3	26	3
Lawyers	175	59	160	58	180	57
Members with military service	117	35	109	31	99	28
Average Age	54	60	55	60	56	62
Length of Service	9 years	11 years	9 years	12 years	10 years	13 years

15. Which of the following statements is supported by the chart?

    (A) It has been difficult for those with military service to gain elective office in Congress.
    (B) African Americans have experienced better representation in Congress than have Hispanics.
    (C) The length of service for those in the House is longer than those in the Senate.
    (D) Advanced education is not necessarily an advantage when running for the House.
    (E) A law degree is not common in Congress.

16. Which of the following groups has made and sustained the highest level of representation?

    (A) Hispanic Americans
    (B) African Americans
    (C) women
    (D) Native Americans
    (E) younger Americans

17. *Wesberry v Sanders*, the "one-man, one vote" Supreme Court decision addressed the problem of

    (A) gerrymandering
    (B) minority-majority districting
    (C) incumbency
    (D) pork barrel legislation
    (E) malapportionment

18. Cloture is a technique used in the Senate to

    (A) discharge a bill from committee
    (B) control nongermane amendments
    (C) stall a bill from passing
    (D) stop a filibuster
    (E) send a strong message to the president

19. A pocket veto is a technique that allows the president to

    (A) kill legislation presented to him within ten days of the adjournment of Congress
    (B) kill legislation without calling attention to his point of view
    (C) communicate his dislike for a bill before it leaves committee
    (D) send a bill back to both houses for further consideration
    (E) veto part of a bill, but allow other parts to become law

20. The franking privilege allows members of Congress to have

    (A) reimbursements for travel expenses
    (B) increased access to the press
    (C) staffers in their home district
    (D) free mailings to constituents
    (E) small gifts from lobbyists

21. Which of the following is most often cited as a strength of the legislative process in the U.S.?

    (A) It is efficient.
    (B) It is generally free of partisan politics.
    (C) It allows for input from many people.
    (D) It generally is not influenced by powerful lobby groups.
    (E) It allows most bills to be passed into law.

22. Which of the following is the main reason the framers created a bicameral legislature?

    (A) to handle the amount of legislation necessary.
    (B) to decentralize power to prevent abuse by elites.
    (C) to divide foreign and domestic policy development.
    (D) to accommodate the factions of the day.
    (E) to represent the rural and urban interests.

23. As compared to the powers outlined in the Constitution, the powers of the modern presidency are

    (A) far greater
    (B) far more restricted
    (C) about the same
    (D) greater in domestic affairs, but about the same in foreign affairs
    (E) greater in foreign affairs, but about the same in domestic affairs

24. Which of the following presidential powers is NOT specifically mentioned in the Constitution?

    (A) power as commander in chief
    (B) power of diplomatic recognition
    (C) power to issue executive orders
    (D) power to sign treaties
    (E) power to appoint ambassadors and other public officers

25. An executive agreement with a foreign head of state is different from a treaty in that

    (A) an executive agreement must be ratified by the Senate
    (B) a treaty must be ratified by the Senate
    (C) an executive agreement is not limited to the president that signed it
    (D) an executive agreement addresses issues that are not very important
    (E) a treaty is among several countries; an executive agreement is between the president and one other head of state

26. Which of the following staff agencies provides members of Congress with advice on the economic effects and probable cost of proposed policies?

(A) Congressional Budget Office
(B) Economic Accounting Office
(C) Office of Technology Assessment
(D) Congressional Research Service
(E) Library of Congress

27. A presidential veto of a legislative bill

(A) is overridden by a 2/3 vote of either house of Congress
(B) is countered by 5 of 9 Supreme Court justices
(C) is overridden by a majority of both houses of Congress
(D) is rarely overridden by Congress
(E) can be challenged by a legislative veto

28. Presidential claims to executive privilege are based on

(A) 1st Amendment rights
(B) "advice and consent" restrictions on the Senate
(C) the Constitutional principle of separation of powers
(D) the Constitutional principle of federalism
(E) the powers given to the president through his election by the people

29. Which of the following is NOT an example of checks and balances of Congress over the executive?

(A) Congressional approval of the budget
(B) Senate approval of presidential appointments
(C) Limitation of the president's powers under executive privilege
(D) Override of the presidential veto of legislation
(E) The Budget Reform and Impoundment Act, 1974

30. The president's main goal in giving his State of the Union message to Congress is usually to

(A) warn Congress not to overspend the budget
(B) challenge recent Supreme Court decisions that might limit his power
(C) set the agenda of issues that the nation and the government should address
(D) explain to the American public how the government plans to spend its money for the fiscal year
(E) communicate to other countries that they should not challenge the power and authority of the United States government

31. The U.S. president currently does not have the line-item veto because

    (A) Congress took the power away from President Clinton.
    (B) the president has never had the power of line-item veto.
    (C) states have protested the line-item veto as an abuse of federalism.
    (D) presidents have not sought the power.
    (E) the Supreme Court ruled the line-item veto unconstitutional.

32. A major criticism of divided government is that it has caused

    (A) an abuse of the constitutional principle of separation of powers.
    (B) an abuse of the constitutional principle of federalism.
    (C) a decline in the policymaking power of the judicial branch.
    (D) gridlock to occur between legislative and executive branches.
    (E) a blurring of policy differences between the two major political parties.

33. "I do not choose to be buried until I am already dead."

                                   Daniel Webster

    Webster made the above comment when he turned down the position of

    (A) vice president
    (B) president
    (C) senator from Massachusetts
    (D) congressional representative from the District of Columbia
    (E) governor of Massachusetts

34. Most public hearings held by Congress to research and gain information regarding possible legislation are conducted by

    (A) conference committees
    (B) the Committee of the Whole
    (C) sub-committees
    (D) the Rules Committee
    (E) ad-hoc committees

35. Historically, vice presidents have been chosen for the party presidential ticket <u>primarily</u> based on

    (A) their qualifications to succeed to the presidency if necessary.
    (B) their ability to lead the Senate as its president.
    (C) the approval of the House of Representatives.
    (D) their ability to help the ticket in terms of experience, ideology, or geography.
    (E) their ability to serve as *president-pro-tempore.*

36. Titles such as "counsel," "assistant to the president", "chief of staff," and "press secretary" are given to people who work in

    (A) top cabinet positions
    (B) independent executive agencies
    (C) government corporations
    (D) the White House Office
    (E) the Executive Office of the President

37. Which of the following is a common criticism of a "circular model" for organizing the White House Office?

    (A) The president can easily become isolated.
    (B) The president tends to rely too heavily on the advice of one or two people.
    (C) It does not provide for a good use of the president's time.
    (D) It tends to be more expensive than the pyramid organization.
    (E) It gives too much power to the chief of staff.

38. The president's Attorney General oversees the

    (A) Department of Defense
    (B) White House Office
    (C) Department of Justice
    (D) Executive Office of the President
    (E) Joint Chiefs of Staff

39. The most important reason that most presidents do not treat their cabinets as advisory bodies is that cabinet secretaries

    (A) are generally appointed from the opposition party
    (B) seek to defend and promote their departments in meetings with the president
    (C) generally dislike one another because most have ambitions to be president
    (D) have everyday access to the president during one-on-one meetings
    (E) do not have much power over decisions that their agency heads make

(Questions 40 and 41 are based on the following quote from a Supreme Court majority opinion):

"Although, among the enumerated powers of government, we do not find the word bank, or incorporation, we find the great powers to lay and collect taxes; to borrow money; to regulate commerce; to declare and conduct a war; and to raise and support armies and navies. …But it may with great reasons be contended, that a government entrusted with such ample powers, …must also be entrusted with ample means for their execution.

The government which has a right to do an act, and has imposed on it the duty of performing that act, must, according to the dictates of reason, be allowed to select the means….

After the most deliberate consideration, it is the unanimous and decided opinion of this Court, that the act to incorporate the Bank of the United States is a law made in pursuance of the constitution, and is a part of the supreme law of the land….

It being the opinion of the Court, that the act incorporating the bank is constitutional…."

40. The decision acknowledged the governmental right to

    (A) impoundment powers
    (B) executive orders
    (C) implied powers
    (D) judicial review
    (E) the pocket veto

41. The quote is from the majority opinion written for

    (A) *McCulloch v. Maryland*
    (B) *Georgia v Peck*
    (C) *Gibbons v Ogden*
    (D) *Cohens v Virginia*
    (E) *Madison v. Marbury*

42. Which of the following is the best explanation for the controversial nature of the electoral college?

   (A) The electoral college does not give states with small populations equal power to large states in selecting the president.
   (B) The electoral college gives too much power to Congress in selecting the president.
   (C) The winner of electoral college votes is not necessarily the winner of the popular vote.
   (D) Electoral college members do not usually vote the same way that people in their states voted in the presidential election.
   (E) Electoral college members do not stay in touch with their state legislatures.

43. Signing statements have been used by presidents to

   (A) provide an interpretation of the law to guide agencies in enacting the law.
   (B) publicly state support or disapproval of Supreme Court decisions.
   (C) inform Congress that they will veto a bill if passed.
   (D) inform Congress of the need for a conference about the bill.
   (E) control the amount of pork projects passed by Congress.

44. The 25th Amendment protects the public from the actions of an incapacitated president by

   (A) an agreement among Congressional leaders and Cabinet members that temporarily removes the president from office.
   (B) an investigation by the Chief Justice, Speaker of the House and Senate Majority Leader.
   (C) an agreement between the vice president and a majority of Cabinet members that the president is disabled.
   (D) a Congressional ethics ruling.
   (E) an agreement among White House staff and Congressional leaders that temporarily removes the president from office.

45. In what way is the bureaucracy of the federal government different from most other large bureaucracies?

   (A) It has more task specialization.
   (B) Its rules are more extensive.
   (C) It has clearer goals.
   (D) It is administered more impersonally.
   (E) It reports to two authorities: the president and Congress.

46. The major power to create, organize, and disband federal agencies is given to

    (A) the president
    (B) the Director of the Office of Management and the Budget
    (C) Congress
    (D) the cabinet secretaries
    (E) the Supreme Court

47. Which of the following is an example of a government corporation?

    (A) Federal Trade Commission
    (B) Security and Exchange Commission
    (C) National Aeronautics and Space Administration
    (D) Tennessee Valley Authority
    (E) Environmental Protection Agency

48. Under the spoils system, appointments to federal jobs were based primarily on

    (A) region
    (B) merit
    (C) the president's whims
    (D) the wishes of Congress
    (E) patronage

49. The Pendleton Act created the

    (A) civil service
    (B) patronage program
    (C) Office of Personnel Management
    (D) Office of Management and the Budget
    (E) Senior Executive Service

50. Which of the following is NOT a power Congress has to control the bureaucracy?

    (A) rewriting legislation
    (B) conducting hearings to oversee the enforcement of laws
    (C) firing the heads of agencies
    (D) approving funds for bureaucratic programs
    (E) redistributing bureau responsibilities

51. Which of the following is an example of a federal independent agency?

    (A) Securities and Exchange Commission
    (B) Federal Trade Commission
    (C) National Labor Relations Board
    (D) National Aeronautics and Space Administration
    (E) Federal Aviation Administration

52. Which of the following positions is NOT a part of the "inner cabinet"?

    (A) secretary of state
    (B) secretary of defense
    (C) secretary of the treasury
    (D) attorney general
    (E) secretary of the interior

53. The United States has a court system at both the federal and state level which is known as a

    (A) double court system
    (B) criminal court system
    (C) appeals system
    (D) dual court system
    (E) two-court system

54. The term "discretionary authority" most aptly defines the policymaking power held by

    (A) Congress
    (B) the president
    (C) the bureaucracy
    (D) the Supreme Court
    (E) state and local governments

55. The 1877 Supreme Court decision in *Munn v. Illinois* gave a significant amount of power to government bureaucracies because it gave them the right to

    (A) challenge the right of the legislature to control their budgets
    (B) hire and fire their own workers
    (C) accept donations from interest groups
    (D) regulate business
    (E) own significant portions of the economy

56. Moving the responsibility of federal programs to the states is known as

    (A) privatization
    (B) devolution
    (C) dual sovereignty
    (D) reduction
    (E) impoundment

57. Which of the following is an important control that the president has on the bureaucracy?

    (A) authorizing funds
    (B) appropriating funds
    (C) declaring bureaucratic acts unconstitutional
    (D) firing bureaucrats
    (E) appointing senior bureaucrats

58. In the United States political system the iron triangle

    (A) describes the relationship between the three branches of government
    (B) explains the power of the executive and legislative branches to combat the courts' power of judicial review
    (C) describes the relationship between the "power cabinets" of State, Defense and Treasury
    (D) describes the close relationship between the bureaucracy, Congress and interest groups
    (E) explains the power of House and Senate committees over the bureaucracy

59. Which of the following is a current restriction that the Hatch Act places on federal employees?

    (A) They may not sign political petitions.
    (B) They may not make political contributions.
    (C) They may not run for political office.
    (D) They may not participate in rallies.
    (E) They may not participate in voter registration drives.

60. A law that imposes a punishment on a person or group without a trial is a

    (A) *ex post facto* law
    (B) bill of Attainder
    (C) habeus corpus
    (D) writ of certiorari
    (E) brief

61. The judicial doctrine based on the practice of deciding court cases with reference to previous decisions is called

   (A) mandamus
   (B) certiorari
   (C) *stare decisis*
   (D) judicial review
   (E) dual sovereignty

62. Which of the following qualifications for becoming a federal judge is directly addressed in Article III of the Constitution?

   (A) Federal judges have no fixed terms of office.
   (B) Federal judges must be at least 35 years old.
   (C) Federal judges must have experience in lower (state and local) courts.
   (D) Federal judges must have lived in the United States for at least 14 Years.
   (E) Federal judges must not hold any type of elected office.

63. The Supreme Court hears most cases as a result of

   (A) original jurisdiction
   (B) concurrent jurisdiction
   (C) *stare decisis*
   (D) appellate jurisdiction
   (E) administrative jurisdiction

64. The power of judicial review was first used in John Marshall's majority opinion expressed in

   (A) *Marbury v. Madison*
   (B) *McCulloch v. Maryland*
   (C) *Gibbons v. Ogden*
   (D) *Barron v. Baltimore*
   (E) the Dred Scott case

65. The "rule of four" refers to the number of

   (A) justices needed to rule a law unconstitutional
   (B) hearings that Congress must hold to review bills
   (C) courts needed to review a case before it reaches the Supreme Court.
   (D) Supreme Court justices needed to approve the review of a case
   (E) experts that must be heard by Congress in public hearings

66. If it became apparent that the number of justices on the Supreme Court needed to be adjusted this must be done by a(n)

    (A) act of Congress
    (B) constitutional amendment
    (C) executive order
    (D) referendum
    (E) joint committee in Congress

67. The Supreme Court decision that ensures that all defendants are provided with an attorney is

    (A) *Miranda v Arizona*
    (B) *Mapp v Ohio*
    (C) *Gideon v Wainwright*
    (D) *Engle v Vitale*
    (E) *Escobedo v Illinois*

68. In which of the following situations might a person be tried for a single criminal act twice?

    (A) It can't happen, since it would be double jeopardy.
    (B) It could happen in cases where more than one person is victimized.
    (C) It would happen if the same action broke both a state and a federal law.
    (D) It could happen if the judge is not objective in his ruling.
    (E) It could happen if the person is not a U.S. citizen.

69. Presidents generally honor the principle of senatorial courtesy in appointing judges to

    (A) the Supreme Court
    (B) U.S. Courts of Appeal
    (C) District Courts
    (D) Tax Court
    (E) Territorial Courts

70. Which of the following best describes the role that political party affiliation plays in a president's selection of federal judges?

    (A) Presidents try to be bipartisan in selecting judges.
    (B) Since judges are supposed to be nonpartisan, party affiliation generally doesn't matter for appointing judges.
    (C) 90% of judicial appointments in modern times have gone to members of the president's political party.
    (D) Party affiliation is important as a selection criterion, but not as important as political ideology.
    (E) Party affiliation is important only if there is a serious question that the Senate won't confirm the nomination.

71. Which of the following is a check of the courts' power of judicial review?

    (A) Congress may pass the bill again with a "super majority" of 2/3 approval.
    (B) A constitutional amendment may be passed.
    (C) A public referendum may overturn the court's decision.
    (D) The president may issue an executive order to overturn the decision.
    (E) The president, along with a 2/3 vote of both the House and Senate, may reject the court's decision.

72. The purpose of the "litmus test" as applied to judicial nominees is to

    (A) determine how long the nominee may want to serve on the court
    (B) provide a geographic balance to the Supreme Court
    (C) gain support of the American Bar Association before the nomination
    (D) determine the views of nominees on an important issue
    (E) maintain diversity of backgrounds on the court

73. Which of the following describes the usual route that a case follows to be brought before the Supreme Court?

    (A) by original jurisdiction, as defined in Article III of the Constitution
    (B) from state supreme courts directly
    (C) from U.S. Courts of Appeal, whose cases almost always go to the Supreme Court
    (D) by writ of certiorari
    (E) referred from the president's desk to the Court

74. If one or more justices of the Supreme Court agree with the majority opinion but for different reasons, those justices will issue a(n)

    (A) per curiam opinion
    (B) dissenting opinion
    (C) status quo opinion
    (D) concurring opinion
    (E) alternative opinion

75. Decisions under the Roberts Court are BEST characterized by which of the following?

    (A) The decisions have been less conservative than before.
    (B) Several conservative justices have controlled the decisions.
    (C) As Chief Justice, Roberts has not been able to write many decisions.
    (D) The majority of the decisions are liberal, with some being quite conservative.
    (E) The decisions have been close, in many cases with a 5–4 majority.

76. The practice of gaining a state's support for a federal judge candidate before a presidential appointment is

    (A) due process
    (B) senatorial courtesy
    (C) state jurisdiction
    (D) state precedent
    (E) judicial review

77. In order to avoid settling disputes more appropriately decided by Congress and the president, the courts have developed the doctrine of

    (A) justiciable dispute
    (B) rule of four
    (C) political questions
    (D) *stare decisis*
    (E) original jurisdiction

78. Cases involving citizens of different states are known as

    (A) federal-question cases
    (B) class-action cases
    (C) political cases
    (D) diversity cases
    (E) judicial review cases

"Where there is ambiguity as to the precise meaning or reach of a constitutional provision, it should be interpreted and applied in a manner so as to least not contradict the text of the Constitution itself."

79. The above statement most clearly reflects the judicial philosophy of

    (A) judicial restraint
    (B) avoiding political questions
    (C) judicial activism
    (D) judicial conservatism
    (E) judicial liberalism

80. Most federal court cases begin in

    (A) district courts
    (B) circuit courts
    (C) legislative courts
    (D) constitutional courts
    (E) courts of appeals

FREE RESPONSE QUESTION

Although public accountability over the United States bureaucratic system is difficult there are institutional ways to hold the bureaucracies accountable.

a)   Explain one reason why public accountability over the bureaucracy is difficult.

b)   Identify and describe two methods used by the executive branch to keep the bureaucracy accountable.

c)   Identify and describe two methods used by Congress to keep the bureaucracy accountable.

NO TESTING MATERIAL PRINTED ON THIS PAGE

GO ON TO THE NEXT PAGE

UNIT FIVE

PUBLIC POLICY

CHAPTER FOURTEEN
POLICY-MAKING

One of government's primary roles is to make policy that will solve society's problems. In the United States all three branches of government and the bureaucracy make policy. Many other organizations try to influence government decisions and programs, including special interest groups, research institutes, corporations, state and local governments, as well as individual citizens.

THE POLICYMAKING PROCESS

The policymaking process regularly makes news headlines, but it is not easy to understand how the overall process works. Every policy has a unique history, but each one generally goes through five basic stages:

1. **Recognizing the problem/agenda setting** – Almost no policy is made unless and until a need is recognized. Many different groups and people may bring a problem or issue to the government's attention through interest group activities or court cases. People within the government itself have their own agendas that they push, including the president, bureaucratic agencies, and members of Congress. Of course, these sources do not agree on which issues are most important, so getting the government to set an agenda that prioritizes problems is quite a challenge.

2. **Formulating the policy** – If enough people agree that government needs to act, then a plan of action must be formulated. At this stage, generally several alternative plans from various political groups are formed. For example, if the issue is gun control, interest groups from both sides will push for different solutions, and reaching a solution almost always involves compromise all around.

3. **Adopting the policy** – In this third stage, the policy becomes an official action by the government. It may take the form of legislation, an executive or bureaucratic order, or a court decision. Policy is often built in a series of small steps passed over time, so this stage may be quite complex.

4. **Implementing the policy** – For an adopted policy to be effective, government must see that it is applied to real situations. For example, if new gun control laws are set in place, government officials must make sure that the general public knows about them. They must also put enforcement in place and see that violators are punished appropriately.

5. **Evaluating the policy** – Evaluation of the good or the harm created by a policy usually takes place over an extended period of time. Policies that may seem sound at the start may have unforeseen negative consequences or unexpected costs. Inevitably, some will call for changes and/or corrections, and others will disagree. The whole process occurs again, starting with recognition – or re-recognition – of the problem. As a result, policymaking is a continuous process, and government at any given time is at various stages in the process with numerous issues under consideration.

ECONOMIC POLICY

How much responsibility should the government have for keeping the United States economy healthy? That question has been answered in many different ways throughout our history. Until the twentieth century the country followed the *laissez-faire* (literally, "to leave alone") policy, which required a free market without any intervention from government. With President Franklin Roosevelt's New Deal era of the 1930s came **Keynesian economics**, or the opposite belief that the government should manage the economy. Today the U.S. economic policy lies somewhere in between – government should regulate and sometimes manage, but should allow a free market whenever possible. Political and business leaders disagree on how much control is enough.

The budgeting of public funds is one of the most important decision making processes of government. Nothing reflects the growth in public policy and the rise of big government more clearly than the increased spending by the federal government. For example, in 1933, the annual federal budget was about $4 billion. Today the annual budget is more than $2.7 trillion, or about 20 percent of the gross domestic product. The **national debt** is about $9 trillion, and in 2007 the **deficit** (amount overspent in a given year) was about $162 billion.

FISCAL POLICY

Fiscal policy affects the economy by making changes in government's methods of raising money and spending it.

Where the Money Comes From

Not surprisingly, most government revenue comes from taxes, but some comes from interest, fees, and borrowing.

- **Federal income taxes** – The income tax is the largest single source of federal revenue today, providing about 45% of the national government's total revenues. It is a **progressive tax** – the higher the income and ability to pay, the higher the tax rate. Not only individuals pay income taxes; corporations do, too. About 14 percent of federal government revenues come from corporate income taxes. Today tax codes are so complex that most ordinary citizens don't understand them. As a result, many critics have called for tax codes to be simplified.

- **Social insurance taxes** – The largest social insurance taxes are for **Social Security** and **Medicare**. Employers apply these taxes to their employees, who are then eligible to receive Social Security benefits when they get older. Social insurance taxes fund the Social Security and Medicare programs. These taxes account for almost 1/3 of the total federal government revenues collected.

- **Borrowing** – The government regularly borrows money – most of it from its own taxpayers – to fund its expenses. **Deficit spending** occurs when the government spends more money than it takes in within any given fiscal year. Starting in the early 1990s Congress began considering required balanced budget amendments/legislation in order to cut the national debt. With increased tax revenues from the economic boom of the 1990s, deficit spending decreased and turned into a surplus, but governments generally borrow more money during wartime than during peace, so the war on terrorism and the war in Iraq put the country back into deficit spending during the early 2000s.

- **Other taxes** – A small percentage of revenue comes from other taxes, such as excise taxes, estate taxes, customs, duties, and tariffs. **Excise taxes** are levied on specified goods and services, such as liquor, gasoline, cigarettes, air travel, and telephones. These are **regressive taxes**, meaning that they are the same for everyone, and are not based on income. **Estate taxes** are levied on the money and property that are inherited when an individual dies, but are generally only levied on large estates. **Customs, duties, and tariffs** are levied on goods imported into the United States.

Where the Money Goes

The government now spends more than $2.7 trillion a year, as provided in the federal budget. Each year the President submits a federal budget for approval by Congress for money to be spent starting in October of that year. Government spends its revenue on many different things, but three major categories are entitlements, national defense, and the national debt.

- **Entitlement programs** – These payments are required by law, and are given to people meeting particular eligibility requirements. The largest programs are Social Security (pensions for older Americans), unemployment insurance, Medicare (medical benefits), and federal retirement pensions. Social Security and Medicare amount to about 41 percent of federal spending per year.
- **National defense** – The second largest amount goes for national defense. Today about 23 percent of the total budget goes for defense which is an increase from 18 percent in 2004. This is in contrast to 28 percent in 1987, when the cold war was still going on. However, the current war on terrorism and the war in Iraq have escalated defense expenditures again, up from about 16% in 2001.
- **National debt** – The third largest amount – about 8 percent – pays interest on the **national debt**, a figure that has also decreased in recent years.

Other expenditures are highway construction, education, housing, and foreign aid.

MONETARY POLICY

Monetary policy is the government's control of the money supply. The government can control how much or how little is in circulation by the amount of money that is printed and coined. If too much money is out there, it tends to cause **inflation**, or the devaluation of the dollar. Too little money in circulation causes the opposite – **deflation** – to occur.

The powerful arm of government that controls the money supply is the **Federal Reserve System**, which is headed by the **Federal Reserve Board**. The board is designed to operate with a great deal of independence from government control. One important way that the "Fed" controls the money supply is by adjusting interest rates – high rates discourage borrowing money, and low ones encourage it.

The Federal Reserve Board's seven members are appointed by the president and are approved by the Senate for 14-year, nonrenewable terms, and the president may not remove them from office before their terms are up. The chair is elected by the board for four years, and may be reelected. The Board heads the Federal Reserve System, which was created by Congress in 1913 to regulate the lending practices of banks. It consists of 12 regional banks, which in turn supervise a total of about 5,000 member banks across the United States.

FOREIGN POLICY

Until the 20th century, the United States was generally guided by an **isolationist foreign policy**, or the philosophy that we should avoid "entangling alliances" (the words of George Washington) whenever possible. Then, in the 20th century our involvement in World War I and World War II thrust us onto the world stage.

In the years after World War II, the United States was guided generally by **containment**, the policy of keeping communism from spreading beyond the countries already under its influence by about 1950. The policy applied to the United States' role in the **cold war**, a struggle between the United States and the Soviet Union for world power. With the collapse of the Soviet Union in 1991, containment no longer made sense, so in the past ten years, the U.S. has been redefining its foreign policy.

We have been active participants in many international organizations, such as the United Nations, but Americans disagree on just how much world involvement is appropriate. And then with the September 11 attacks on the World Trade Towers and the Pentagon, the United States finds itself spearheading an international war on terrorism. These developments conjure up the old questions within a very different set of circumstances. How actively should we fight terror? What, if any, are the limits? President Bush's decision to invade Iraq in 2003 to remove Saddam Hussein from power was controversial, and remains so, especially as the cost of the war escalated.

FOREIGN POLICY GOALS

To try to redefine foreign policy under the new set of circumstances brought about in 2001, we can begin with the Department of State, whose primary duty has always been the security of the nation. State Department goals include:

- Protecting national security
- Providing international leadership in developing world peace
- Insuring a balance of power; keeping aggressive nations from overpowering weaker ones
- Cooperating with other nations in solving international problems
- Promoting human rights and democratic values
- Fostering cooperative foreign trade and globalization of trade through international organizations

These goals are both national and international in nature, and the 2001 attacks on the World Trade Towers and the Pentagon confirm the fact that national and international interests are not easily separated any more. President George W. Bush used a policy of preemption to justify the war in Iraq, or the principle of attacking before being attacked. A major reason for invading Iraq presented by the Bush administration was to locate and destroy weapons of mass destruction within the country's borders. However, such weapons were never found during the U.S. occupation of the country.

WHO MAKES FOREIGN POLICY?

Many people and organizations within government have a hand in setting United States foreign policy. The main objective of foreign policy is to use **diplomacy** – conferences, meetings, and agreements – to solve international problems. They try to keep problems from developing into conflicts that require military settlements.

- **The President** – The leader in foreign policy is almost always the president. Presidents, or their representatives, meet with leaders of other nations to try to peacefully solve international problems. According to the Constitution, presidents sign treaties with other nations with the "advice and consent" of the Senate. So the Senate, and to a lesser extent, the House of Representatives, also participate in shaping foreign policy. Presidents may also make **executive agreements** with other heads of state that do not require Senate approval.

- **The Secretary of State** – As the head of the State Department, the secretary is the chief coordinator of all governmental actions that affect relations with other countries. The State Department also includes the **Foreign Service**, which consists of ambassadors and other official U.S. representatives to more than 160 countries. Ambassadors and their staffs set up embassies in the countries and serve as the major American presence in their respective assigned countries. They protect Americans abroad and are responsible for harmonious relationships with other countries.

- **The National Security Council** – As part of the Executive Office of the President, the Council helps the president deal with foreign, military, and economic policies that affect national security. Its members are the president, the vice president, the secretary of state, the secretary of defense, and any others that the president designates. The national security adviser coordinates the Council, and often has as much influence as the secretary of state, depending on his or her relationship to the president.

- **The Central Intelligence Agency** – One of the most famous of all government agencies, the CIA gathers, analyzes, and transmits information from other countries that might be important to the security of the nation. Although the CIA is best known for its participation in "spy" cases and "top secret" investigations, much of its work is public and routine. The CIA director is appointed by the president and confirmed by the Senate.

With the passage of a major intelligence bill in late 2004, intelligence gathering was altered significantly. The bill created a national intelligence director, who certainly will play a major role in shaping foreign policy in the future.

MILITARY POLICY

Until 1947 the Cabinet-level official most directly responsible for military policy was called the secretary of war. The name changed to "secretary of defense," and the department that this official heads has more federal employees than any other in the government. The Department of Defense is headquartered in the Pentagon, where about 25,000 military and civilian personnel work. The secretary of defense is always a civilian, and he supervises three large military departments – Army, Navy, and Air Force.

Under the Constitution, the president is commander-in-chief of the armed forces, and he has used that authority to order American military forces into combat on many occasions. During peacetime, his most important military powers are those he exercises through the secretary of defense in managing the Department of Defense. The president and secretary of defense make important decisions regarding the military budget and distribution of funds among the military services.

The most important military advisory body to the secretary of defense is the **Joint Chiefs of Staff**. Its five members are the chiefs of staff of the three military departments, the commandant of the Marines, and a chair. All of the service chiefs are appointed by the president and must be confirmed by the Senate. Only the secretary of defense, however, sits on the president's cabinet and on the National Security Council.

SOCIAL POLICY

The preamble to the Constitution states that "We the People of the United States, in Order to create a more perfect Union, establish Justice.... promote the general Welfare...do ordain and establish this Constitution…" Social policy is set with this important charge in mind.

The interpretation of the government's responsibility for the welfare of its citizens has changed over time and remains controversial today. The government currently assumes major responsibilities in three key social policy areas: health care, welfare, and education.

Health Care

Health care is controversial today with regard to the issue of a national health insurance program. In 1993 Congress defeated President Bill Clinton's proposed plan to provide all citizens with basic insurance coverage for doctor fees, hospitalization, and prescription drugs. On the other hand, most people accept government's role in medical research and regulating food and drugs. **The Public Health Service** researches, gathers information, and monitors health care. **The Food and Drug Administration** regulates the labeling and processing of most foods, drugs, and cosmetics. The **Center for Disease Control (CDC)** gained a new importance during the 2001 Anthrax scare following the September 11 attacks on the World Trade Towers and the Pentagon. The CDC continued to gain attention with the outbreak of "mad cow disease" when it reported the first case in the U.S. (Texas) in 2005. The agency provides updates on the disease in North America, the most recent in December, 2007 regarding Canadian cattle and the effects in the United States market. The CDC website also carries travel advisories regarding the problems of the disease for Americans traveling outside of the United States.

Welfare

To many Americans, the phrase "welfare" – right out of the preamble to the Constitution – often conjures images of irresponsible recipients who take welfare payments from the government instead of working. In truth, most Americans during their lifetimes will be the recipients of government welfare. The most extensive single welfare program is **Social Security**, a social insurance plan for the elderly, poor, and disabled. Employees and employers contribute to a fund through payroll taxes, and virtually everyone who contributes for at least ten years is eligible for payments. Most Americans support the program as long as it's called "Social Security," and not "welfare." Other public assistance programs include Medicare, Medicaid, Aid to Families with Dependent Children, and food stamps.

Social Security became a target for reform after President George W. Bush's State of the Union Address in February 2005. President Bush warned that the system would soon become bankrupt as the "Baby Boom" generation begins to retire, and he suggested establishing private accounts for younger people to ensure that money would be available to them when they retired. Democrats and some Republicans criticized the plan because money put into private accounts would further deplete the trust fund that is set aside to pay future benefits. Suggested reforms to avoid future bankruptcy included reduced benefits, higher taxes, taxes on upper income groups, and delayed age for retirement. The downturn in the economy that began in 2007 has forced the idea of **privatization** of Social Security to be dropped, at least temporarily.

Education

Public education is generally regarded as the responsibility of states and local communities, so the federal government's role in this area is limited. Today most federal funds go to higher education, primarily in the form of student loans and grants. Since the 1950s the federal government has provided funds for public education grades 1-12, particularly for programs to upgrade science, language, and mathematics. Other programs, such as **Head Start** for preschoolers, focus on helping underprivileged children. However, the federal government today funds less than 10 percent of the total amount spent on education in the United States. A recent initiative by President George W. Bush is **No Child Left Behind (NCLB)**, a comprehensive program that sets standards and schedules for testing, curriculum, and teacher qualifications. The program has been controversial, partly because it has imposed unfunded mandates on the states.

REGULATORY POLICY

The U.S. government first began regulating individuals, businesses, and its own agencies during the late 1800s. Since then, the government's regulatory role has grown rapidly, so that today most activities are regulated in some way by the federal government. Important regulatory activities of the government include:

- **Regulating business.** The national government began regulating business in the late 1800s in order to eliminate **monopolies**, businesses that have exclusive control of an industry. Government now regulates a wide array of business practices, including elimination of competition and fraudulent product offerings.

- **Regulating labor.** Labor regulations became a major focus of the government during the 1930s. Then as now, most labor policies have been made to protect the American worker. The government has promoted equal employment opportunities, safe and sanitary workplace standards, and fair bargaining practices between employer and workers.

- **Regulating energy and the environment.** Energy policies are coordinated by the **Department of Energy**, created in the late 1970s in the wake of worldwide oil and gas shortages. A major concern of energy policy makers is maintaining a supply of cheap energy that the country depends on for most of its activities. Many are alarmed by the country's dependence on Middle-Eastern oil, and others keep a watchful eye on depletion of U.S. natural resources and damage to the environment. Environmental policy, on the other hand is the responsibility of many different government departments and agencies. Especially important is the **Environmental Protection Agency**, which enforces policies on water and air pollution, pesticides, radiation, and waste disposal.

Many different people take part in setting U.S. public policy. Some groups that form close links to individual citizens participate in policy making, particularly interest groups, the media, and political parties. Within the government itself, all three branches have a say, and in any one area, policies are usually set by any number of people having input at many points in the process.

IMPORTANT DEFINITIONS AND IDENTIFICATIONS:

- Center for Disease Control
- Central Intelligence Agency
- Cold War
- containment
- customs, duties, tariffs
- deficit
- deficit spending
- deflation
- diplomacy
- entitlement programs
- Environmental Protection Agency
- estate taxes
- executive agreements
- Federal Reserve Board
- Federal Reserve System
- fiscal policy
- Food and Drug Administration
- Foreign Service
- Head Start
- inflation
- isolationism foreign policy
- Joint Chiefs of Staff
- Keynesian economics
- laissez-faire policy
- Medicare
- monetary policy
- monopolies
- national debt
- National Security Advisor
- National Security Council
- No Child Left Behind
- preemption
- privatization
- progressive tax
- Public Health Service
- regressive tax
- social insurance taxes
- Social Security

UNIT FIVE QUESTIONS

1. The Food and Drug Administration is primarily responsible for which of the following with regard to U.S. government policy?

   (A) Setting the price levels of food and drugs.
   (B) Regulating the labeling and processing of food and drugs.
   (C) Providing information to Congress about the supply of food and drugs.
   (D) Cooperating with charities to help provide low-cost food and drugs to the poor.
   (E) Providing food and drugs to areas during a national crisis or natural disaster.

2. All of the following government officials advise the president with regard to foreign policy EXCEPT:

   (A) Secretary of Defense
   (B) Secretary of State
   (C) Secretary of Commerce
   (D) Secretary of Treasury
   (E) Secretary of Transportation

3. The amount that the government overspends in a budget year is called

   (A) public debt
   (B) private debt
   (C) the deficit
   (D) fiscal excess
   (E) progressive spending

4. An example of social insurance taxes is a(n)

   (A) personal income tax
   (B) corporate income tax
   (C) social security tax
   (D) sales tax
   (E) tariff on imports

5. The largest source of government revenue comes from

   (A) Excise taxes
   (B) Entitlement taxes
   (C) Customs duties
   (D) Corporate taxes
   (E) Progressive income taxes

6. Which of the following is the most common way that Americans have influenced the government's policy-making process?

   (A) Participating in interest groups
   (B) Meeting with members of Congress
   (C) Writing to the president
   (D) Testifying before congressional committees
   (E) Refusing to pay their taxes

7. During which era of U.S. history was the foreign policy of containment most influential?

   (A) The time when Theodore Roosevelt was president
   (B) The New Deal Era
   (C) Before and during World War II
   (D) The Cold War era
   (E) The post-Cold War era

8. No Child Left Behind is a federal program that

   (A) improved health standards in the nation
   (B) increased welfare payments to help poor families
   (C) standardized education goals
   (D) increased federal tax benefits for parents
   (E) provided more funding for college scholarships to help the poor

9. Which of the following was the foreign policy applied by President George W. Bush in the time period following the attacks of September 11, 2001?

   (A) Isolationism
   (B) Containment
   (C) Détente
   (D) Internationalism
   (E) Preemption

10. Its members are the president, the vice president, the secretary of state, the secretary of defense, and any others that the president designates. The body is called the

   (A) National Security Council
   (B) Department of Defense
   (C) Central Intelligence Agency
   (D) Council of Economic Advisers
   (E) Joint Chiefs of Staff

11. Which of the following is an example of monetary policy?

   (A) Entitlement programs
   (B) Deficit spending
   (C) Excise taxes
   (D) Inflationary controls
   (E) National defense

12. Which of the following policy areas does NOT have its own separate cabinet level department in the federal bureaucracy?

   (A) Transportation
   (B) Commerce
   (C) Defense
   (D) Education
   (E) The census

13. Which of the following is MOST responsible for the projected bankruptcy of the Social Security system?

   (A) Inflationary conditions requiring higher benefits for all retirees
   (B) Higher tax rates for low-income wage earners
   (C) The pressure put on the system as the baby boomers retire
   (D) Added benefits for widows and orphans
   (E) Increased mandatory contributions from the states

14. Which of the following policy areas is considered to be primarily the responsibility of state and local governments?

   (A) Defense
   (B) Labor relations
   (C) Education
   (D) Social Security
   (E) Medicare

15. The most important advantage of executive agreements in policy-making for the president is that

   (A) interest groups usually always approve of them.
   (B) a filibuster is not possible when Congress debates them.
   (C) they do not need Senate approval as do treaties.
   (D) the House of Representatives is not required to "advise and consent" to them.
   (E) it is only necessary to gain Congressional leadership approval.

FREE RESPONSE QUESTION

Although the allocations vary from year to year, the federal spending budget of the United States government typically includes many expenditures that are "built in," mandatory, and difficult to change. These expenditures hinder the creation of new policies.

a) Identify two types of mandatory expenditures and explain why each is difficult to change.

b) Using your knowledge of U.S. politics, identify one non-budgetary factor that prevents the creation of new policies AND explain how this factor hinders new policies.

NO TESTING MATERIAL PRINTED ON THIS PAGE

UNIT SIX

CIVIL LIBERTIES AND CIVIL RIGHTS

CHAPTER FIFTEEN
CIVIL LIBERTIES

A respect for civil liberties and civil rights is one of the most fundamental principles of the American political culture. The founders were very concerned with defining and protecting liberties and rights, and their efforts are reflected in the Declaration of Independence, the Constitution, and the Bill of Rights. Civil liberties and rights have continued to evolve through the years by means of additional amendments (particularly the Fourteenth), court decisions, and legislative actions.

THE DECLARATION OF INDEPENDENCE

"We hold these truths to be self-evident; that all men are created equal, that they are endowed by their Creator with certain unalienable rights, that among these are life, liberty, and the pursuit of happiness. That, to secure these rights, governments are instituted among men, deriving their just powers from the consent of the governed."

Thomas Jefferson, 1776

The Declaration clearly reflects the founders' belief that governments are responsible for protecting the "unalienable rights" of "life, liberty, and the pursuit of happiness." Since people are clearly capable of abusing the "natural rights" of others, the government must protect the rights of its citizens.

THE ORIGINAL CONSTITUTION

Most of the framers believed that the basic "natural rights" were guaranteed by the original Constitution before the Bill of Rights was added. Rights specifically mentioned in the body of the Constitution are:

- writ of *habeas corpus*
- no bills of attainder
- no *ex post facto* laws
- trial by jury in federal courts in criminal cases
- protection as citizens move from one state to another
- no titles of nobility
- limits on punishment for and use of the crime of treason
- no religious oaths for holding federal office
- guarantee of republican government for all states

THE WRIT OF HABEAS CORPUS

"The privilege of the Writ of *Habeas Corpus* shall not be suspended, unless when in Cases of Rebellion or Invasion the public Safety may require it."

Article One, Section Nine
The Constitution of the United States

Habeas corpus literally means "produce the body." The writ is a court order requiring government officials to present a prisoner in court and to explain to the judge why the person is being held. Suspension of *habeas corpus* is a right of Congress, since the passage above appears in Article One, which defines the powers of Congress.

Originally, the writ was only a court inquiry regarding the jurisdiction of the court that ordered the individual's confinement, but today it has developed into a remedy that a prisoner can formally request. A federal judge may order the jailer to show cause why the person is being held, and the judge may order the prisoner's immediate release.

The Supreme Court under Chief Justice Rehnquist has severely limited the use of *habeas corpus* partly because prisoners on death row have used it to delay their executions, sometimes for years. Supporters of *habeas corpus* believe that judges should be allowed to use their own judgment in issuing the writs because they are protecting constitutional rights.

EX POST FACTO LAWS AND BILLS OF ATTAINDER

The Constitution forbids both national and state governments from passing ***ex post facto laws***. An *ex post facto* law is a retroactive criminal law that affects the accused individual negatively. Such laws may make an action a crime that was not a crime when committed, or they may increase punishment for a crime after it was committed. On the other hand, the restriction does not apply to penal laws that work in favor of the accused.

A bill of attainder is a legislative act that punishes an individual or group without judicial trial. The Constitution forbids them because the founders believed that it is the job of the courts, not Congress, to decide that a person is guilty of a crime and then impose punishment.

THE BILL OF RIGHTS

The overwhelming majority of court decisions that define American civil liberties are based on the Bill of Rights, the first ten amendments added to the Constitution in 1791. Even though most of the state constitutions in 1787 included separate bills of rights for their citizens, the original Constitution mentioned only the rights listed above. These rights were scattered throughout the articles, with most of the attention focused on defining and limiting the powers of the branches of government, not on preserving individual rights. Many people were widely suspicious of these omissions, and in order to gain ratification, the founders agreed to add ten amendments in 1791, the **Bill of Rights**.

- The **First Amendment** guarantees freedom of speech, press, assembly and petition. In addition, it prohibits Congress from establishing a national religion.
- The **Second Amendment** allows the right to bear arms.
- The **Third Amendment** prohibits the quartering of soldiers in any house.
- The **Fourth Amendment** restricts searches and seizures ("the right of the people to be secure in their persons, houses, papers, and effects").
- The **Fifth Amendment** provides for grand juries, restricts eminent domain (the right of the government to take private property for public use), and prohibits forced self-incrimination and double jeopardy (being tried twice for the same crime).
- **Amendment Six** outlines criminal court procedures.
- **Amendment Seven** guarantees trial by jury in civil cases that involve values as low as twenty dollars.
- **Amendment Eight** prevent excessive bail and cruel and unusual punishment.
- The **Ninth Amendment** allows that Amendments 1-8 do not necessarily include all possible rights of the people.
- The **Tenth Amendment** reserves for the states any powers not delegated to the national government specifically in the Constitution. (reserved powers).

OTHER SOURCES OF CIVIL LIBERTIES AND CIVIL RIGHTS

The Constitution and the Bill of Rights form the basis of American values concerning civil liberties and civil rights, but they have been supplemented through the years by other amendments, court decisions, and legislative action.

THE FOURTEENTH AMENDMENT

Civil rights are also protected by the **Fourteenth Amendment**, which protects violation of rights and liberties by the state governments.

"All persons born or naturalized in the United States, and subject to the jurisdiction thereof, are citizens of the United States and of the State wherein they reside. No State shall make or enforce any law which shall abridge the privileges or immunities of citizens of the United States; nor shall any State deprive any person of life, liberty, or property, without due process of law; nor deny to any person within its jurisdiction the equal protection of the laws."

Amendment Fourteen, Section One

Although the Fourteenth Amendment was originally passed in the post-Civil War era specifically to protect the rights of ex-slaves, the famous Section One protects many citizens," rights from abuse by state governments. Whereas the Bill of Rights literally applies only to the national government, the Fourteenth Amendment is intended to limit the actions of state governments as well. Section One includes:

- a citizenship clause that protects **"privileges and immunities"**
- a **due process clause** that prohibits abuse of "life, liberty, or property"

- an **equal protection clause** that has been an important basis of the modern civil rights movement

One important consequence of the court's interpretation of the Fourteenth Amendment is the **incorporation** of the Bill of Rights into the due process clause of that amendment so as to make them apply to the states. The Bill of Rights originally only limited the powers of the federal government, and in ***Barron vs. Baltimore*** (1833) the U.S. Supreme Court ruled that the Bill of Rights did not apply to state laws. It was assumed that Bills of Rights in state constitutions would protect individuals from abuse by state laws. However, the 14th Amendment nationalized the nature of civil rights with this statement:

"No State shall...deprive any person of life, liberty, or property, without due process of law."

Incorporation happened gradually over time through individual court decisions that required states to protect most of the same liberties and rights that the Bill of Rights protects from federal abuse. The gradual application of the Bill of Rights to the states is known as **selective incorporation**. These changes are reflected in numerous court decisions made between 1925 and 1969. Two examples of cases that reflect incorporation are:

- ***Gitlow v. New York*** (1925) – Benjamin Gitlow was arrested and found guilty of breaking a New York state sedition act when he passed out pamphlets that supported socialism and overthrow of the government. Gitlow believed that his freedom of speech was violated, and the case was appealed to the Supreme Court. Even though the Court did not declare the New York law unconstitutional, the majority opinion stated that "fundamental personal rights" such as freedom of speech were protected from infringement by states by the Due Process Clause of the Fourteenth Amendment.

- ***Gideon v. Wainwright*** (1963) – Clarence Gideon appealed the decision of a Florida court to send him to prison for breaking and entering a pool hall. He based his appeal on the right to counsel (guaranteed in the Sixth Amendment) – because in the original trial he could not afford to hire a lawyer and was not provided one by the state court. The Supreme Court ruled in his favor, again incorporating the right to council into the Due Process Clause of the Fourteenth Amendment to require states to provide counsel to anyone charged with a felony who was too poor to afford a lawyer.

COURT DECISIONS

The Supreme Court continues to shape the definition and application of civil rights and civil liberties. Although the court has always played an important role in the protection of civil rights and civil liberties, it has been particularly active in the modern era since about 1937. The Supreme Court sets precedents that influence legislation and subsequent court decisions. The Court's influence is based largely on **judicial review**, the power to judge the constitutionality of a law or government regulation.

LEGISLATIVE ACTION

The Constitution, the Bill of Rights, and the Fourteenth Amendment protect individuals from actions of government, but court decisions and legislation protect individuals from discriminatory actions by private citizens and organizations. Legislative action is an essential component of the modern civil rights era, although the courts took the earliest initiatives.

The activist court of the 1960s set precedents that broadly construe the commerce clause, which gives Congress the power to regulate interstate and foreign commerce. As a result, through laws like the **Civil Rights Act of 1964**, the legislature has played a major role in combating discrimination.

The Constitution, the Bill of Rights, the Fourteenth Amendment, Supreme Court decisions, and legislative actions all define the nature of civil rights and civil liberties in American society, but issues arise which constantly cause reinterpretations of the sources. Conflicts arise largely because issues often involve one citizen's or group's rights versus another's.

FIRST AMENDMENT LIBERTIES

"Congress shall make no law respecting an establishment of religion or prohibiting the free exercise thereof; or abridging the freedom of speech, or of the press; or the right of the people peaceably to assemble, and to petition the Government for a redress of grievances."

The First Amendment
The Constitution of the United States

The **First Amendment** protects several basic liberties: freedom of religion, speech, press, petition, and assembly. Interpretation of the amendment is far from easy, as court case after court case has tried to define the limits of these freedoms. The definitions have evolved throughout American history, and the process continues today.

FREEDOM OF RELIGION

The 1st Amendment protects freedom of religion in two separate clauses: the **"establishment" clause**, which prohibits the government from establishing an official church, and the **"free exercise" clause** that allows people to worship as they please. Surprisingly, the First Amendment does not refer specifically to the "separation of church and state" or a **"wall of separation."** Those phrases evolved later, probably from letters written by Thomas Jefferson, but the First Amendment does prohibit the establishment of a government sponsored religion, such as the Anglican Church in England.

The Establishment Clause

The *Everson v. Board of Education* case in 1947 challenged a New Jersey town for reimbursing parents for the cost of transporting students to school, including local parochial schools. The plaintiffs claimed that since the parochial schools were religious, publicly financed transportation costs could not be provided for parochial students. The challenge was based on the establishment clause. The court in this case ruled against the plaintiffs, claiming that busing is a "religiously neutral" activity, and that the reimbursements were appropriate. However, the majority opinion declared that states cannot support one religion above another.

Aid to church-related schools has been challenged as a violation of the establishment clause. In 1971 in *Lemon v. Kurtzman*, the Supreme Court ruled that direct state aid could not be used to subsidize religious instruction. The Court's opinion stated that government aid to religious schools had to be secular in purpose, and that "an excessive government entanglement with religion" should be avoided. However, in recent years the Court has relaxes restrictions on government aid to religious schools. For example, in 1997 the Supreme Court overturned *Aquilar v. Felton*, a 1985 decision that ruled unconstitutional state aid for disadvantaged students who attend religious schools.

A current establishment clause issue is that of **school vouchers**, money provided by the government to individuals that allows them to "purchase" education at any school, public or private. School districts in several states, including Florida, Ohio, and Wisconsin, have experimented with voucher programs. In 2002 the Supreme Court held that the Cleveland voucher system was constitutional, although almost all the students used the vouchers to attend religious schools.

The most controversial issue of the separation of church and state has been school prayer. The first major case was *Engle v. Vitale* (1962). In this case, the Court banned the use of a prayer written by the New York State Board of Regents. It read, "Almighty God, we acknowledge our dependence upon Thee, and we beg Thy blessings upon us, our parents, our teachers, and our country." Later decisions overturned laws requiring the saying of the Lord"s Prayer and the posting of the Ten Commandments in classrooms. In 1985, *Wallace v. Jaffree* banned Alabama"s **"moment of silence"** law that provided for a one-minute period of silence for "meditation or voluntary prayer."

In recent years prayer outside the classroom has become an issue, with student-initiated prayer at graduation ceremonies and sports events at its focus. In 2000 the Supreme Court affirmed a lower court ruling that school prayer at graduation did not violate the establishment clause, but that prayer over loud speakers at sports events did.

In 2005 the court ruled on the public display of framed copies of the Ten Commandments in public schools and courthouses. In *McCreary County v ACLU* the American Civil Liberties Union challenged these displays in three counties in Kentucky as a violation of the First Amendment Establishment Clause. The Supreme Court agreed that the purpose of the displays was to promote religion and as such were unconstitutional. However, a similar case in Texas had a different outcome. In *Van Orden v Perry* (2005) a monument of the Ten Commandments, located on the grounds of the state capitol, was also challenged as a violation of the Establishment Clause. The Court ruled that the Texas display had a more historical meaning and was, therefore, constitutional.

The Free Exercise Clause

The free exercise clause does not allow any laws "prohibiting the free exercise of religion." The courts have interpreted the 14th Amendment to extend the freedom to protection from state governments as well. Religions sometimes require actions that violate the rights of others or forbid actions that society thinks are necessary. The Supreme Court has never allowed religious freedom to be an excuse for any type of behavior. It has consistently ruled that people have the absolute right to believe what they want, but not necessarily the right to religious practices that may harm society.

Some outlawed practices have been polygamy, the use of poisonous snakes in religious rites, and prohibiting medical treatment to children based on religious beliefs. *Oregon v Smith* (1990) dealt with the use of peyote, a strong hallucinogen drug, by the members of the Native American Church. The Supreme Court ruled that prohibiting the use of the drug was not a violation of the Free Exercise Clause because religious beliefs do not excuse a person from following laws prohibiting certain conduct. The Court stated that allowing exceptions "would open the prospect of constitutionally required exemptions from civic obligations of almost every conceivable kind" such as paying taxes and vaccination requirements. Despite this ruling allowing states to prohibit the use of peyote, courts in other states have upheld its use in religious ceremonies. For example, in 2004 the Utah Supreme Court ruled that peyote can be used even by non-Native Americans for religious purposes. On the other hand, courts have disallowed some government restrictions of religious exercise, such as forcing flag salutes and requiring Amish parents to send their children to school after eighth grade.

Protection of Religious Pluralism

Religious pluralism occurs when a society has citizens that practice many types of religious beliefs. Conflicts are normal when the country tries to protect the people's ability to worship as they please while not forcing their religious beliefs on others. The courts often must decide whether actions or decisions force others to live by the rules of any one religion, indicating that the "wall of separation" has been violated. Courts have also been concerned about whether or not violations intentionally promote a particular religious belief. Challenges to community Nativity scenes have resulted in different interpretations by the Court. In *Lynch v Donnelly* (1984), the Court ruled that the city's nativity display was one among others involving such items as Santa Claus and a "Seasons Greetings" sign. The court ruled that it reflected the "historic origins of the holiday and had legitimate secular purposes." However, in *Allegheny v ACLU* (1989) the Court ruled a Nativity scene inside a courthouse did violate the Establishment Clause by displaying a sign stating, "Glory to God for the birth of Jesus Christ." Violations of the Establishment Clause have been found in the use of school prayer at football games (*Santa Fe Independent Schools v Doe* in 2000) and during the school day (*Abington School District v Schemp* in 1963). However, the tax exempt status of churches was upheld in *Walz v Tax Commission of City of New York* (1970) since it does not advance or inhibit religion because it applies to all religions. In *Hein v Freedom from Religion Foundation* (2007) President George W. Bush's Faith-Based and Community Initiative was challenged under the Establishment Clause but the Court disallowed the case, ruling that the Freedom from Religion Foundation had no standing to sue since it had suffered no direct injury.

FREEDOM OF SPEECH

Citizens of modern America almost take for granted the responsibility of the government to guarantee freedom of speech. In reality, the definition of freedom of speech has changed dramatically over the years, with an ever-increasing emphasis on protection of free speech, often at the expense of other liberties and rights. Until recently, especially during times of war and crisis when national security is at stake, the government has passed laws that control free speech.

Free Speech v. National Security

Early in United States history the government almost certainly did not put high priority on its responsibility to protect freedom of speech. John Adams, when faced with an international crisis that threatened war with France, saw that Congress passed the **Sedition Act of 1798**, making it a crime to write, utter, or publish anti-government statements with the "intent to defame." The Federalists, who favored strong government authority and emphasized order at the expense of liberty, believed that the First Amendment did not forbid punishing newspapers for libel. The Anti-Federalists did NOT argue that the press should be free of government controls; they protested the act on the grounds that state, not federal government should have control. Thomas Jefferson, a prominent Anti-Federalist, allowed the twenty-year limitation of the Act to run out during his presidency, and the Act died during peace time with little protest.

Presidents, such as Abraham Lincoln during the Civil War, continued to support the governmen's right to restrict freedom of speech during national security crises through the 19th century and into the 20th. During World War I, the U.S. Congress passed two controversial laws that restricted freedom of speech: The **Espionage Act of 1917** and the **Sedition Act of 1918**.

The Espionage Act of 1917 forbid false statements that intended to interfere with the U.S. military forces or materials to be mailed if they violated the law or advocated resistance to government. The Sedition Act of 1918 forbid individuals to utter, print, write or publish language intended to incite resistance to the U.S. government. Under the mandate of the Sedition Act, thousands were arrested and convicted, and some were deported from the country.

The most famous Supreme Court case that resulted from the World War I restrictions was *Schenck v. U.S.* (1919) Charles Schenck, a socialist who mailed circulars to young men urging them to resist the military draft, was convicted of violating the Espionage Act. The Supreme Court upheld his conviction, with Oliver Wendell Holmes writing the precedent-setting opinion that any language that directly caused an illegal act was not protected by the First Amendment. Holmes distinguished between language that was merely critical of the government and that which was directly a "clear and present danger" to national security. The **"clear and present danger"** test became a standard by which to balance national security and freedom of speech.

Even before the U.S. entered World War II, Congress passed the **Smith Act**, intending to protect the country from the influence of Nazism and Communism. The Act contained two clauses:

- punishment for willfully advocating the overthrow of the government
- punishment for membership in a group that advocated the overthrow of government (the membership clause)

A few cases were tried dealing with wartime behavior, but the real impact of the Smith Act came after World War II was over with the fear of Communist espionage in the Red Scare, or McCarthyism. The U.S. experienced a dramatic reaction to the Cold War, fueled by the fear that communists were infiltrating the U.S. government and passing security secrets to the Russians. The **Internal Security Act of 1950** required Communist organizations to register and to publish membership lists. Many were questioned by congressional committees and many were arrested.

By the late 1950s, with McCarthyism subsiding and a new Supreme Court under the direction of Earl Warren, the Court leaned more and more toward freedom of speech. No laws were passed restricting speech during the Vietnam War, and the **_Brandenburg v. Ohio_** (1969) case established that speech would have to be judged as inciting "imminent" unlawful action in order to be restricted. The case involved a Ku Klux Klan leader convicted of attempting to incite mob action when he said "We"ll take the (expletive deleted) street later." The conviction was overturned by the Supreme Court because Brandenburg did not call for an **"imminent" action**.

Restrictions on Free Speech

Today, the following forms of speaking and writing are not granted full constitutional protection:

1) **Libel**, a false written statement that attacks another person's character, is not automatically protected, although it is very hard to sue for libel. Public figures must prove that a statement is not only false but that it intended "actual malice," a condition that is very hard to define.

2) **Obscenity** is not protected, but the Court has always had a difficult time defining obscenity. The current Court leaves local governments to decide restrictions for hard-core pornography, but if they choose to restrict it, they must meet some strict constitutional tests. One common reaction has been for a local government to establish areas where pornography can and can't be sold. A new issue concerns pornography on the internet. In 1997 the Supreme Court ruled the **Communications Decency Act** unconstitutional because it infringed too much on free speech.

3) **Symbolic speech**, an action meant to convey a political message, is not protected because to protect it would be to allow many illegal actions, such as murder or rape, if an individual meant to send a message through the action. The Court made an exception to the action of flag-burning in ***Texas v. Johnson*** (1989), when it declared that the Texas law prohibiting flag desecration was unconstitutional. Since flag-burning has no other intent than to convey a message, the Court has ruled that it does not incite illegal actions. Symbolic speech includes advocacy of illegal actions, as well as "fighting words," or inciting others to commit illegal actions. In 2003 the Supreme Court ruled that a Virginia law that prohibited the burning of a cross with "an intent to intimidate" did not violate the First Amendment. The Court reasoned that a burning cross is an instrument of racial terror so threatening that it overshadows free speech concerns.

SECOND AMENDMENT RIGHTS

In the case ***District of Columbia v Heller*** (2008) the Supreme Court reviewed, for the first time since 1939, the right of Americans to own guns for personal use. The case involved a challenge to the most restrictive gun law in the United States. The Washington, D. C. law banned registration of handguns, required licenses for all pistols, and required all legal firearms to be kept unloaded and disassembled or trigger-locked. The question in the case focused on whether the 2nd Amendment protects the use of guns for personal use or if it only applies to the use of guns for militia purposes. In a close decision (5-4) the court ruled that the 2nd Amendment protects an individual right to own a gun for personal use, including keeping a gun at home for self-defense. According to Justice Scalia, writing for the majority, the decision was not intended to state that all gun control laws were unconstitutional, only that this law was too restrictive. "The court's opinion should not be taken to cast doubt on long standing prohibitions on the possession of firearms...." The Court "finds support in the historical tradition of prohibiting the carrying of dangerous and unusual weapons." This case, combined with the shooting tragedy at Virginia Tech, which resulted in many student deaths, caused Congress, with the support of President Bush, to develop a gun control law restricting the ownership of guns by those suffering from mental illness. It required gun stores to restrict the sale of the guns to those who were registered. Because many states could not afford to maintain proper records, the bill provided $1.3 billion to help states develop programs to register this information. The legislation even gained the support of the National Rifle Association, a group that consistently works to prevent gun control legislation. However, the law does contain a familiar loophole. Just as in previous gun-control laws, gun shows are exempt from the law, meaning that a person suffering from mental illness may still buy a gun at a gun show. Congress has plans to review closing this loophole but, as of early 2009, has not done so yet.

PRIVACY RIGHTS

The phrase **"right to privacy"** does not appear anywhere in the Constitution or the Bill of Rights. The idea was first expressed in the 1965 *Griswold v. Connecticut* case in which a doctor and family-planning specialist were arrested for disseminating birth control devices under a little-used Connecticut law that forbid the use of contraceptives. The Supreme Court ruled against the state, with the majority opinion identifying "penumbras" – unstated liberties implied by the stated rights – that protected a right to privacy, including a right to family planning.

The most important application of privacy rights came in the area of abortion as first ruled by the Court in *Roe v. Wade* in 1973. Jane Roe (whose real name was Norma McCorvey) challenged the Texas law allowing abortion only to save the life of a mother. Texas argued that a state has the power to regulate abortions, but the court overruled, forbidding any state control of abortions during the first three months of a pregnancy and limiting state control during the fourth through sixth months. The justices cited the right to privacy as the liberty to choose to have an abortion before the baby was viable. The *Roe v. Wade* decision sparked the controversy that surrounds abortion today.

Since the late 1980s the Supreme Court has tended to rule more conservatively on abortion rights. For example, in *Webster v. Reproductive Health Services* (1989) the Court upheld a Missouri statue that banned the use of taxpayer-supported facilities for performing abortions. In *Planned Parenthood v Casey* (1992), the Court upheld a Pennsylvania law that required pre-abortion counseling, a waiting period of twenty-four hours, and for girls under eighteen, parental or judicial permission. In 2000 the court reviewed a Nebraska act that banned "partial birth" abortion, a procedure that could only take place during the second trimester of a pregnancy. The Court declared the act unconstitutional because it could be used to ban other abortion procedures. The majority opinion also noted that the law did not include protection of the health of the pregnant women. In 2003, the U.S. Congress passed a national law similar to the Nebraska act called the Partial-Birth Abortion Act which was immediately challenged in court. The challenge involved whether the law permitted the procedure in order to protect the health of the mother. In *Gonzalez v Planned Parenthood* (2007) the Court ruled that the federal law did not violate the due process clause of the 5th Amendment. The court stated that to require an exception whenever "medical uncertainty" exists would be "exacting a standard to impose on the legislative power…to regulate the medical profession."

RIGHTS OF DUE PROCESS

The **due process** clauses in the Fifth and Fourteenth Amendment forbid the national and state governments to "deny any person life, liberty, or property without due process of law." Although the Supreme Court has refused to define precisely what is meant by due process, it generally includes both **procedural due process** that gives an individual a fair hearing or formal trial and **substantive due process** (fundamental fairness). Although due process is most often associated with the rights of those accused of crimes, it is required for protecting property rights as well.

PROPERTY RIGHTS

The founders saw the government as not only the protector of property but also the potential abuser of property rights.

The Fifth Amendment allows the government the right to **eminent domain** (the power to claim private property for public use), but the owner must be fairly compensated. The Court has interpreted this clause to be a direct taking of property, not just a government action that may result in a property losing value, such as a rezoning regulation. Also, the government and the property owner sometimes interpret "just compensation" differently. In such a case, the courts are the final arbitrators.

Eminent domain became controversial in *Kelo v New London*, *Ct.* (2005). The city of New London used the power of eminent domain to seize private property and sell it to a private developer in order to create jobs and increase the city's tax base. The property owners involved challenged the sale of their land to private developers as "public use". The Supreme Court ruled that the act did qualify as "public use" as it was not done to benefit a certain group of private individuals but followed an economic plan that benefited the community. The Court stated that the 5th Amendment did not require a "literal" public use, but could involve a "broader and more natural interpretation of public use…". In reaction, many states passed laws or constitutional amendments restricting the use of eminent domain. Some of the restrictions involved limiting land use, requiring public hearings as part of the process and better clarification in the meaning of "just compensation".

THE FOURTH AMENDMENT AND SEARCH AND SEIZURE

Freedom from **"unreasonable search and seizure"** is guaranteed by the Fourth Amendment. To prevent abuse by police, the Constitution requires that searches of private property are permissible only if "probable cause" exists that indicates that a crime may have taken place.

An important limitation was set on police searches by *Mapp v. Ohio*, a 1961 case in which the police broke into the home of Dollree Mapp, a woman under suspicion for illegal gambling activities. Instead, they found obscene materials and arrested Mapp for possessing them. She appealed her case, claiming that the Fourth Amendment should be applied to state and local governments, and that the evidence had been seized illegally and should not be used against her at trial. The police, she claimed, had no probable cause for suspecting her for the crime she was arrested for. The court ruled in her favor, thus establishing a precedent for 4th Amendment rights.

FIFTH AMENDMENT RIGHTS

The Fifth Amendment forbids self-incrimination, stating that no one "shall be compelled to be a witness against himself." The rights for protection against self-incrimination originated from a famous 1966 Court decision *Miranda v. Arizona*. Ernesto Miranda was arrested as a prime suspect in the rape and kidnapping of an eighteen year old girl. During a two hour questioning by the police, he was not advised of his constitutional right against self-incrimination nor his right to counsel. His responses led to his conviction, but the Supreme Court reversed it, and set the modern **Miranda Rights:** to remain silent, to be warned that responses may be used in a court of law, and to have a lawyer present during questioning. Evidence obtained in violation of the Miranda warning is inadmissible under the exclusionary rule.

A very important principle related to both the 4th and 5th Amendments is the **exclusionary rule**, which upholds the principle that evidence gathered illegally cannot be used in a trial. Critics of the exclusionary rule, including former Chief Justice William Rehnquist, express doubts that criminals should go free just because of mistakes on the part of the police. However, the Courts continue to apply the exclusionary rule. Those that support the exclusionary rule believe that it is necessary to safeguard essential civil liberties. At times a more modified version of the rule, known as the **good-faith exception**, has been permitted by the courts. Courts recognize that minor mistakes may occur while gathering evidence, but that the evidence may still be used in the trial. For instance, if the police can prove that the evidence would have been discovered in another way, evidence gathered with an incomplete search warrant may be accepted by the courts. Justification for use of the good faith exception is usually based on the "overriding considerations of public safety" that may be necessary in a case.

THE EIGHTH AMENDMENT AND CRUEL AND UNUSUAL PUNISHMENT

The 8th amendment prohibits **"cruel and unusual punishments,"** a concept rooted in English law. By far, the most controversial issue that centers on the 8th Amendment is capital punishment, or the practice of issuing death sentences to those convicted of major crimes.

In general, states are allowed to pursue their own policies regarding capital punishment. The Supreme Court ruled on the death penalty in 1972 in *Furman v. Georgia.* Even then, it did not judge capital punishment to be cruel and unusual punishment. It simply warned the states that the death penalty was to be carried out in a fair and consistent way.

RIGHT VS. RIGHT

Most of us think of civil rights and liberties as principles that protect freedoms for all of us all the time. However, the truth is that rights listed in the Constitution and the Bill of Rights are usually *competing* rights. Most civil liberties and rights court cases involve the plaintiff's right vs. another right that the defendant claims has been violated. For example, in 1971, the New York Times published the "Pentagon Papers" that revealed some negative actions of the government during the Vietnam War. The government sued the newspaper, claiming that the reports endangered national security. *The New York Times* countered with the argument that the public had the right to know and that its freedom of the press should be upheld. So, the situation was national security v. freedom of the press. A tough call, but the Court chose to uphold the rights of *The Times*.

TERRORISM AND CIVIL LIBERTIES

The passage of the Patriot Act, approximately a month after the terrorist attacks on the World Trade Center on September 11, 2001, has raised questions about how far the government can go in its investigation and prosecution of individuals accused of acts of terror. Concerns have centered on the role of court orders in permitting the government to gain telephone taps and monitor internet communications along with the due process rights of detainees.

The Bush administration preferred use of military courts rather than civil courts to conduct the trials of suspected terrorists, causing many to be concerned about the procedures used in the trials. A military trial is conducted by a commission of military officers who can operate in secret if classified information is used in evidence. If the accused is convicted, the appeal must go through the secretary of defense and the president, not a civilian court. The lack of transparency in the process worries those who fear for the loss of civil rights of the accused. In order to address this problem, beginning in 2002, those labeled by the administration as "unlawful combatants" captured in Afghanistan and other countries were held in detention at the U. S. military base at Guantanamo Bay, Cuba. The detainees demanded access to the civilian courts to challenge the legality of their confinement.

The following is a summary of cases heard by the Supreme Court regarding the rights of Guantanamo Bay detainees:

- *Rasul v Bush* (2004) – The court ruled that the principle of habeas corpus requires that terrorist detainees must have access to federal courts if held in territory that is functionally part of the U. S.
- *Hamdi v Rumsfeld* (2004) – The court ruled that a U.S. citizen held as an enemy combatant is entitled to due process. Hamdi was arrested in Afghanistan and detained in a Virginia prison. As a citizen Hamdi had the right to contest his detention before a neutral authority.
- *Hamdan v Rumsfeld* (2006) – In a strike against the government the courts maintained their jurisdiction over pending cases. The court held that the military commissions were improperly established by the president, without Congressional authorization, and that they lacked the protections required by the Geneva Conventions. In a response to this decision Congress passed the Military Commissions Act of 2006 granting the president authorization to strip the federal courts of jurisdiction over pending as well as new cases. In February 2007, the Court of Appeals for the District of Columbia ruled that the law has stripped the right of habeas corpus from detainees.
- *Boumediene et al. v Bush* (2008) – The court delivered another decision against the government when it ruled that the prisoners at Guantanamo Bay have a constitutional right to go to federal court to challenge their continued detention. The decision did leave open "the extent of showing required of the government" at the habeas corpus hearing to justify a prisoner"s continued detention, the handling of classified evidence and the degree of due process to which the detainees are entitled.

Despite the Court rulings against the administration, by early 2009, 270 detainees were still being held. As the new administration took over under President Barack Obama, cases concerning these detainees were still undecided. Many critics have demanded that the prison at Guantanomo Bay be shut down, an issue left to be decided by the new administration.

IMPORTANT DEFINITIONS AND IDENTIFICATIONS:

- *Aquilar v. Felton*
- *Barron vs. Baltimore*
- bills of attainder
- Bill of Rights
- *Brandenberg. v. Ohio*
- *Boumediene et al. v Bush*
- clear and present danger test
- Communications Decency Act
- cruel and unusual punishment
- due process clause of the 5th and 14th Amendments
- *District of Columbia v Heller*
- eminent domain
- *Engle v. Vitale*
- equal protection clause
- Espionage Act of 1917
- establishment clause
- *Everson v. Board of Education*
- *ex post facto* laws
- exclusionary rule
- First Amendment rights
- Fourteenth Amendment
- *Furman v. Georgia*
- free exercise clause
- *Gideon v. Wainwright*
- *Gitlow v. New York*
- *Gonzalez v Planned Parenthood*
- good-faith exception
- *Griswold v. Connecticut*
- *habeas corpus*
- *Hamdi v Rumsfeld*
- *Hamdan v Rumsfeld*
- imminent action
- Internal Security Act of 1950
- judicial review
- *Kelo v New London, Connecticut*
- *Lemon v. Kurtzman*
- libel
- *Mapp v. Ohio*
- *McCreary County v. ACLU*
- *Miranda v. Arizona*
- Miranda Rights
- moment of silence
- obscenity
- *Oregon v Smith*
- *Planned Parenthood v Casey*
- privileges and immunities clause
- procedural due process
- *Rasul v Bush*
- religious pluralism
- right to counsel
- right to privacy
- *Roe v. Wade*
- *Schenck v. U.S.*
- school vouchers
- Sedition Act of 1798
- Sedition Act of 1918
- selective incorporation
- Smith Act
- substantive due process
- symbolic speech
- *Texas v. Johnson*
- unreasonable search and seizure
- *Van Orden v Perry*
- Wall of Separation
- *Wallace v. Jaffree*
- *Webster v. Reproductive Health Services*

CHAPTER SIXTEEN
CIVIL RIGHTS

One of the most influential Constitutional clauses during the mid to late 20th century has been the equal protection clause of the Fourteenth Amendment that forbids any state to "deny to any person within its jurisdiction the equal protection of the laws." This clause has not been interpreted to mean that everyone is to be treated the same, but that certain divisions in society, such as sex, race, and ethnicity may be suspect categories, and that laws that make distinctions that affect these groups will be subjected to especially strict scrutiny by the courts. In recent years, these **suspect categories** have been expanded to include discrimination based on age, disability, and sexual preference.

CIVIL RIGHTS FOR RACIAL AND ETHNIC MINORITIES

The United States has always been home to many different racial and ethnic groups that have experienced varying degrees of acceptance into American society. Today major racial and ethnic minorities include African Americans, Latinos, Asians, and Native Americans.

EQUALITY FOR AFRICAN AMERICANS

The history of African Americans includes 250 years of slavery followed by almost a century of widespread discrimination. Their efforts to secure equal rights and eliminate segregation have led the way for others.

After the Civil War, civil rights were guaranteed for former slaves in the Fourteenth and Fifteenth Amendments. However, many discriminatory laws remained in states across the country, and the states of the defeated Confederacy passed **Jim Crow laws**, which segregated blacks from whites in virtually all public facilities including schools, restaurants, hotels, and bathrooms. In addition to this *de jure* (by law) segregation, strict *de facto* (in reality) segregation existed in neighborhoods in the South and the North.

The 1896 court decision *Plessy v. Ferguson* supported the segregation laws. Homer Plessy sued the state of Louisiana for arresting him for riding in a "whites only" railroad car. The Court ruled that the law did not violate the equal protection clause of the 14th Amendment, as Plessy claimed. The majority opinion stated that segregation is not unconstitutional as long as the facilities were substantially equal. This **"separate but equal"** doctrine remained the Court's policies until the 1950s.

The Modern Civil Rights Movement

In 1909 the National Association for the Advancement of Colored People **(NAACP)** was founded to promote the enforcement of civil rights guaranteed by the Fourteenth and Fifteenth Amendments. The NAACP struggled for years to convince white-dominated state and national legislatures to pass laws protecting black civil rights, but they made little progress until they turned their attentions to the courts. The NAACP decided that the courts were the best place to bring about change, and they assembled a legal team that began to slowly chip away at the "separate but equal" doctrine.

From the mid-1930s to about 1950, the NAACP focused its attention on requiring that separate black schools actually be equal to white schools. Finding little success with this approach, **Thurgood Marshall**, an NAACP lawyer for Linda Brown in ***Brown v. Board of Education of Topeka*** in 1954, argued that separate but equal facilities are "inherently unequal" and that separation had "a detrimental effect upon the colored children." The Court overturned the earlier Plessy decision and ruled that "separate but equal" facilities are unconstitutional. Following this landmark case was over a decade of massive resistance to desegregation in the South, but organized protests, demonstrations, marches, and sit-ins led to massive de jure desegregation by the early 1970s.

The rights of racial minorities were further protected by the **Civil Rights Act of 1964**, the **24th Amendment**, and the **Voting Rights Act of 1965**. The 1964 act banned racial discrimination in public facilities and voter registration and allowed the government to withhold federal funds from states and local areas not complying with the law. The 24th Amendment banned paying a tax to vote (the poll tax) – a practice intended to keep blacks from voting. The 1965 act outlawed literacy tests and allowed federal officials to register new voters. As a result, the number of registered black voters increased dramatically, and today registration rates of African Americans are about equal to those of whites. The Johnson Administration also set up as part of the "Great Society" an **Office of Economic Opportunity** that set guidelines for equal hiring and education practices. To comply with the new guidelines, many schools and businesses set up quotas (a minimum number of minorities) for admission or employment.

School Integration

Schools were not integrated overnight after the *Brown* decision, and active resistance continued through the early 1960s. In 1957 Arkansas Governor Orville Faubus used the state's National Guard to block the integration of Central High School in Little Rock. President Dwight Eisenhower responded by federalizing the Arkansas National Guard and sending in 500 soldiers to enforce integration. In 1962 James Meredith, an African American student, was not allowed to enroll at the University of Mississippi, prompting President John F. Kennedy to send federal marshals to protect Meredith.

To break down de facto school segregation caused by residential patterns, courts ordered many school districts to use **busing** to integrate schools. Students were transported from areas where they lived to schools in other areas to achieve school integration. The practice proved to be controversial, but the courts upheld busing plans for many years. However, by the late 1990s and early 2000s federal courts had become increasingly unwilling to uphold busing or any other policies designed to further integration. For example, in 2001 a federal court determined that the Charlotte-Mechlenburg school district in North Carolina no longer had to use race-based admission quotas because they had already achieved integration. However, courts still take de facto school segregation seriously, and have challenged the plans of two school districts in recent years.

In 2000 the Jefferson County Board of Education (Louisville, Kentucky) had been released from court-ordered integration, and a new program was put in place that emphasized school choice, school capacity and racial diversity. *Meredith v Jefferson County Board of Education* (2007) challenged the plan on the basis that it violated the Equal Protection Clause of the 14th Amendment. In Seattle, another school choice plan had been developed to achieve racial diversity in the absence of court-ordered busing. In this plan, race could be considered for admission to a school in order to reach a 60% non-white and 40% white school population that reflected the population composition of the district. *Parents Involved in Community Schools v Seattle School District #1* challenged the plan based on the Equal Protection Clause of the 14th Amendment. In both of these cases Chief Justice Roberts, writing for the majority, stated that "the best way to stop discrimination on the basis of race is to stop discriminating on the basis of race." The Court stated that both cases stressed demographic goals rather than "any demonstrable educational benefit from racial diversity". Neither school district plan considered any qualification of the students other than race. However, in his concurring opinion, Justice Kennedy clarified the possible use of racial considerations to achieve racial diversity in public high schools. He stated that "public schools may sometimes consider race to ensure educational opportunity."

Today de facto school segregation still exists, especially in cities, where most African American and Hispanic students go to schools with almost no non-Hispanic whites. So by the early years of the 21st century, the goal of integration expressed in *Brown v. Board of Education of Topeka* in 1954 has not been realized.

RIGHTS FOR NATIVE AMERICANS

Of all the minorities in the United States, Native Americans are one of the most diverse. Almost half of the nearly 2 million people live on **reservations**, or land given to them as tribes by treaties with the U.S. government. 308 different tribes are formally registered with the government, and among them, almost 200 languages are spoken. Enrolled members of tribes are entitled to certain benefits (such as preferred employment or acceptance to college) administered by the Bureau of Indian Affairs of the Department of the Interior. The benefits are upheld by the Supreme Court as grants not to a "discrete racial group, but rather, as members of quasi-sovereign tribal entities."

Poor living conditions and job opportunities on reservations have been the source of growing Native American militancy. Tribes have demanded more autonomy and fewer government regulations on reservations. Some recent cases have involved the right of tribes on reservations to run and benefit from gambling operations that the government has regulated. Some tribes are demanding better health care facilities, educational opportunities, decent housing, and jobs.

Article I, Section 8 grants Congress full power under the commerce clause to regulate Indian tribes. Congress abolished making treaties with the tribes in 1871, but until recent times tribal governments were weak, many reservations were dissolved, and many tribes severed their relationship with the U.S. government. During the past twenty years, both the tribes and the government have shown revived interest in interpreting earlier treaties in a way to protect the independence and authority of the tribes. With the backing of the **Native American Rights Fund** (funded in part by the Ford Foundation), more Indian law cases have been brought in the last two decades than at any time in our history. Colorado elected the first Native American (Ben Nighthorse Campbell) to Congress in 1992.

LATINO RIGHTS

Latinos not only compose the fastest growing minority group in the United States today but, according to U. S. Census 2006 estimates, they are also the largest minority group in the United States. Compared to 33.9 million African Americans, the approximately 44.3 million Latinos may be divided into several large subgroups:

- **Mexican Americans** – About 28 million are Mexican Americans who live primarily in the Southwestern United States: Texas, New Mexico, Arizona, and California. Traditionally, Mexican Americans are strong supporters of the Democratic Party.

- **Puerto Ricans** – The second largest group consists of 3.9 million Puerto Ricans, living primarily in northern cities, such as New York and Chicago. Since Puerto Rico is a commonwealth of the United States, many Puerto Ricans move back and forth between island and homeland.

- **Cubans** – A third group has come since the early 1960s from Cuba, many fleeing to Florida from Castro's regime. The immigration has continued over the years. While in 2006 the Census estimated only 1.5 million Cubans were living in the United States, in many areas of southern Florida, Cuban Americans have now become the majority group. In contrast to Mexican Americans, Cubans tend to be politically conservative and support the Republican Party.

- **Central and South American countries** – A rapidly growing number are emigrating from political upheaval in Central American countries, such as Nicaragua and Guatemala. As political unrest in these areas continues, people are coming to live near relatives already in the United States.

A major issue for Latinos centers on English as a Second Language education in U.S. public schools. Latino children often find language a barrier to success in school, and schools have struggled to find the best ways to educate them. Supporters of ESL education believe that Spanish instruction should be provided and encouraged, whereas critics claim that such education hampers the learning of English, a necessary skill for success in the United States. In recent years, bilingual programs established in the 1960s have come under increasing attack. In 1998, California residents passed a ballot initiative that called for the end of bilingual education in the state. After the courts backed the initiative, the states of Arizona and Massachusetts also banned bilingual education.

Latinos, like blacks, have become increasingly involved in politics, and by the 1998 election 19 Latinos were members of the House of Representatives but none served in the Senate. The number of Hispanics in the House and Senate increased by the 111th Congress (2009-2011) with 31 serving in the legislature (28 in the House and 3 in the Senate). With the resignation of Supreme Court Justice David Souter President Obama nominated Sonia Sotomayer, of Puerto Rican descent, to the Supreme Court in the first year of his presidency. When confirmed by the Senate she became the first Hispanic to serve on the Supreme Court.

THE RIGHTS OF ASIAN-PACIFIC ISLANDERS

About 10 million Americans are of Asian origin, a number that is rapidly increasing. Asian Americans come from many different countries with different languages and customs. About 40 per cent of our immigrants now are from Asia, mostly from the Philippines, China, Taiwan, Korea, Vietnam, Cambodia, Pakistan, and India. The Chinese were the first major group of Asians to come to the United States, attracted by expansion in California and the opportunities to work in mines.

Until recently, Asians were severely limited by U.S. immigration policies. Discriminatory immigration and naturalization restrictions were placed on the Chinese in 1882, and remained in place until after World War II. In 1906 The San Francisco Board of Education excluded all Chinese, Japanese, and Korean children from neighborhood schools. During World War II, Japanese Americans on the West Coast were placed in internment camps because of the fear that they would conspire with a Japanese attack from the Pacific Ocean. A major influx of Asians began in response to new U.S. immigration laws passed in the 1960s, which based immigration quotas more on occupation and education than on region of origin. Immigration policies now favor many Asians, especially those with high educational and professional qualifications enforced by current immigration laws.

A number of groups have come at least partly as a result of Cold War politics since World War II. Koreans are a growing group, concentrated in southern California, Hawaii, Colorado, and New York City. Korean businesses have been the object of violent attacks, such as in the 1992 Los Angeles riots and separate, more recent incidents in New York City. The most recent arrivals are refugees from the political upheavals in Vietnam, Laos, and Cambodia.

Some estimates suggest that by 2050 as many as 10 percent of all Americans will be of Asian-Pacific Islands origins.

WOMEN AND EQUAL RIGHTS

Before the 1970s the Court interpreted the equal protection clause of the Fourteenth Amendment very differently for women than it did for blacks. Whereas the legal tradition clearly intended to keep blacks in a subservient position, the legal system claimed to be protecting women by treating them differently.

In the late eighteenth century, not only were women denied the right to vote, but they had few legal rights, little education, and almost no choices regarding work. The legal doctrine known as **coverture** deprived married women of any identity separate from that of their husbands. Circumstances began to change in the mid-nineteenth century.

THE SUFFRAGE MOVEMENT

A meeting in Seneca Falls, New York in 1848 is often seen as the beginning of the women's **suffrage** (right to vote) **movement**. The meeting produced a *Document of Sentiments* modeled after the Declaration of Independence signed by 100 men and women that endorsed the movement.

It took 72 years till the goal of voting rights was reached. With the passage of the **Nineteenth Amendment** in 1920, the suffrage movement that had begun in the early 1800s came to a successful end. The Amendment was brief and to the point: "The right of citizens of the United States to vote shall not be denied or abridged by the United States or by any State on account of sex."

However, other legal rights were not achieved until the late 20th century, partly because the Courts sought to protect women from injustice. In 1908 the Court upheld an Oregon law that limited female (but not male) laundry workers to a ten-hour workday. The Court claimed that "The two sexes differ in structure of body, in the functions to be performed by each, in the amount of physical strength, in the capacity for long-continued, labor, particularly when done standing...." So, biological differences justified differences in legal status, an attitude reflecting protective paternalism.

THE MODERN WOMEN'S RIGHTS MOVEMENT

Other legal rights were not addressed until the 1970s, when the women's movement questioned the Court's justification for different treatment of the sexes under the law. A unanimous Court responded by setting down a new test, the **reasonableness standard**: a law that endorses different treatment "must be reasonable, not arbitrary, and must rest on some ground of difference having a fair and substantial relation to the object of the legislation so that all persons similarly circumstances shall be treated alike."

The "reasonableness" standard was much looser than the **"strict scrutiny" standard** used to judge racial classifications (which are "suspect" classifications): some distinctions based on sex are permitted and some are not. For example, a state cannot set different ages at which men and women are allowed to buy beer, nor can girls be barred from Little League baseball teams, and public taverns may not cater to men only. However, a law that punishes males but not females for statutory rape is permissible, and states can give widows a property-tax exemption not given to widowers. Other practices generally endorsed by the court but now being challenged are the acceptability of all-boy and all-girl public schools and the different rates of military officer promotions (men generally have been promoted earlier than women).

Women and the Military Draft

One of the most controversial issues defining women's rights is the implication of equal rights for the military draft. Should women be treated differently than men regarding military service? The Supreme Court decided in ***Rostker v. Goldberg*** (1981) that Congress may require men but not women to register for the draft without violating the due-process clause of the Fifth Amendment. However, other laws passed by Congress regarding differential treatment in the military have recently been challenged. For many years Congress barred women from combat roles, but in 1993, the secretary of defense opened air and sea combat positions to all persons regardless of sex. Only ground-troop combat positions are still reserved for men.

The Equal Rights Amendment

The controversial issues surrounding the military draft contributed to the ultimate failure of the **Equal Rights Amendment**, which read "Equality of rights under the law shall not be denied or abridged by the United States or any State on account of sex." Congress passed this amendment in 1972, but it ran into trouble in the ratification process. By 1978, thirty-five states had ratified, three short of the necessary three-fourths. Many legislators and voters worried that the ERA would require women to be drafted for combat duty. Meanwhile, the time limit for ratification ran out, the Republican Party withdrew its endorsement, and Congress has not produced the two-thirds majority needed to resubmit it to the states.

Abortion Rights

Roe v. Wade (1973) broke the tradition of allowing states to decide the availability of abortions within state boundaries. In this case the Court struck down a Texas law that banned abortion except in cases when the mother's life was threatened. The Court argued that the due-process clause of the Fourteenth Amendment implies a "right to privacy" that protects a woman's freedom to "choose" abortion or not during the first three months (trimester) of pregnancy. States were allowed freedoms to regulate during the second and third trimesters.

The decision almost immediately became controversial, with those supporting the decision calling themselves **"pro-choice"** and those opposing **"pro life."** Although the Roe decision still holds, its critics still fight for its reversal. The Court has declared unconstitutional laws that require a woman to have the consent of her husband, but it has allowed states to require underage girls to have the consent of her parents. In the 1989 *Webster v. Reproductive Health Services* case, the Court upheld some state restrictions on abortions (such as a twenty-four hour waiting period between request for and the performance of an abortion), but the Court has since refused to overturn Roe.

Discrimination in the Workplace

Since the 1960s laws have been passed that protect women against discrimination in the workplace. **Title VII** of the Civil Rights Act of 1964 prohibits gender discrimination in employment, and has been used to strike down many previous work policies. In 1978, Congress amended Title VII to expand the definition of gender discrimination to include discrimination based on pregnancy. The Supreme Court later extended Title VII to include **sexual harassment**, which occurs when job opportunities, promotions, and salary increases are given in return for sexual favors.

One of the most important recent issues regarding women's rights is **"equal pay for equal work."** In 1983, the state Supreme Court of Washington ruled that its government had discriminated for years against women by not giving them equal pay for jobs of "comparable worth" to those that men held. This doctrine of **comparable worth** requires that a worker be paid by the "worth" of his or her work, not by what employers are willing to pay. Although the system is difficult to implement, many large companies have adopted sophisticated job evaluation systems to determine pay scales for jobs within their structures

The Supreme Court ruling in a pay discrimination case, ***Ledbetter v Goodyear Tire & Rubber Company*** (2007), had less to do with women's rights and more to do with the timing of the claim. Lilly Ledbetter learned, through an anonymous note, that she was paid less than men in her position, even those with less seniority. She won a jury verdict, but Goodyear challenged it based on Title VII of the Civil Rights Act, 1964. The law stated that pay discrimination suits had to be brought within 180 days "after the alleged unlawful employment practice occurred." Ms. Ledbetter's challenge did not occur within the time limit. The Supreme Court upheld the 180 day period of the Civil Rights Act, citing the increasing difficulty for employers to defend their practices as time passes. Justice Ruth Bader Ginsberg dissented in the case stating that secrecy in the workplace regarding salaries makes it difficult for employees to discover the discrepancy within 180 days. She suggested "the legislature may act to correct this…reading of Title VII." In 2009 the legislature did just that as the Lilly Ledbetter Fair Pay Act was passed. On January 29, 2009 it became the first law signed by President Barack Obama. The new law states that pay discrimination occurs with each paycheck, effectively eliminating the strict 180 day time period in the original law.

OTHER CIVIL RIGHTS MOVEMENTS

The gains made by racial groups, ethnic groups, and women have motivated others to organize efforts to work for equal rights. Three of the most active are older Americans, the disabled, and homosexuals. All three groups have organized powerful interest groups, and all have made some progress toward ensuring their rights.

RIGHTS FOR OLDER AMERICANS

The baby boomers born after World War II are now swelling the ranks of Americans over 50, and with their numbers, discrimination against older Americans has gained the spotlight. A major concern is discrimination in the workplace.

Congress has passed several age discrimination laws, including one is 1975 that denied federal funds to any institution discriminating against people over 40. The Age

Discrimination in Employment Act raised the general compulsory retirement age to 70. Since then, retirement has become more flexible, and in some areas compulsory retirement has been phased out entirely.

One of the most influential interest groups in Washington is the American Association of Retired Persons (**AARP**). With more than 30 million members, the organization successfully lobbies Congress to consider the rights of older Americans in policy areas such as health, housing, taxes, and transportation.

RIGHTS FOR DISABLED AMERICANS

Disabled Americans make up about 17 percent of the population, and they have organized to fight discrimination in education, employment, rehabilitation services, and equal public access.

The first rehabilitation laws were passed in the late 1920s, but the most important changes came when the Rehabilitation Act of 1973 added disabled people to the list of groups protected from discrimination.

Two important anti-discrimination laws are:

- **The Education for All Handicapped Children Act of 1975** – This law gave all children the right to a free public education.

- **The Americans with Disabilities Act (ADA)** – This law, passed in 1990, extended many of the protections established for racial minorities and women to disabled people. However, beginning in 1999, the Supreme Court has issued a series of decisions that effectively limit the scope of ADA, excluding conditions such as nearsightedness and carpal tunnel syndrome as disabilities.

These laws have been widely criticized because they require expensive programs and alterations to public buildings. Activists for the movement criticize the owners of public buildings and the government for not enforcing the laws consistently.

HOMOSEXUAL RIGHTS

In the last two decades, homosexuals have become much more active in their attempt to gain equal rights in employment, education, housing, and acceptance by the general public. In recent years several well-organized, active interest groups have worked to promote the rights of homosexuals and lobby for issues such as AIDS research funding. Many cities have banned discrimination, and many colleges and universities have gay rights organizations on campus.

Despite, these changes, civil rights for homosexuals is still a controversial issue, as reflected in 1993 by the resistance to the Clinton administration's proposals to protect gay rights in the military. The resulting "don't ask, don't tell" policy has not resolved the ambiguous status of gays in the military, and the Supreme Court has not yet ruled on its constitutionality.

The Supreme Court first addressed homosexual rights in 1986 when it ruled in ***Hardwick v. Georgia*** that Georgia's law forbidding homosexual relations was constitutional. The Court based its decision on **original intent** (the intent of the founders), noting that all 13 colonies had laws against homosexual relations, as did all 50 states until 1961. Most recently, in *Romer v. Evans* (1996) the Court provided some support to homosexuals when it struck down a Colorado amendment to the state constitution that banned laws protecting homosexuals. In the majority opinion, Justice Anthony Kennedy wrote that "a bare desire to harm a politically unpopular group cannot constitute a legitimate governmental interest." The Court reversed *Hardwick v. Georgia* in 2003 with ***Lawrence v. Texas***, when it held that laws against sodomy violate the due process clause of the 14th amendment. In the words of the Court,

> "The liberty protected by the Constitution allows homosexual persons the right to choose to enter upon relationships in the confines of their homes and their own private lives and still retain their dignity as free persons."

Currently, a controversial topic is state recognition of homosexual marriages and "civil unions." After courts in Massachusetts upheld the right in that state in 2004, a number of homosexual marriages were conducted in other areas of the country, including San Francisco and New York City. In reaction, by 2006 nineteen states passed initiatives which banned recognition of homosexual marriages. In 2008 three states included restrictions against gay marriage on their ballots. Although laws exist in Florida and Arizona banning gay marriage, voters in both states approved constitutional amendments prohibiting it. Part of the motivation for this action in both states was to prevent court action questioning the constitutionality of the laws.   Passage of California Proposition 8 in 2008 also banned recognition of gay marriage. The vote in California was the first to ban gay marriage in a state where it had previously been legal. Court rulings in California and Florida had contradicted the public vote. In California the state supreme court had previously ruled that gay marriage was constitutional while the Florida court ruling overturned a state law banning gays from adopting children. In some instances a clear difference exists between court interpretations and the results of recent ballot initiatives which indicate that the issue of gay marriage will remain controversial.

REVERSE DISCRIMINATION

By the 1970s the focus of concern turned to racial balance as opposed to mere nondiscrimination, or **equality of opportunity vs. equality of result**. Do civil rights require merely the absence of discrimination, or do they require that steps be taken to insure that blacks and whites enroll in the same schools, work in the same jobs, and live in the same housing?

The Courts helped define the issue in the 1978 ***Bakke v. California*** case that questioned the quota practices of the University of California medical school at Davis. Bakke, a white student denied admission to the school, sued the state, claiming **reverse discrimination**, since minorities with lesser qualifications were admitted to the medical school. In a divided decision, the court ruled in Bakke's favor, declaring strict quotas unconstitutional although allowing race as one criterion for admission to a public institution.

Many cases followed that further defined reverse discrimination. Two examples are:

- *United Steelworkers v. Weber* (1979) – Kaiser Aluminum was sued for reverse discrimination in its hiring practices. This time the courts ruled that a private company could set its own policies, and the government could not forbid quotas in the case.
- *Richmond v. Croson* (1989) – The court struck down the city of Richmond's plan to subcontract 30% of its business to minority companies, but the decision was bitterly opposed by three members of the Court.

In 2003 in two cases involving policies at the University of Michigan, the Supreme Court's ruling supported the constitutionality of affirmative action programs and the goals of diversity. The Court struck down the university's plan for undergraduate admission, saying that it amounted to a quota system. However, they upheld the plan used by the law school, which took race into consideration as part of a broad consideration of applicants' backgrounds.

As the United States continues to become a more and more diverse country, the nature of civil rights issues for minority groups certainly will change. Despite the changes, the pursuit of equality undoubtedly will remain a constant in the American political culture.

IMPORTANT DEFINITIONS AND IDENTIFICATIONS:

- AARP
- *Bakke v. California*
- *Brown v. Board of Education of Topeka*
- busing
- Civil Rights Act of 1964
- comparable worth
- coverture
- de facto segregation
- de jure segregation
- *Document of Sentiments*
- equal pay for equal work
- Equal Rights Amendment
- equality of opportunity
- equality of result
- *Hardwick v. Georgia*
- Jim Crow laws
- *Lawrence v. Texas*
- *Ledbetter v Goodyear Tire & Rubber Co.*
- *Meredith v Jefferson County Board of Education*
- NAACP
- Native American Rights Fund

- Nineteenth Amendment
- Office of Economic Opportunity
- original intent
- *Parents Involved in Community Schools v Seattle School District # 1*
- *Plessy v. Ferguson*
- pro-choice v. pro-life
- reasonableness standard
- reservations
- reverse discrimination
- *Richmond v. Croson*
- *Roe v. Wade*
- *Roster v. Goldberg*
- separate but equal doctrine
- sexual harassment
- suffrage movement
- suspect categories
- Thurgood Marshall
- Title VII
- *United Steelworkers v. Weber*
- Voting Rights Act of 1965
- 24th Amendment

UNIT SIX QUESTIONS

1. Which of the following court decisions helped to define citizen protection against illegal search and seizure?

   (A) *Gitlow v New York*
   (B) *Near v Minnesota*
   (C) *Mapp v Ohio*
   (D) *Griswold v Connecticut*
   (E) *Sullivan v New York*

2. Which of the following rights was guaranteed in the body of the original Constitution?

   (A) Freedom of speech
   (B) Right to bear arms
   (C) Protection against unreasonable searches and seizures
   (D) Trial by jury in civil cases
   (E) No *ex post facto* laws

3. The concept that evidence illegally obtained by police may not be used in a trial is known as the

   (A) evidence rule
   (B) exclusionary rule
   (C) certiorari rule
   (D) *habeas corpus* rule
   (E) indictment rule

(Questions 4 and 5 are based on the following quote):

> "No State shall make or enforce any law which shall abridge the privileges or immunities of citizens of the United States; nor shall any State deprive any person of life, liberty, or property, without due process of law; nor deny to any person within its jurisdiction the equal protection of the laws."

4. This famous quote is from

   (A) The *Federalist Papers*
   (B) 14th Amendment
   (C) 5th Amendment
   (D) The Articles of Confederation
   (E) Article II of the Constitution

5. The quote has been used by courts as a basis for

   (A) Incorporation of the Bill of Rights
   (B) Application of the 1st Amendment to the federal government
   (C) Guaranteeing the right to trial by jury in federal courts
   (D) Denying the right to vote to minorities
   (E) Restricting the practice of corporal punishment for federal crimes

6. The "wall of separation" referred to by Thomas Jefferson describes a principle set up in the

   (A) Elastic (or necessary and proper) clause of Article I
   (B) Establishment clause of the 1st Amendment
   (C) Free expression clause of the 1st Amendment
   (D) Due process clause of the 5th Amendment
   (E) "cruel and unusual punishment" clause of the 9th Amendment

7. The "clear and present danger" test set by *Schenck v U.S.* has become a standard by which to balance national security and

   (A) freedom of religion
   (B) freedom to assemble
   (C) freedom of speech
   (D) the right to be free in your "person"
   (E) eminent domain

8. In the past, de jure segregation usually resulted from

   (A) housing patterns.
   (B) court decisions.
   (C) state and local laws or actions and regulations.
   (D) national laws and regulations.
   (E) actions by civil rights interest groups.

9. In regard to the rights of detainees at Guantanamo Bay, the Supreme Court has upheld the

   (A) removal of detainees from Cuba to the United States for civil trial.
   (B) constitutionality of military tribunal trials for suspects.
   (C) exclusion of constitutional protections of noncitizens.
   (D) the right of habeas corpus for all detainees regardless of their national origins.
   (E) right of the president to rescind habeas corpus during national emergencies.

10. What tendency has the Supreme Court reflected since the late 1980s in ruling on abortion rights?

    (A) The Court has widened abortion rights beyond the definition given in *Roe v Wade* (1973).
    (B) The Court has passed a number of decisions that contradict *Roe v Wade*.
    (C) The Court has upheld *Roe v Wade*, but it has also supported some state restrictions to abortion rights.
    (D) The Court has reversed *Roe v Wade*, and now allows states to pass laws than ban abortions.
    (E) The Court has avoided ruling on abortion rights altogether in recent years.

11. Congressional elections in 1992 changed the membership of Congress by increasing the number of

    (A) Liberal Republicans
    (B) Political Independents and Third Party candidates
    (C) Naturalized American Citizens
    (D) Minorities and Women
    (E) Conservative Republicans

12. The Supreme Court decision in *Engle v Vitale*, 1962, was based on personal protections in the

    (A) 1st Amendment
    (B) 4th Amendment
    (C) 5th Amendment
    (D) 6th Amendment
    (E) 8th Amendment

13. The decision issued by the *Supreme Court in Brown v Board of Education of Topeka* in 1954 led most directly to

    (A) the establishment of the "separate but equal" doctrine
    (B) a great decline in the de facto school segregation
    (C) equal opportunities for blacks in employment
    (D) a great decline in de jure school segregation
    (E) greater access to school vouchers in poor urban communities

14. Citizen protections under the Bill of Rights have been applied to the states through court interpretations of the

    (A) Bill of Attainder
    (B) Necessary and Proper Clause
    (C) Full Faith and Credit Clause
    (D) 14th Amendment
    (E) Supremacy Clause

15. Which of the following is the best description of the immigration patterns of Asians to the U.S.?

    (A) Asians have almost always immigrated in large numbers to the United States.
    (B) Asians immigrated to the United States in large numbers during the 19th century.
    (C) Asian immigration was restricted severely between the 1880s and 1960s, but has since increased dramatically.
    (D) Asian immigration has always been seriously restricted so that very few have settled in the United States.
    (E) Asians have generally had little interest in immigrating to the United States, so their numbers have always been small.

16. The fastest growing minority group in the United States is currently

    (A) African Americans
    (B) Asians
    (C) Native Americans
    (D) Latinos
    (E) Pacific Islanders

"Equality of rights under the law shall not be denied or abridged by the United States or any State on account of sex."

17. The statement above is known as the

    (A) 19th Amendment
    (B) 14th Amendment
    (C) 15th Amendment
    (D) Equal Rights Amendment
    (E) *Document of Sentiments*

Use the following chart for questions 18 and 19.

STRICTER LAWS ON ABORTION

	1987		1993		2003	
	Favor	Oppose	Favor	Oppose	Favor	Oppose
Republicans	48%	46%	45%	48%	50%	44%
Democrats	40%	52%	28%	64%	25%	70%
Independent	38%	55%	24%	69%	32%	61%
Men	38%	53%	28%	64%	35%	57%
Women	44%	50%	34%	58%	36%	58%

Pew Research Center

18. The chart above reflects which of the following trends?

   (A) Independents consistently favored stricter abortion laws from 1987 – 2003.
   (B) Partisan divisions between Republicans and Democrats over abortion became more evident in the 1990s and remained apparent in 2003.
   (C) Republicans and Independents reflected the same views on abortion laws in the 1990s.
   (D) By 1993 Democrats were evenly divided over their support for stricter laws over abortion.
   (E) Independents, Republicans and Democrats substantially weakened their support for stricter abortion laws from the 1980s through 2003.

19. The chart reflects which of the following gender attitudes toward stricter abortions laws?

   (A) Men and Republicans closely reflected the same attitudes about abortion laws in 2003.
   (B) Women, more than men, opposed stricter laws on abortion from 1987 through 2003.
   (C) Men gradually increased their support of stricter laws on abortion from 1987 to 2003.
   (D) The gender gap over abortion in 1987 gradually disappeared by 2003.
   (E) Women and Democrats closely reflected the same attitudes about abortion laws in 2003.

20. In the 2003 cases involving admissions policies at the University of Michigan, the Supreme Court rulings

    (A) overturned the constitutionality of affirmative action programs.
    (B) supported the constitutionality of affirmative action programs.
    (C) declared quota systems constitutional in some cases.
    (D) supported the university's policies in both cases.
    (E) overturned the previous court ruling in *Bakke v California*.

FREE RESPONSE QUESTION

When the civil rights of political minorities have been denied, they have responded by using several methods to advance their civil rights.

(A) Discuss one specific civil right that has been denied to one specific minority group.

(B) Discuss one specific civil right that has been denied to a second specific minority group.

(C) Using two of the following, explain how each has been used by the minority groups identified in A and B to gain civil rights.

Interest Groups
Equal Protection Clause
Litigation

NO TESTING MATERIAL PRINTED ON THIS PAGE

GO ON TO THE NEXT PAGE

PART II

SAMPLE EXAMINATIONS

SAMPLE EXAMINATION ONE

Directions: Each of the questions or incomplete statements below is followed by five suggested answers or completions. Select the one that is best in each case.

1. In contrast to the modern day members of Congress, members in early U.S. history

   (A) were better educated
   (B) stayed in their jobs for longer periods of time
   (C) generally served for shorter periods of time
   (D) were younger and less informed about important political issues
   (E) generally were more representative of the working class

(Questions 2 and 3 refer to the quote below):

"But when a long train of abuses and usurpations, pursuing invariably the same object, evinces a design to reduce them under absolute despotism, it is their right, it is their duty, to throw off such government..."

2. The quotation is found in

   (A) the Declaration of Independence
   (B) Article I of the Constitution
   (C) the 1st Amendment
   (D) *Federalist #10*
   (E) *Common Sense*

3. The quotation reflects acceptance of John Locke's principle of

   (A) equality in the state of nature
   (B) federalism
   (C) the social contract
   (D) separation of powers
   (E) majoritarianism

UNITED STATES NATIONAL VOTER TURNOUT IN FEDERAL ELECTIONS	
Election Year	**Voter Turnout (percentage)**
1968 Presidential election	60.8%
1970 Mid-term election	46.6%
1980 Presidential election	52.6%
1982 Mid-term election	39.8%
1992 Presidential election	55.1%
1994 Mid-term election	38.8%
2004 Presidential election	55.3%
2006 Mid-term election	43.6%

Federal Elections Commission

4. The data in the table above supports which of the following statements?

   (A) American voters turn out in basically the same numbers for all elections.
   (B) American voters believe it is important to vote in mid-term elections.
   (C) American voters historically turn out in higher number for presidential election than mid-term elections.
   (D) American voters turned out in higher numbers for elections in the 1980s and 1990s than for elections since 2000.
   (E) In 2004 American voters turned out in record numbers for the presidential election.

5. Which of the following government officials would NOT be subject to impeachment?

   (A) the president
   (B) the vice president
   (C) a judge that sits on a federal District Court
   (D) a Supreme Court justice
   (E) a U.S. senator

6. Judicial independence in the United States political system is encouraged by the

    (A) length of terms served by federal judges.
    (B) fact that the president's appointments must be evenly divided between the Republicans and Democrats.
    (C) use of the American Bar Association to reccomend salary increases.
    (D) constitutional amendment process.
    (E) bureaucratic decisions that carry out laws and court decisions.

7. A presidential advisory body that focuses on military affairs is the

    (A) Joint Chiefs of Staff
    (B) White House Staff
    (C) Ways and Means Committee
    (D) Appropriations Committee
    (E) Foreign Affairs Committee

8. Logrolling is a controversial but common practice followed in

    (A) Congress
    (B) executive branch agencies that help shape the budget
    (C) federal courts
    (D) the White House Office
    (E) most governors' offices

9. Which of the following was banned by the Bipartisan Campaign Reform Act of 2002?

    (A) individual contributions to individual candidates
    (B) interest group contributions to congressional candidates
    (C) PAC money to presidential candidates
    (D) soft money to national parties
    (E) federal government contributions to presidential candidates

10. Title VII of the Civil Rights Act of 1964 directly addresses

    (A) racial discrimination in public places
    (B) voting rights for minorities
    (C) gender discrimination in employment
    (D) the rights of non-citizens residing in the U.S.
    (E) women's reproductive rights

(Questions 11 and 12 are based on the following chart):

How Much Does the Government Listen to the People 1964-2000?								
	1964	**1968**	**1976**	**1980**	**1988**	**1996**	**2000**	**2004**
Not Much	24	29	33	41	28	22	20	21
Some	38	42	54	49	57	63	63	63
A Good Deal	32	23	11	8	13	15	16	16
Don't Know, Depends	6	6	3	2	2	0	1	1

Scores in Percentages
Source: The National Election Studies

11. Which of the following BEST describes the trends shown on the chart?

(A) The highest percentage of Americans that believed the government listened to the people "not much" of the time was the period of 1996-2004.
(B) Between 1988 and 2004 Americans generally believed that the government listens to public opinion only some of the time.
(C) Between 1964 and 2004 Americans became less willing to commit to an answer to the question of whether or not the government listens to the people.
(D) Between 1964 and 1980 Americans gained confidence in the government's attention to people's opinions about government and politics, but they lost confidence between 1980 and 2000.
(E) In all years, Americans were most likely to respond "a good deal" to the question of how much the government listens to people's opinions.

12. The trend shown on the chart was most likely would result in

(A) low voter turnout
(B) voter dissatisfaction
(C) White House scandals
(D) closer media scrutiny of the White House
(E) increasing American political efficacy

13. What effect does a plurality (winner-take-all) election system generally have on the political party system?

(A) The plurality election system generally results in a multi-party system.
(B) The plurality election system generally encourages political parties to be more ideological and less practical.
(C) The plurality election system generally results in an apathetic electorate with few loyalties to political parties.
(D) The plurality election system generally results in a political system that is dominated by two broad-based parties.
(E) The plurality election system generally results in a one-party system with lesser parties that occasionally challenge the status quo.

14. Which of the following is the BEST description of the power of the House Rules Committee?

(A) Its members determine the rules that govern the ethical behavior of members of Congress.
(B) Its members decide which committee assignments new representatives receive.
(C) Its members generally have power over leadership decisions made by the speaker and the majority leader.
(D) Its members generally determine assignment of bills to standing committees.
(E) Its members set rules for debate when bills are presented to the House floor.

15. Which of the following has the LEAST accountability to the public?

(A) House of Representatives
(B) Senate
(C) bureaucracy
(D) state legislature
(E) the vice president

16. What type of political system by its definition divides policy-making powers between the central government and sub-units?

(A) representative democracy
(B) direct democracy
(C) unitary system
(D) confederation
(E) federal system

17. The Three-fifths Compromise at the Constitutional Convention was intended primarily to solve disputes between

    (A) Thomas Jefferson and Alexander Hamilton
    (B) Britain and the United States
    (C) East and West
    (D) North and South
    (E) merchants and farmers

18. A Supreme Court justice who writes a concurring opinion for a Court decision usually does so because (s)he

    (A) agrees with the majority opinion as well as with the reasons given by the justice that writes the majority opinion
    (B) agrees with the majority opinion but disagrees with the reasons given by the justice who writes the majority opinion
    (C) wishes to express his/her reasons for disagreeing with the majority opinion
    (D) is neutral on the decision and wants to explain why
    (E) must abstain from voting in the case because of personal conflicts of interest

19. Gridlock is a direct consequence of the political system characteristic of

    (A) federalism
    (B) separation of powers
    (C) popular sovereignty
    (D) judicial review
    (E) constitutionalism

20. Blue Dog Democrats are members of Congress who shares a common

    (A) concern for pollution issues
    (B) concern for global warming
    (C) interest in equal rights for minorities
    (D) support for fiscal conversatism
    (E) support for the right-to-life

21. The 22nd Amendment (1952) affects the presidency in which of the following ways?

    (A) It requires Congressional approval in order to replace a vice-president that dies or resigns.
    (B) It limits the president to two elected terms.
    (C) It mandates that the president explain the reason(s) for vetoing a bill.
    (D) It requires the president to gain approval from the senators of a state before appointing federal judges in their state.
    (E) It requires Congress to gain presidential approval before sending a Constitutional amendment to the states for ratification.

22. Which of the following powers does the Constitution prohibit to the states but allow the national government?

    (A) taxation of imports
    (B) taxation of income
    (C) funding of local governments
    (D) taxation of exports
    (E) police power

23. In contrast to voters in the general election, voters in primary elections

    (A) care more about the future of the country
    (B) are more likely to vote for candidates with more moderate views
    (C) tend to vote for more liberal candidates
    (D) tend to vote for more conservative candidates
    (E) tend to have more partisan political views

24. Which of the following is an example of an *in forma pauperis* case?

    (A) *Dartmouth v Woodward*
    (B) *Engle v Vitale*
    (C) *Gideon v Wainwright*
    (D) *Gibbons v Ogden*
    (E) *Marbury v Madison*

25. Which of the following is NOT an accurate description of the members of Congress?

    (A) Most are white males.
    (B) The average age is 57 representatives and 63 years old for senators.
    (C) Most members have college degrees.
    (D) As many as 1/3 are non-Christians.
    (E) Most come from the upper-middle class or higher.

26. The "revolving door" describes a practice in which

    (A) government officials quit their jobs to take positions as lobbyists or consultants to businesses
    (B) minority candidates for jobs are interviewed but never hired
    (C) pollsters illegally interview voters as they are leaving polling sites
    (D) elected officials spend so much time trying to get reelected that they don't have time to govern
    (E) politically prominent officials are appointed to important judicial posts

27. Political Action Committees (PACS) are important to the United States political process primarily because they

    (A) identify possible federal judicial appointments for the president.
    (B) organize voter mobilization campaigns at the grassroots level.
    (C) raise money for political campaigns.
    (D) recruit possible candidates for state and local office.
    (E) create "issue ads" for presidential candidates.

28. The main function of a congressional conference committee is to

    (A) appropriate money to fund legislative initiatives
    (B) negotiate with the president's office in shaping final legislation
    (C) consider special legislation that doesn't fall under the responsibility of standing committees
    (D) decide the standing committee assignments for new members of Congress
    (E) hammer out differences between House and Senate versions of the same bill

29. Which of the following types of groups have the LEAST number of restrictions on their campaign contributions?

    (A) 527s
    (B) PACs
    (C) public interest groups
    (D) corporate interest groups
    (E) political parties

30. The "marble cake" analogy is often used to describe

    (A) dual sovereignty
    (B) dual federalism
    (C) cooperative federalism
    (D) divided government
    (E) segregation plans presented to the courts during the 1960s

31. The type of primary that requires all voters to previously identify a party preference is known as a/an

    (A) open primary
    (B) run-off primary
    (C) blanket primary
    (D) closed primary
    (E) presidential-preference primary

32. Which of the following court cases is mismatched with the right that it addresses?

    (A) *Texas v. Johnson;* symbolic speech
    (B) *U.S. v. Schenck:* freedom of speech
    (C) *Miranda v. Arizona:* protection from self-incrimination
    (D) *Everson v. Board of Education:* freedom of religion
    (E) *Roe v. Wade:* protections from search and seizure

33. Which of the following is the BEST explanation for the breakup of the "Solid South" that began in the 1950s?

    (A) Southerners became more prosperous during the last half of the 20th century.
    (B) The Democratic Party endorsed a civil rights platform that many southerners did not agree with.
    (C) Blacks began to vote in record numbers, as the civil rights movement began to protect their voting rights.
    (D) The Republican Party carried out a strong campaign directed at capturing southern voters.
    (E) People from other parts of the country began moving into the South in larger and larger numbers.

34. Which of the following eligible voters are LEAST likely to vote?

    (A) young voters with low education levels
    (B) blue collar union members
    (C) middle-class African Americans
    (D) mid-western rural residents
    (E) Catholic voters

ELECTORAL VOTES 1992	
CANDIDATE	**NUMBER OF ELECTORAL VOTES**
George H.W. Bush	200
William J. Clinton	268
Ross Perot	70

35. In the hypothetical election result above, according to the Constitution, the winner of the presidential race would be decided by

    (A) a special bi-partisan committee
    (B) a run-off election
    (C) the Supreme Court
    (D) the Senate
    (E) the House of Representatives

36. The 1978 case that set precedents for later rulings on reverse discrimination was

    (A) *Lawrence v. Texas*
    (B) *Bakke v. California Board of Regents*
    (C) *Hardwick v. Georgia*
    (D) *Rostker v. Goldberg*
    (E) *Brown v. Topeka*

37. Which of the following conducts most of the research for Congress regarding proposed bills?

    (A) Committee of the Whole
    (B) Rules Committee
    (C) Office of Management and Budget
    (D) the sub-committee that the bill is assigned to
    (E) cabinet department that will be responsible for the policy

38. Alexander Hamilton believed that the Constitution should be broadly interpreted so that the national government represents "the supreme law of the land" (Article Six), and that its powers should be broadly defined and liberally construed. This view of the Constitution is known as

    (A) loose construction
    (B) majoritarianism
    (C) nullification
    (D) strict construction
    (E) dual federalism

39. Which of the following is the LEAST likely to serve in an active advisory capacity to the president?

    (A) the cabinet
    (B) the White House Office
    (C) the National Security Council
    (D) the Office of Management and Budget
    (E) the National Economic Council

40. All of the following are major players in the process of determining the annual federal budget EXCEPT:

    (A) congressional appropriations committees
    (B) congressional budget committees
    (C) the chief justice of the Supreme Court
    (D) the president
    (E) the Office of Management and the Budget

41. In the United States due process protection of citizens has primarily been clarified by

    (A) court decisions
    (B) congressional action
    (C) presidential action
    (D) presidential decrees
    (E) bureaucratic actions

42. Which of the following presidential appointments does NOT require Senate confirmation?

    (A) Secretary of Commerce
    (B) press secretary
    (C) ambassador to France
    (D) US Representative to the UN
    (E) administrative head of the Environmental Protection Agency

43. The most common route that a case follows to the Supreme Court is through a(n)

    (A) writ of habeus corpus
    (B) writ of mandamus
    (C) writ of certiorari
    (D) *amicus curiae* brief
    (E) *stare decisis* agreement

44. The budget process for the federal government best illustrates the principle of

    (A) federalism
    (B) divided government
    (C) bipartisan cooperation
    (D) separation of powers
    (E) checks and balances

45. The constitutional provisions for the electoral college were seriously questioned in recent U.S. political history during the

    (A) early Democratic primaries before the election of 2004
    (B) House hearings for the impeachment of President Bill Clinton
    (C) court proceedings that addressed ethics charges against Speaker of the House Tom DeLay
    (D) presidential election of 2000
    (E) Supreme Court deliberations for *Texas vs. Johnson*

46. In recent elections pollsters have found that churchgoers

    (A) have similar voting patterns to those of non-churchgoers
    (B) are more likely to vote Republican than non-churchgoers are
    (C) are more likely to vote Democratic than non-churchgoers are
    (D) are more likely to vote for third party candidates than non-churchgoers are
    (E) are less likely to go to the polls to vote than non-churchgoers are

47. When nominating federal judges, a president must be most directly concerned with the candidate's acceptability to the

    (A) Senate
    (B) House of Representatives
    (C) Supreme Court
    (D) Cabinet
    (E) American Bar Association

48. Party conventions are held to officially nominate candidates for the offices of president and vice president and to

   (A) name the party chairman
   (B) design a party platform
   (C) decide party campaign strategy
   (D) determine how to fund the upcoming presidential election
   (E) approve leaders for the party organizations at the state level

Reprinted with permission, "Minneapolis Star Tribune"

49. Which of the following best illustrates the point being made in the cartoon above?

   (A) Moderate Republicans that do not support President Bush's policies will be punished by the Republican Party.
   (B) People who support abortion rights and other "leftist" positions try to masquerade as moderates.
   (C) Extremists that advocate dangerous policies try to hide behind happy faces.
   (D) Extremist policies are now out of date and need to be updated to moderate positions that best suit current needs of the country.
   (E) The Republican Party has been taken over by right-wing politicians, who try to disguise themselves as moderates.

50. Which of the following presidents is usually credited with beginning the modern conservative movement that promoted reducing federal responsibility for social policy?

    (A) Richard Nixon
    (B) Jimmy Carter
    (C) Ronald Reagan
    (D) George H. W. Bush
    (E) Bill Clinton

51. A procedure permitting voters to reject or approve an act of the state legislature is known as a(n)

    (A) line-item vote
    (B) open vote
    (C) mandate
    (D) referendum
    (E) public vote

52. Which of the following is the LEAST likely to be a criterion considered by a presidential candidate in choosing a vice presidential running mate?

    (A) region
    (B) age
    (C) popular base support
    (D) experience in the judicial system
    (E) party subgroup appeal

53. The 1936 polls that predicted that Alf Landon would beat Franklin Roosevelt by a landslide in the presidential election were in error primarily because they

    (A) did not account for people's lack of knowledge about the candidates
    (B) worded their questionnaires in ways that distorted the results
    (C) did not have an accurate random sample
    (D) conducted straw polls
    (E) overestimated their sampling errors

54. Which of the following is most often associated with a conservative political ideology?

    (A) support for government assistance to the poor
    (B) opposition to faith-based initiatives in policy-making
    (C) belief in "rugged individualism"
    (D) a progressive taxation system that taxes the rich at higher rates than the middle class
    (E) support for a national government-sponsored healthcare program

55. Which of the following rights is protected by the 1st Amendment to the Constitution?

    (A) freedom of speech
    (B) right to remain silent
    (C) right to counsel
    (D) *habeas corpus*
    (E) freedom from unreasonable search and seizure

56. According to the Commerce Clause, Congress may

    (A) tax the exports of computers to Mexico.
    (B) review a garbage collection monopoly given by the city of Omaha.
    (C) regulate the sale and transportation of tomatoes within the state of Florida.
    (D) set requirements regarding the shippment of apples from Washington state to California.
    (E) regulate the sale of alcohol in the city of New Orleans.

57. Interest groups are most likely to influence the election process by

    (A) nominating candidates to stand for office.
    (B) conducting voter mobilization drives for favorable candidates and parties.
    (C) conducting elections at the local level.
    (D) working only with legislatures.
    (E) focusing their efforts on the elections of state judges.

58. The Constitution grants the House of Representative the right to

    (A) confirm presidential appointments to executive positions.
    (B) initiate all impeachment proceeding.
    (C) approve treaties with other nations.
    (D) remove agency head and other top bureaucrats from office.
    (E) override objections by the Senate to proposed legislation.

59. *United States v. Nixon, Nixon v. Fitzgerald,* and *Jones v. Clinton* were all cases that focused on the issue of

    (A) sexual misconduct by the president.
    (B) impoundment of funds.
    (C) the legislative veto.
    (D) military powers of the president.
    (E) executive privilege.

60. During the confirmation process Supreme Court justice nominees usually experience a "litmus test" which means that they must

    (A) be memberts of the party that controls the Senate.
    (B) answer questions about their religious beliefs.
    (C) live in a particular region of the country to maintain regional balance on the Court.
    (D) respond correctly to questions regarding an important issue of the time.
    (E) take a written test that measures their knowledge of constitutional provisions.

FREE RESPONSE QUESTIONS

<u>Section II</u>
Time – 100 minutes

Directions: You have 100 minutes to answer all four of the following questions. Unless the directions indicate otherwise, respond to all parts of all four questions. It is suggested that you take a few minutes to plan and outline each answer. <u>Spend approximately one-fourth of your time (25 minutes) on each question</u>. In your response, use substantive examples where appropriate. Make certain to number each of your answers as the question is numbered below.

1. Political participation in the United States can take place in various forms.

   a) Other than voting, identify two ways that Americans participate politically.
   b) Explain one impact that the first type of political participation you identified in (a) might have on the political system.
   c) Explain one impact that the second type of political participation you identified in (a) might have on the political system.
   d) Explain one reason why voter turnout among young people is traditionally lower than voter turnout among older people.

2. The delegates that attended the Constitutional Convention held many different views about what government structure and functions should be included in the Constitution.

   a) Identify and explain two different issues that caused disagreement among delegates to the Constitutional Convention.
   b) For each of the issues you identified in (a), identify and describe a compromise made by the delegates at the Constitutional Convention.
   c) Describe one Constitutional provision that resulted from a compromise at the Convention that was amended later in history and explain why it was amended.

3. Once elected presidents have found that it is difficult to fulfill campaign promises and policy preferences.

   a) Identify and explain two formal checks that other branches may use to challenge presidential goals.
   b) Explain two methods (formal or informal) that the president may use to overcome opposition to his policy goals.
   c) Explain one reason that modern presidents (since 1945) have often found it easier to reach their goals than have presidents of the past.

AMERICAN VIEWS REGARDING THE NEED FOR A THIRD PARTY

	Parties Adequate	Third Party Needed
June, 2008	47	47
January, 2008	40	55
June, 2007	33	58
January, 2007	40	51
January, 2006	48	48
January, 2005	50	43
January, 2004	56	40

Number in percentages
Source: Gallup.com

Question: In your view, do the Republican and Democratic parties do an adequete job of representing the American people, or do they do such a poor job that a third major party is needed?

4. a) Using the data in the chart above, describe the changes in the attitudes of American citizens toward the need for a third party in the American political system.

    b) Identify and explain two formal impediments to the development of third parties in the United States.

    c) Describe two contributions that third parties have made to the American political system.

SAMPLE EXAMINATION TWO

Time - 45 minutes
60 Questions

Directions: Each of the questions or incomplete statements below is followed by five suggested answers or completions. Select the one that is best in each case.

1. Which of the following is a common result of gerrymandering?

   (A) The party that controls the state legislature gains an electoral advantage.
   (B) Third parties gain electoral advantages.
   (C) Voter participation increases dramatically.
   (D) Polling agencies have trouble predicting the outcome of elections.
   (E) The opposition party makes marginal gains in the state legislature.

2. Which of the following types of elections in the United States generally bring out the LOWEST voter turnout?

   (A) presidential elections
   (B) national level midterm elections
   (C) Republican primary elections for presidential candidates
   (D) local elections
   (E) Democratic primary elections for presidential candidates

3. Presidential vetoes are rarely overturned. However, in which of the following scenarios would a presidential veto most likely be overturned?

   (A) The president has a contentious relationship with the cabinet.
   (B) The majority of the Supreme Court justices have different political views from the president.
   (C) The proposed legislation affects only a small number of people, and the opposing party holds the majority in the Senate.
   (D) The proposed legislation is controversial, and "divided government" is in place.
   (E) The majority of the representatives and senators are members of the same party as the president.

295

4. A concurring opinion is issued by the Supreme Court when

   (A) a justice votes with the majority but for different reasons
   (B) a justice disagrees with the majority opinion
   (C) no justices disagree with the majority opinion
   (D) justices want to clarify the meaning of the majority opinion
   (E) justices want to clarify the meaning of the dissenting opinion

5. Which of the following events most directly inspired the Constitutional Convention to meet together in 1787?

   (A) the defeat of the British at Yorktown
   (B) the signing of the Declaration of Independence
   (C) the publication of *The Federalist Papers*
   (D) the publication of *Common Sense*
   (E) Shay's Rebellion

6. Presidential elections in the United States are conducted according to the rules of the electoral college. These rules often impact presidential campaigns because

   (A) presidential candidates tend to focus their campaigns on states where the election appears to be very close.
   (B) presidential candidates waste a lot of time campaigning in states that have few electoral votes.
   (C) presidential candidates tend to campaign only in urban areas.
   (D) in general, presidential candidates tend to campaign more in states in the east, and states in the west are ignored.
   (E) Congressional candidates are much less likely to benefit from the popularity of presidential candidates than they would if the president were directly elected.

7. Recent efforts to reform the United States electoral process have centered on

   (A) opening the process to encourage the development of a third political party.
   (B) reducing the importance of the electoral college.
   (C) controlling the influence of campaign contributions.
   (D) reducing the influence of lobbyists on members of Congress.
   (E) controlling the amount of negative campaign ads used by candidates.

(Questions 8 and 9 are based on the following chart):

American Political Participation 1996-2004			
Type of political involvement	**Percentage**		
	1996	**2000**	**2004**
Watched the campaign on television	74%	82%	86%
Voted in election	73%	73%	77%
Read about campaign in newspaper	55%	56%	67%
Listened to campaign radio programs	38%	38%	51%
Tried to influence how others vote	28%	34%	48%
Wore a button or put a sticker on the car	10%	10%	21%
Gave money to help a campaign	8%	9%	13%
Attended a political meeting	5%	5%	7%
Worked for a party or candidate	2%	3%	3%

Source: The National Election Studies, Center for Political Studies, University of Michigan

8. What patterns of American political participation does the chart reflect?

    (A) Most people that watched the campaign on television also read about the
        campaign in newspapers and listened to campaign radio programs.
    (B) Most citizens who voted tried to influence how others voted.
    (C) Except for voting, Americans are more likely to passively participate in
        campaigns than become actively involved.
    (D) Most Americans work for a party or candidate at some point in their lifetime.
    (E) Most Americans don't really care about politics.

9. The chart above is constructed from citizens' responses to questions. Which of the
   following is the BEST argument for viewing the responses with some doubts as to
   their reflection of actual participation?

    (A) Statistics show that many more than 3% of eligible voters work for parties or
        candidates during campaigns.
    (B) The actual number that voted in the elections 1996-2004 was no better than 55%;
        73% - 77% said they voted.
    (C) Studies show that newspaper readerships about campaigns are higher than the
        percentages shown on the chart.
    (D) Since most people do a lot of channel surfing, it is doubtful that numbers of
        those watching the campain on television is accurate for the elections indicated.
    (E) Based on common observation, the figures for wearing buttons and putting
        stickers on cars is obviously too low for the elections indicated.

10. The federal courts have ruled in recent years that government restrictions on flag burning are unconstitutional because they abuse

    (A) freedom of pure speech
    (B) the right to privacy
    (C) freedom of symbolic speech
    (D) due process
    (E) equal protection

11. Which body in the House of Representatives is most directly responsible for setting the parameters for debate and the proposal of amendments to bills on the floor?

    (A) the majority leadership
    (B) the majority and minority leadership combined
    (C) the standing committee that marked up the bill
    (D) the Rules Committee
    (E) the Committee on Committees

12. Laws that maintained segregation and discrimination in public places in the U.S. were prohibited by

    (A) *Gideon v Wainwright*
    (B) *Miranda v Arizona*
    (C) *Plessy v Ferguson*
    (D) the Civil Rights Act of 1964
    (E) the Equal Opportunity Act

13. The founders decided that voter qualifications should be

    (A) based on universal manhood suffrage
    (B) left for the individual states to decide
    (C) the same for national, state, and local elections
    (D) based on property ownership
    (E) open to all, regardless of gender or race

14. The Constitution dictates which of the following with regard to voting?

    (A) Setting federal residency requirements for all voters.
    (B) Setting an age requirement for all voters.
    (C) The type of ballot used in federal elections.
    (D) Determining a minimum education level for voters.
    (E) Determining when a convicted felon may be able to vote once released from prison.

15. "Creeping categorization" of federal grants usually results in

    (A) increasing control of state governments in determining how federal money is spent
    (B) revenue sharing, a situation in which responsibility for spending money is shared between the state and federal governments
    (C) separating of money approved by the House of Representatives from that approved by the Senate
    (D) increasing control by the national Congress over how states spend federal money
    (E) decreasing the number of unfunded mandates that Congress is able to impose of the states

16. The Fourteenth Amendment to the Constitution helped to clarify

    (A) voting rights for African Americans
    (B) voting rights for women
    (C) protections of civil rights from abuse by states
    (D) the role of Congress in regulating interstate trade.
    (E) the ability of aliens to own property in the United States

17. Which of the following is NOT a theoretical advantage of federalism?

    (A) The public usually has a clear understanding of each level of government's responsibility.
    (B) Various approaches are used at the state level to solve problems that may be examined and utilized by other states.
    (C) Increased government efficiency is possible since local governments are responsible for local issues and the federal government is responsible for national issues.
    (D) More opportunities exist for political involvement because citizens have more access points at different levels of government.
    (E) It is seen as the best way to handle the diverse problems of a large country.

18. Which of the following groups is usually most directly involved in organizing primary elections?

    (A) national party leaders
    (B) the electoral college
    (C) the national Congress
    (D) the president and the cabinet
    (E) state and local party leaders

By permission of Steve Benson and Creators Syndicate, Inc.

19. Which of the following best represents the point being made in the cartoon above?

    (A) Earmarks are a positive way to pass legislation.
    (B) Republicans use earmarks more than Democrats.
    (C) The public approves of Congressional use of earmarks.
    (D) The use of earmarks is a practice of both political parties.
    (E) Congress, not the president, is the source of earmarks.

20. In order to insure that a sample accurately represents a population, a researcher must follow the principle of

    (A) margin of error
    (B) straw polling
    (C) group benefits
    (D) random sampling
    (E) accurate franking

21. Which of the following is a liberal political belief?

    (A) healthcare benefits tied to the workplace
    (B) free market principle for businesses
    (C) low taxes
    (D) support for faith-based initiatives
    (E) crime fighting by curing social and economic reasons for crimes

(Questions 22 and 23 are based on the following table):

STATE OF OHIO VOTER BALLOT 1996
President: William Clinton, Democrat Robert Dole, Republican
House District #12 Joseph Thomason, Democrat Gilbert Stephens, Republican
Senate Richard Stegeman, Democrat Ronald Johnson, Republican

22. In the election above, if a person voted for William Clinton, Joseph Thomason and Ronald Johnson the ballot would be an example of a

    (A) party ticket
    (B) straight ticket
    (C) split ticket
    (D) similar ticket
    (E) dominant ticket

23. If the results of the election matched the voter choices above what kind of government would result?

    (A) parliamentary government
    (B) divided government
    (C) partisan government
    (D) executive dominated government
    (E) bandwagon government

24. Which of the following people would be MOST likely to have control over the way the president spends his time?

    (A) the secretary of state
    (B) the attorney general
    (C) the vice president
    (D) the chief of staff
    (E) the national security advisor

25. Constitutional amendments may be formally proposed by

    (A) the president
    (B) state courts
    (C) bureaucracies
    (D) Congress
    (E) interest groups

26. Congressional district boundaries are reset every 10 years based on the

    (A) average number of voters for the past decade for each district.
    (B) results of the Bureau of the Census study.
    (C) study results of each of the state legislatures.
    (D) poll results of the House Rules Committee.
    (E) House Bipartisan Committee report on District Boundaries.

27. The right of members of Congress to send mail to their constituents at the government's expense is called

    (A) executive privilege
    (B) statutory power
    (C) the franking privilege
    (D) the spoils system
    (E) logrolling

28. The main intent of most gerrymandering is to

    (A) equalize the number of constituents that each representative actually represents
    (B) increase the number of minority candidates that win congressional races
    (C) decrease the number of minority candidates that win congressional races
    (D) elect more Democrats to the House
    (E) create districts that give candidates from one party an advantage over candidates from the other

(Questions 29 and 30 are based on the following chart):

PARTISAN DIFFERENCES IN GOVERNMENT TRUST September 8 - 11, 2008			
	Democrat	**Independent**	**Republican**
Federal gov't., domestic problems	35%	39%	69%
Federal gov't., international problems	39%	50%	83%
Executive	14%	33%	83%
Legislative	61%	44%	36%
Judicial	59%	62%	86%

Gallup Poll

29. Which of the following statements is supported by the table above?

(A) Independents trust the executive more than Democrats and Republicans do.
(B) All political groups consistently gave the judicial branch a high level of trust.
(C) Republicans felt that the legislature could be trusted equally to the executive branch.
(D) Democrats generally trusted all branches of government more than Independents and Republicans.
(E) All groups felt that the federal government may be trusted to handle domestic problems.

30. Which of the following is a result of the presidential primary system?

(A) A decline in voter turnout in the general election.
(B) An increase in the cost of campaigns for the candidates.
(C) An increase the importance in political parties in the selection process.
(D) A decline in voter registration drives by interest groups.
(E) An increase in the number of young voters.

31. Which of the following is NOT addressed directly in the First Amendment?

(A) the rights of citizens to petition the government for redress of grievances
(B) freedom of the press
(C) freedom of speech
(D) the protection of the rights of those accused of committing a crime
(E) free exercise of religion

32. All of the following traditionally provide advice to Congress regarding proposed legislation EXCEPT:

    (A) Interest Groups
    (B) Bureaucracies
    (C) Congressional Staffers
    (D) Public Hearings
    (E) State legislatures

33. The court case that helped set the precedent that evidence seized during an illegal search is excluded in a state criminal trial against the accused was

    (A) *Mapp v. Ohio*
    (B) *Gideon v. Wainwright*
    (C) *Miranda v. Arizona*
    (D) *Gitlow v. New York*
    (E) *Tinker v. Des Moines*

34. Which of the following is a presidential power directly identified in the Constitution?

    (A) to lead the president's political party
    (B) to be responsible for impoundment of funds
    (C) to exercise executive privilege
    (D) to veto legislative proposals by Congress
    (E) to exercise emergency powers

35. Which of the following is an accurate statement about voting behavior in the United States?

    (A) College students are more likely to vote than older voters.
    (B) Black Americans are more likely to vote than are Latino Americans.
    (C) Men are more likely to vote than women are.
    (D) First-time voters are more likely to vote than those that have had the right for a long time.
    (E) Citizens with college degrees are more likely to vote than those with only high school degrees.

36. The U.S. system of checks and balances allows

    (A) the president to remove the speaker of the House of Representatives
    (B) Congress to require the president to spend all funds allocated by Congress
    (C) the Supreme Court to declare a law unconstitutional
    (D) the Supreme Court to remove members of Congress from office
    (E) Congress to remove a cabinet member from office

37. Which of the following presidential actions requires consent by the Senate?

    (A) removal of agency heads from their positions
    (B) appointment of ambassadors
    (C) executive agreements
    (D) executive orders
    (E) presidential pardons

38. Supporters of the line-item veto believe it is one way to limit

    (A) the Senate's power to block popular bills from the House of Representatives.
    (B) unpopular Supreme Court decisions.
    (C) the ability of states to ignore federal mandates.
    (D) the number of pork projects included in legislative bills.
    (E) the ability of the president to impound funds.

39. The development and approval of the United States budget primarily involves

    (A) the Ways and Means Committees of the House and Senate
    (B) the House of Representatives and the president
    (C) the Treasury Department and Congress
    (D) the president and both houses of Congress
    (E) the president, the House and the Supreme Court

40. An example of entitlement spending in the federal budget is

    (A) Social Security payments
    (B) interest payments on the national debt
    (C) defense spending
    (D) salaries of federal bureaucrats
    (E) environmental programs

41. The doctrine of selective incorporation refers to

    (A) the Department of Homeland Security extending the responsibility of defending the country from terrorist attacks to the states.
    (B) Supreme Court decisions that require legislation to be adequately funded by the annual budget.
    (C) a Congressional requirement that the president spend all of the money appropriated for government programs.
    (D) Supreme Court decisions that have gradually extended the requirements of the Bill of Rights to the states.
    (E) the process states use in applying for federal grants.

42. Political efficacy refers to the

    (A) number of voters that turn out for mid-term elections.
    (B) acceptance of Supreme Court decisions.
    (C) the extent to which citizens feel government officials respond to their views and demands.
    (D) the way that the House and Senate work together to solve problems over bills.
    (E) the amount of votes that separate the winners and losers in elections.

43. Which of the following court cases is most closely associated with protection of the right to privacy?

    (A) *Plessy v. Ferguson*
    (B) *Lemon v. Kurzman*
    (C) *Roe v. Wade*
    (D) *Texas v. Johnson*
    (E) *Furman v. Georgia*

44. If Supreme Court justices are struggling with the doctrine of original intent in a particular case, they are concerned about

    (A) the initial purpose of a law as it was passed by Congress
    (B) the intentions in committing a crime of a person convicted of a felony
    (C) the nature of the case as it was first presented to a lower court
    (D) the slant that the lawyers on both sides are trying to put in place
    (E) the intention of the framers as they put together the original Constitution

45. Filibusters are used to deliberately slow down the policymaking process by

    (A) Representatives in the house who wish to bring a bill to the floor.
    (B) Senate members of the minority party who wish to prevent a vote on the floor.
    (C) An opponent of a bill who insists that bills have bureaucratic approval before they can become laws.
    (D) A lobbyist who forces public hearings on certain legislation.
    (E) An opponent of the bill requiring Supreme Court Review before consideration.

46. Which of the following groups is BEST represented by political action committees (PACs) in Washington?

    (A) farmers
    (B) labor unions
    (C) public interest groups
    (D) civil rights groups
    (E) businesses

47. Which of the following is NOT a difference between the House of Representatives and the Senate?

    (A) Size of the constituencies of members
    (B) Direct election of the members of each house
    (C) Length of term of members
    (D) Membership size
    (E) Role in the impeachment process

48. The amount that the federal government spends over its budget in any given year is called

    (A) a deficit
    (B) the national debt
    (C) fiscal spending
    (D) monetary spending
    (E) negative amortization

49. Consider this question asked in a political opinions questionnaire: "Do you think that people generally consider the Democrats or the Republicans more conservative or wouldn't you want to guess about that?"

    Which principle of political polling was the researcher focusing on with the addition of "or wouldn't you want to guess about that?"

    (A) Samples must accurately represent the population they are measuring.
    (B) People do not like to admit that they lack knowledge about a political issue.
    (C) Wording must be objective and free of emotion.
    (D) A research project must be cost efficient to be useful.
    (E) Sampling error must be carefully constructed and made known when polling results are announced.

50. Third party candidates have affected recent U.S. elections by

    (A) increasing the voter turnout by drawing previously disaffected voters into the election.
    (B) developing their own media outlets to gain public attention.
    (C) forcing the federal government to adjust election laws to make it easier for them to run for congressional office.
    (D) confusing voters by discussing frivolous issues.
    (E) using PACs and interest groups to disrupt the smooth operation of the major parties.

51. Which of the following cabinet positions is primarily responsible for advising the president regarding foreign affairs?

    (A) Secretary of Defense
    (B) Secretary of Commerce
    (C) Secretary of State
    (D) National Security Advisor
    (E) Attorney General

52. Which of the following is an accurate statement regarding political liberalism?

    (A) Married people generally have more liberal political views than unmarried.
    (B) Protestants generally have more liberal political views than Catholics.
    (C) Women generally have more liberal political views than men.
    (D) Latinos generally have more liberal political views than blacks.
    (E) Southerners generally have more liberal political views than northeasterners.

53. The civil service was created primarily to guarantee

    (A) proper qualifications of those working in the bureaucracy.
    (B) properly qualified candidates for congressional office.
    (C) protection of voter rights from abuse by state governments.
    (D) promotion of government employees based on patronage.
    (E) a high level of competence of those serving as Congressional staffers.

54. All of the following are examples of independent regulatory agencies EXCEPT:

    (A) Federal Reserve Board
    (B) Securities and Exchange Commission
    (C) Interstate Commerce Commission
    (D) Executive Office of the President
    (E) National Labor Relations Board

55. Since its passage, the War Powers Resolution of 1973 has had little effect in

    (A) reducing the deployment of national guard troops without a governor's approval.
    (B) requiring that all military funding be approved only through special legislation.
    (C) shifting the responsibility for waging and funding war to the president.
    (D) restricting the president's power to activate military troops.
    (E) restricting the ability of the president to deploy U.S. troops without a formal declaration of war.

56. According to the 25th Amendment, what can be done if a president is disabled, either physically or mentally, but refuses to give up his office?

    (A) Nothing can be done officially, but the vice president is expected to fill in.
    (B) If the vice president and cabinet determine that the president is disabled, the vice president may become acting president.
    (C) Congress may vote to remove the president permanently and replace him with the vice president.
    (D) The speaker of the house takes the president's position, and the *president pro tempore* of the Senate takes the vice president's position.
    (E) The vice president becomes acting president after he has informed Congress of his intentions.

57. The House Rules Committee is important to the legislative process when

    (A) a bill is reported to the sub-committees for consideration.
    (B) preparations for public hearings of a bill are being made.
    (C) the House must conference with the Senate over the wording of a bill.
    (D) the president vetoes a bill and the House reconsiders the bill.
    (E) a bill is referred to the floor for debate.

58. If a committee chair in the House of Representatives steps down or is not reelected, which of the following people would most likely replace him/her?

    (A) a colleague from the same state or region
    (B) the person selected by a vote of the majority party members in the House
    (C) the person appointed by the president to fill the role
    (D) the majority party member of the committee with the most seniority
    (E) the minority party member of the committee with the most seniority

59. The "rule of four" is a tradition that sets the number of

    (A) Supreme Court justices needed to bring a case up from the lower courts for consideration
    (B) times that a member of Congress can miss an important vote without being censured by his/her colleagues
    (C) times that a bill can be presented to the legislature before it is permanently barred
    (D) agencies needed to lodge a formal complaint against the Office of Management and the Budget with the president
    (E) resolutions that may be presented to Congress within any given month

60. Under which of the following chief justices was the Supreme Court both liberal and activist?

(A) William Howard Taft
(B) Charles Evans Hughes
(C) Harlan Fiske Stone
(D) Earl Warren
(E) William Rehnquist

FREE RESPONSE QUESTIONS

Section II
Time – 100 minutes

Directions: You have 100 minutes to answer all four of the following questions. Unless the directions indicate otherwise, respond to all parts of all four questions. It is suggested that you take a few minutes to plan and outline each answer. <u>Spend approximately one-fourth of your time (25 minutes) on each question</u>. In your response, use substantive examples where appropriate. Make certain to number each of your answers as the question is numbered below.

Kal, The Economist, CartoonArts International

1. a) Describe the cartoon's message regarding the use of the presidential veto.
   b) Explain how the use of the veto is usually a more important power of the president during periods of divided government.
   c) Describe one formal way the legislature can challenge veto.
   d) Describe one informal way the legislature can challenge a presidential veto.

2. The presidential electoral system in the United States has changed significantly in recent years.

   a) Describe two ways that the increasing use of state primaries has changed the presidential electoral system.
   b) Identify and explain two reasons why control of the electoral process has shifted from the political party to the presidential candidate.
   c) Identify and explain one impact that the shift of control to the presidential candidates has had on the electoral process.

3. The principle of "checks and balances" is reflected in many provisions of the United States Constitution.

   a) Discuss the main purpose of checks and balances, as viewed by the founders.
   b) Describe one check that the legislative branch has on the court system.
   c) Describe one check that the executive branch has on the court system.
   d) Explain one limitation that the legislature has on its power to check the court system.
   e) Explain one limitation that the executive branch has on its power to check the court system.

4. The development and implementation of the United States budget involves both the executive and legislative branches.

   a) Describe two ways that the executive branch shapes the budget process.
   b) Describe two ways that the legislature shapes the budget process.
   c) Explain two ways Congress may continue to monitor the implementation of the budget after it has been passed into law.

SAMPLE EXAMINATION THREE

Section One

Time - 45 minutes
60 Questions

Directions: Each of the questions or incomplete statements below is followed by five suggested answers or completions. Select the one that is best in each case.

1. Which of the following has been the most frequently used method to amend the Constitution?

    (A) Amendments were proposed by a 2/3 vote of each house of Congress and ratified by at least 3/4 of the state legislatures.
    (B) Amendments were proposed by a 2/3 vote of each house of Congress and ratified by specially called conventions in at least 3/4 of the states.
    (C) Amendments were proposed by a national constitutional convention requested by at least 2/3 of state legislatures and ratified by at least 3/4 of the state legislatures.
    (D) Amendments were proposed by a national constitutional convention and ratified by specially called conventions in at least 3/4 of the states.
    (E) Amendments were proposed by 2/3 of each house of Congress, ratified by 2/3 of the state and signed by the president.

2. A primary election in which voters may decide when they enter the voting booths which party's primary they wish to participate in is called

    (A) an open primary
    (B) a runoff primary
    (C) delegate selection only primary
    (D) a closed primary
    (E) a binding presidential preference primary

3. Which of the following is the most usual criterion that a presidential nominee applies when selecting a vice-presidential running mate?

    (A) balance and appeal to the party's ticket
    (B) amount of personal wealth the running mate has
    (C) ability to work effectively with senators
    (D) ideological compatibility
    (E) knowledge of domestic policy issues

313

4. The political organization whose primary focus is to raise campaign funds to support favored candidates is

   (A) an interest group
   (B) the Federal Election Commission
   (C) a political action committee
   (D) a political party
   (E) a political caucus

5. All adults 18 years or older were able to vote after the passage of the

   (A) Voting Rights Act of 1965
   (B) Civil Rights Act of 1964
   (C) 19th Amendment
   (D) 26th Amendment
   (E) 27th Amendment

6. The main responsibility of a conference committee in Congress is to

   (A) negotiate with the president in order to avoid presidential vetoes
   (B) hold hearings on proposed legislation
   (C) assign new members to standing committees
   (D) decide what rules will be placed on proposed legislation on the floor
   (E) reconcile differences between House and Senate versions of a bill

7. A difference between the House of Representatives and the Senate in passing legislation is that

   (A) members of the House use caucuses to track the progress of legislation.
   (B) Standing committees are only used in the Senate to review legislation.
   (C) the House sets limits on debate through the Rules Committee.
   (D) public hearings on revenue bills may only be held in the House.
   (E) the Senate Majority Leader has more control over the process than does the Speaker of the House.

The Powers not delegated to the United States by the Constitution, nor prohibited by it to the States, are reserved to the States respectively, or to the people.

10th Amendment

8. The 10th Amendment above protects which of the following principles?

(A) Checks and balances
(B) Separation of Powers
(C) Judicial Review
(D) Federalism
(E) Equal Protection

9. Charles Beard's famous interpretation of the Constitution contends that the major conflicts and compromises resulted from the clash of

(A) owners of land as property, and owners of business or commercial interests
(B) elitists and populists
(C) supporters of creating a strong central government, and supporters of state rights
(D) eastern elites and western settlers
(E) wealthy and middle class delegates to the Constitutional Convention

10. Which of the following groups were granted the right to vote during the 19th century?

    I. non-property owning white males
   II. former slaves
  III. women
   IV. 18-21 year olds

(A) I only
(B) I and II only
(C) I, II, and III only
(D) I, II, III, and IV
(E) I and III only

11. James Madison argues in his *Federalist Papers* that violence and chaos is most likely to erupt in a political system that is a(n)

(A) direct democracy
(B) representative democracy
(C) authoritarian regime
(D) monarchy
(E) oligarchy

(Questions 12 and 13 are based on the following cartoon:)

By permission of Steve Benson and Creators Syndicate, Inc.

12. Which of the following is the message conveyed in the cartoon?

    (A) Taxpayers generally approve of pork spending by Congress.
    (B) Congress sees its role as protecting taxpayers from unnecessary pork spending.
    (C) Congress is unconcerned about the costs of pork legislation passed onto the taxpayer.
    (D) Special interests are not concerned with getting favors from members of Congress.
    (E) Special interests prefer to work with state legislatures rather than the U.S. Congress.

13. According to the cartoon a problem with pork legislation is that

    (A) the increased cost of pork legislation makes it difficult for special interest groups to represent their members.
    (B) there are not enough pork projects to help the taxpayers.
    (C) taxpayers' demand for more pork projects cause budgetary problems for Congress to solve.
    (D) Congress may limit beneficial pork legislation due to the increased costs to the taxpayers.
    (E) pork legislation benefits Congress and special interests more than taxpayers.

Questions 14 and 15 are based on the following chart:

Strength of Partisanship 1984-2004											
	'84	**'86**	**'88**	**'90**	**'92**	**'94**	**'96**	**'98**	**'00**	**'02**	**'04**
Independent/ Apolitical	13	14	12	12	13	12	10	12	13	9	10
Leaning Independent	23	21	25	24	27	25	26	24	28	28	29
Weak Partisan	35	37	32	34	32	33	34	34	27	33	28
Strong Partisan	29	28	31	30	29	30	30	29	31	31	33

Question: "Generally speaking, do you usually think of yourself as a Republican, a Democrat, and Independent, or what?"

14. Which of the following best describes the trend reflected in the chart?

    (A) More people identified themselves as Independent between 1984 and 2004.
    (B) Significantly fewer people identified themselves as Strong Partisan between 1984 and 1992 than did those between 1994 and 2004.
    (C) Throughout the time period the percentage of those identifying themselves as Independent/Apolitical remained relatively stable.
    (D) The percentage of those identifying themselves as Strong Partisan increased from 1984 to 1992 and then dropped off significantly by 2004.
    (E) The percentage of those Leaning Independent consistently rose during the time period.

15. The information in the chart most clearly implies that

    (A) Successful candidates for office were likely more liberal between 1984 and 2004.
    (B) Successful candidates could be strongly partisan between 1984 and 2004.
    (C) Due to the increased percentage of apolitical citizens the percentage of voters would be low from 1984-2004.
    (D) Both parties had to reach out to independent voters in order to win elections.
    (E) The most successful party from 1984-2004 would have remained true to its base rather than compromising with others.

16. The doctrine of comparable worth has been applied to combat discrimination against

    (A) racial and ethnic minorities in schools
    (B) homosexuals in housing
    (C) women in the work force
    (D) the physically disabled in public places
    (E) women in sports competition

17. A very important principle that holds that evidence gathered illegally cannot be used in a trial is called

    (A) the exclusionary rule
    (B) the right to privacy
    (C) the clear and present danger test
    (D) eminent domain
    (E) unenumerated rights clause

18. Which of the following best describes divided government between 1969 and 2009?

    (A) Republicans have controlled the presidency, and the Democrats have controlled Congress.
    (B) Democrats have controlled the presidency, and the Republicans have controlled Congress.
    (C) Divided government persisted throughout the entire period.
    (D) Both President Clinton and President George W. Bush experienced periods of divided government.
    (E) The Republicans have always controlled both branches, with Democrats serving as the loyal opposition.

19. Which structure in the U.S. political system is best understood by viewing its functioning through a "grass roots" model?

    (A) interest groups
    (B) Congress
    (C) political parties
    (D) the presidency
    (E) the Supreme Court

20. The major focus of the "devolution revolution" as it began during the 1990s was

    (A) federal funding for highways
    (B) education
    (C) the welfare system
    (D) federal and state income taxes
    (E) the environment

21. An example of a constitutional power of the U.S. president is

    (A) head of his/her political party
    (B) chief communicator
    (C) chief legislator
    (D) commander-in-chief
    (E) regulator of interstate commerce

22. In order to change the number of justices on the Supreme Court

    (A) the Constitution must be amended
    (B) Congress must pass the proper legislation
    (C) the president must propose and the Senate approve of the change
    (D) the Supreme Court must approve of legislation passed by Congress
    (E) the president must propose change and ¾ of the states must approve of the change

23. The leading proponent of a strong centralized government at the Constitutional Convention was

    (A) Patrick Henry
    (B) Benjamin Franklin
    (C) Thomas Jefferson
    (D) John Adams
    (E) Alexander Hamilton

24. In order to insure that a sample accurately represents a population, a researcher must follow the principle of

    (A) margin of error
    (B) random sampling
    (C) group benefits
    (D) straw polling
    (E) accurate franking

25. "Creeping categorization" is a phrase that describes the tendency for

    (A) the federal government to push responsibility for welfare programs to the states
    (B) bills passed by Congress to accumulate complicated provisions
    (C) government agencies to set up complex procedures based on division of labor
    (D) block grants to gradually become categorical grants
    (E) states to have conflicting categories for defining the commerce clause

26. *Amicus curaie* briefs are usually prepared by

    (A) subcommittee chairmen in Congress to simplify marking up of bills
    (B) the OMB Director to help the president understand budget requests
    (C) federal judges to explain why they ruled as they did
    (D) agency bureaucrats for subcommittee hearings
    (E) interest groups for judges/justices that hear a case in which they have an interest in the outcome

27. *Tinker v DeMoines* (1969) and *Texas v Johnson* (1989) were court cases involving which of the following principles?

    (A) freedom of religion
    (B) the death penalty
    (C) trial by jury
    (D) symbolic speech
    (E) search and seizure

28. In *Lopez v United States* (1995) the Court strengthened state power by

    (A) allowing states to set minimum wage requirements.
    (B) allowing state to control alcohol within their borders.
    (C) permitting states to use the death penalty as they see fit.
    (D) permitting states to regulate gun zones around schools.
    (E) giving states exclusive authority over public education.

29. Which of the following individuals is the most likely to vote?

    (A) A person, aged 18-30.
    (B) A regular churchgoer.
    (C) A Southerner.
    (D) A person who lives in a rural area.
    (E) A person with a college degree.

30. Which of the following has become significantly more important in recent years as a means for candidates to gain national office?

    (A) support from party leaders
    (B) support from people who already hold national elected office
    (C) support from delegates to the national conventions
    (D) selection by voters in a series of state primaries
    (E) official endorsements by the editors of major newspapers

31. Which of the following federal government programs is the most significant budgetary concern due to its current size and projected growth?

    (A) Head Start
    (B) entitlement programs
    (C) disability plans for war veterans
    (D) federal funding for interstate highways
    (E) preservation of land as national parks

32. Which of the following is true of female candidates for national public office?

    (A) Female voters are more likely to vote for female candidates than male voters are.
    (B) Female candidates are more likely to run as Democrats than as Republicans.
    (C) Fewer women run for national political office today than 10-20 years ago.
    (D) Just as many women run as Republicans for public office as Democrats.
    (E) Female candidates are more likely to run against other female candidates than against men.

33. Which of the following voters would be MOST likely to vote for Republicans rather than Democrats?

    (A) an unmarried city dweller from the northeast
    (B) a middle aged laborer active in his labor union
    (C) a black teacher from the southeast
    (D) a white businessman from a small Midwestern town
    (E) a young Asian college professor from urban California

34. The "Neo-Con" movement that developed in the early 21st century is most focused on the issue of

    (A) global terrorism
    (B) social security reform
    (C) rights of the unborn
    (D) international trade
    (E) the natural environment

35. Which of the following was responsible for doubling the size of the electorate in the United States?

   (A) the 15th Amendment
   (B) the 19th Amendment
   (C) the Civil Rights Act of 1964
   (D) the Voting Rights Act of 1965
   (E) the 26th Amendment

36. Which of the following statements best describes an important change in presidential power since its creation in the Constitution?

   (A) Presidential power over domestic policy has decreased due to Congressional control over the legislative agenda.
   (B) Presidential power over domestic policy has increased due to the use of the line-item veto.
   (C) Presidential power over the budget has decreased due to the increased influence of the Office of Management and Budget.
   (D) Presidential power over foreign policy has decreased due to the restrictions of the War Powers Act.
   (E) Presidential power over foreign policy has increased due to the difficulty of Congress has in coming to a consensus.

37. Which of the following ways could Congress respond if the Supreme Court finds a law that it passes unconstitutional?

   (A) Congress could override the Court's decision by a 2/3 majority of both houses.
   (B) Congress could replace justices with younger, more agreeable ones.
   (C) Congress could convince the president to veto the Court's decision.
   (D) Congress could appeal the Court's Decision to the District of Columbia Court of Appeals.
   (E) Congress could pass another law, similar to the old one, but one that respected the objections of the justices.

38. In contrast to those of the House of Representatives, rules that govern the conduct of business in the Senate are

   (A) subject to the whims of the vice president
   (B) much less elaborate and structured
   (C) much more elaborate and structured
   (D) more likely to be determined by the majority party
   (E) much more dependent on input from the president

111th Congress Profile 2009-2011		
Membership Characteristics	**House of Representatives (Numbers)**	**Senate (Numbers)**
Male	357	83
Female	78	17
African Americans	41	1
Hispanics	27	3
Asian/Pacific Islanders	7	2
Native Americans	1	0
Republicans	178	40
Democrats	257	58
Independents	0	2

39. Which of the following is the most likely scenario to result from the statistics in the chart above?

   (A) The Republicans will have the support necessary to prevent policy measures they oppose.
   (B) Young members will be able to take significant power from older members.
   (C) Ethnic and racial minority groups will have significantly more power in the Senate than the House.
   (D) Women will likely wield more power over policy than other minority groups.
   (E) Hispanics will likely wield more power over policy than African Americans.

40. Which of the following make it difficult for minor party candidates to win the presidency?

   I.   The lack of diverse interests in the U. S. that would support more than two parties
   II. The electoral college winner-take-all rule
   III. The strict rules candidates must meet in qualifying for the national ballot
   IV. The amount of money needed to run a national campaign

   (A) I and II only
   (B) II, III, and IV only
   (C) III, and IV only
   (D) II, and IV only
   (E) I, II, III and IV

41. The changing role of women in U.S. politics has been evidenced in recent years by

    (A) the appointment of two women to the Supreme Court since 2005.
    (B) serious consideration of women candidates for president and vice president in 2008.
    (C) the growing influence of "hockey-moms" in the 2008 campaign.
    (D) the reintroduction of the Equal Rights Amendment to Congress in 2006.
    (E) the recapture of the White House by the Republicans in 2004.

42. Problems that exist between the House and Senate regarding legislation must be handled by the

    (A) Standing Committee
    (B) Judiciary Committee
    (C) Ways and Means Committee
    (D) Conference Committee
    (E) Appropriations Committee

43. The process by which political values are passed to the next generation is called political

    (A) articulation
    (B) socialization
    (C) aggregation
    (D) adjudication
    (E) diffusion

44. An important advantage that an incumbent has over a challenger when running for national public office is that the incumbent

    (A) almost always gets an endorsement from the president
    (B) usually receives more campaign contributions
    (C) benefits from the positive view that most people have of Congress
    (D) receives campaign funds from the government
    (E) is usually better qualified for the office

45. Which of the following best describes a feature that political parties have in common with interest groups?

    (A) They both run candidates for national office.
    (B) They both express detailed but narrow policy alternatives.
    (C) They both lobby members of Congress.
    (D) Neither has much input into the budget process for the national government.
    (E) They both link citizens to the political process.

46. What has been the most usual outcome of a presidential veto?

    (A) Congress will usually compromise with the president rather than let the veto stand.
    (B) The constitutional provisions for overriding vetoes make it very difficult for Congress to accomplish.
    (C) The House is usually able to gain the votes to override the veto but the Senate rarely is able to do so.
    (D) Presidents are usually able to gain public approval through the use of the media preventing an override of the veto.
    (E) Presidents are likely to send any attempt to override their vetoes for constitutional consideration by the Supreme Court.

47. Which of the following is the BEST description of the way that most cases make their way to the U.S. Supreme Court?

    (A) Most cases are selected by the Chief Justice of the Supreme Court.
    (B) Most are defined by Article III of the Constitution as cases that the Supreme Court must hear.
    (C) The Department of Justice directs most of its cases to the Supreme Court.
    (D) The Supreme Court usually takes cases that the president recommends to the justices.
    (E) The Supreme Court justices have only a few restrictions on the cases that they choose to hear.

Use the following quote for question #48.

"Among the numerous advantages promised by a well constructed Union, none deserves to be more accurately developed than its tendency to break and control the violence of faction. ...By a faction I understand a number of citizens, whether amounting to a majority or minority of the whole, who are united and actuated by some common impulse of passion, or of interest, adverse to the rights of other citizens, or to the permanent and aggregate interests of the community."

James Madison
Federalist #10

48. Modern-day versions of Madison's factions include all of the following groups EXCEPT:

    (A) National Organization of Women
    (B) American Association of Retired Persons
    (C) Labor Unions
    (D) Chamber of Commerce
    (E) National Security Council

49. Which of the following is an example of a party realignment?

    (A) A majority of voters in a specific region switches its support to another party.
    (B) Political parties come together to solve an issue of public policy.
    (C) A presidential candidate chooses a vice-presidential candidate from another party.
    (D) The various parties come together to support a judicial candidate.
    (E) Party leadership switch views on key important issues.

50. *Munn vs. Illinois* is a case that established the principle of

    (A) the right for government to regulate business
    (B) selective incorporation
    (C) the right to privacy
    (D) the right to freedom from cruel and unusual punishment
    (E) national supremacy

51. After the president develops the budget for the federal government, the next step is

    (A) review and approval by the General Accounting Office
    (B) review and approval by the Congressional Conference Committee
    (C) review by the president's cabinet for comments
    (D) submission to the Office of Management and Budget for its consideration
    (E) submission to the Congress for its consideration

52. The judiciary upheld the constitutionality of the Civil Rights Act of 1964 based upon the constitutional provision of the

    (A) power to tax and spend
    (B) "necessary and proper" clause
    (C) establishment clause
    (D) commerce clause
    (E) due process clause

53. Which of the following court cases promoted the selective incorporation of freedom of speech?

    (A) *Mapp v. Ohio*
    (B) *Gitlow v. New York*
    (C) *U.S. v. Schenck*
    (D) *Gideon v. Wainwright*
    (E) *Roe v. Wade*

By permission of Chip Bok and Creators Syndicate, Inc.

54. The cartoon above reflects which situation from the 2008 election?

   (A) Hillary Clinton's broad-based support as the Democratic vice-presidential candidate.

   (B) The criticism of Hillary Clinton as the first woman to make a serious run for the presidency.

   (C) The problem John McCain had in defending his age as a presidential candidate.

   (D) The possible damage the Democratic Party had to overcome after a long divisive primary.

   (E) The belief that Sarah Palin actually hurt John McCain's chance to win the presidency due to her inexperience.

Newspapers and Civic Life March, 2008			
	A lot	Some	Not much/Not at all
18-39 years old	41%	31%	24%
40-64 years old	42%	32%	24%
65+ years old	51%	26%	21%

"Closure of local paper would hurt civic life."   Pew Research Center

55. Which of the following statements is reflected in the chart above?

(A) Newspapers are no longer important as a form of news.
(B) Newspapers are the most important source of news for Americans.
(C) In contrast to other age groups, a higher percentage of 40 – 64 year olds believes that newspapers are very important to civic life.
(D) In contrast to other age groups, a higher percentage of citizens 65 or older believe that newspapers are very important to civic life.
(E) A majority of people in all age groups believe that newspapers are important to civic life.

56. Which of the following would most likely be chosen to serve as Chairman of the Senate Appropriations Committee in 2009?

(A) A Republican with 15 years in the Senate and 5 years service on the Appropriations Committee.
(B) A Republican with 10 years in the Senate and 10 years service on the Appropriations Committee.
(C) An Independent with 17 years in the Senate and 12 years service on the Appropriations Committee.
(D) A Democrat with 20 years in the Senate and 4 years service on the Appropriations Committee.
(E) A Democrat with 13 years in the Senate and 7 years service on the Appropriations Committee.

57. The federal law that first created the civil service system to ensure a more qualified bureaucratic system is the

(A) Personnel Management Act
(B) Federal Employment Act
(C) Pendleton Act
(D) Sherman Act
(E) Progression Act

58. The president's primary channel for communicating with the media, the press secretary, is a part of the

    (A) Executive Office of the President
    (B) White House Office Staff
    (C) Department of Health and Human Services
    (D) Office of Special Counsel
    (E) General Service Administration

59. The Supreme Court has ruled against the use of the legislative veto that was part of the Immigration and Nationality Act based on the principle of

    (A) popular sovereignty
    (B) federalism
    (C) separation of powers
    (D) national supremacy
    (E) due process

60. Suppose that the president suffered a debilitating stroke and was unconscious for some time. The government's response would be guided most directly by

    (A) Article I of the Constitution
    (B) Article II of the Constitution
    (C) the 2nd Amendment
    (D) the 22nd Amendment
    (E) the 25th Amendment

FREE RESPONSE QUESTIONS

<u>Section II</u>
Time – 100 minutes

Directions: You have 100 minutes to answer all four of the following questions. Unless the directions indicate otherwise, respond to all parts of all four questions. It is suggested that you take a few minutes to plan and outline each answer. <u>Spend approximately one-fourth of your time (25 minutes) on each question</u>. In your response, use substantive examples where appropriate. Make certain to number each of your answers as the question is numbered below.

Toles © 1993 The Washington Post. Reprinted by permission of Universal Press Syndicate. All rights reserved.

1. a)   Explain the main point that the cartoon makes about presidential power.
   b)   Describe one disadvantage the president has in executing legislation passed by Congress.
   c)   Describe one advantage the bureaucracy has over the president in executing legislation.
   d)   Explain one way the president may overcome the disadvantage you identified in (b).
   e)   Explain one way the president may overcome the bureaucratic advantage you identified in (c).

2. Split-ticket voting has often occurred in national and state elections in the United States.

    a)   Define split-ticket voting.
    b)   Identify and explain two reasons why a citizen might cast a split-ticket vote.
    c)   Identify and explain one reason that the practice of split-ticket voting has become more common in many state and national elections since 1968.

3. The Framers of the Constitution divided the federal government's power in several ways.

    a)   Define separation of powers. Define bicameralism.
    b)   Explain two limitations that separation of powers places on one institution of the federal government.
    c)   Describe two limitations that bicameralism places on one institution of the federal government.

4. In contrast to many other democracies, the United States has a two-party system.

    a)   Identify and explain three factors that encourage a two-party system in the United States.
    b)   Identify and explain one implication for the political system should the United States adopt a multi-party system.

NO TESTING MATERIAL PRINTED ON THIS PAGE

GO ON TO THE NEXT PAGE

SAMPLE EXAMINATION FOUR

Directions: Each of the questions or incomplete statements below is followed by five suggested answers or completions. Select the one that is best in each case.

1. According to one version of elite theory, new political leaders are recruited primarily

   (A) from leading political families
   (B) through a merit-based education system
   (C) from sub-units of the government, such as states
   (D) through direct vote by the people
   (E) from many diverse, competing interest groups

2. In recent elections pollsters have found that married voters

   (A) have similar voting patterns to those of unmarried voters
   (B) are more likely to vote Republican than unmarried voters are
   (C) are more likely to vote Democratic than unmarried voters are
   (D) are more likely to vote for third party candidates than unmarried voters are
   (E) are more likely to go to the polls to vote than unmarried voters are

3. The U.S. Constitution is based on the political philosophy of the "social contract theory" of

   (A) Thomas Jefferson
   (B) Benjamin Franklin
   (C) Thomas Hobbs
   (D) John Locke
   (E) John Adams

4. The Lilly Ledbetter Law (2009) provided significant protection for

   (A) women against domestic violence
   (B) immigrants from being deported without a hearing
   (C) the states against unjustified lawsuits
   (D) women against wage discrimination in the workplace
   (E) the rights of illegal immigrant children to a free education while in the United
   States

5. Many Anti-Federalists criticized the Constitution because they believed that it

   (A) did not create a strong central government
   (B) should include a bicameral legislature
   (C) did not adequately protect individual liberties
   (D) should be more specific about the relationship between state and local
   governments
   (E) did not specifically define the power of judicial review

© Kirk Anderson, www.kirktoons.com

6. Which of the following best illustrates the point being made in the cartoon above?

   (A) The public does not pay attention to the press.
   (B) Newspapers are not a credible source of information to the public.
   (C) The internet is becoming an important source of political information.
   (D) Newspaper reporting is motivated more by profit incentives than by the desire to
   report the news.
   (E) Newspapers are more important as a source of news than the radio is.

7. "Dealignment" is a political process in which

    (A) voters shift their allegiance from one political party to another
    (B) interest groups give money to candidates from both political parties
    (C) state and local party officials do not support decisions made by national party officials
    (D) third parties take votes away from the two major parties
    (E) party identification weakens and voters prefer to call themselves "independents"

8. The court decision in *Gibbons v Ogden* (1824) strengthened

    (A) the executive's role in foreign policy.
    (B) the constitutional right of Congress to regulate interstate commerce.
    (C) the Supreme Court's ability to review state supreme court decisions.
    (D) Congressional ability to create a national bank.
    (E) the role of states in regulating voter requirements.

(Questions 9 and 10 are based on the following quote):

> "But the most common and durable source of factions, has been the various and unequal distribution of property. Those who hold, and those who are without property, have ever formed distinct interests in society…The regulation of these various and interfering interests forms the principal task of modern legislation."

9. The quote above is taken from

    (A) Article I of the Constitution
    (B) the Declaration of Independence
    (C) *Common Sense*
    (D) the 1st Amendment of the Constitution
    (E) *The Federalist #10*

10. The quote is used by the author to argue that

    (A) the Constitution should be ratified by the states
    (B) the legislative branch should be stronger than the executive branch
    (C) judicial review is intended in Article III of the Constitution
    (D) the American colonies should break away from England
    (E) individual rights should be guaranteed in the Constitution

11. Which of the following has been a consistent third party presidential candidate from 1996-2008?

    (A) Ron Paul
    (B) Ralph Nader
    (C) Michael Huckabee
    (D) George Wallace
    (E) Ross Perot

12. Super delegates are

    (A) non-voting delegates representing territories at the Democratic National Convention.
    (B) party leaders in both parties that work out the details of the platforms during their conventions.
    (C) members of Congress that aid the Speaker of the House and the Majority Leader of the Senate.
    (D) Democratic party elites that automatically become delegates to the national party convention without being elected.
    (E) members of Congressional committees that run the public hearings.

13. Which of the following is the best description of the relationship between an interest group and a PAC?

    (A) Interest groups run candidates for public office; PACs do not.
    (B) Interest groups and PACs compete for federal money to support their causes.
    (C) PACs are subject to regulation by the Federal Election Commissions; interest groups are not.
    (D) Political action committees (PACs) are the political arms of interest groups that raise funds to contribute to favored candidates or political parties.
    (E) Interest groups often hire PACs to coordinate their efforts to influence political policy-making by raising funds and devising campaign strategies.

14. A primary that restricts voters to only those that are declared members of a specific party is known as a/an

    (A) blanket primary
    (B) open primary
    (C) closed primary
    (D) preliminary primary
    (E) caucus primary

15. The rules that govern the conduct of the House of Representatives are

    (A) less restrictive than those in the Senate
    (B) more restrictive than those in the Senate
    (C) mostly designed to restrict the power of the House leadership
    (D) mostly designed to restrict the power of the president
    (E) almost identical to the rules that govern the Senate

16. Which of the following is a concurrent power of both national and state governments?

    (A) regulation of interstate commerce
    (B) the right to mobilize an army
    (C) taxation of exports
    (D) establishment and maintenance of court systems
    (E) diplomatic relations with foreign nations

17. Which of the following was a successful method used by the National Association for the Advancement of Colored People in order to gain civil rights?

    (A) Litigating cases in federal court.
    (B) Lobbying state legislatures.
    (C) Pressuring for executive orders.
    (D) Litigating cases in state courts.
    (E) Pressuring foreign governments.

18. Which of the following is a check that the president has on the judiciary?

    (A) He may alter the structure of the court system.
    (B) He has the power to appoint federal judges.
    (C) He has the power to remove federal judges.
    (D) He decides the length of their terms of office.
    (E) He may challenge judicial decisions by referring them to Congress for a vote.

19. Which of the following is a liberal political belief?

    (A) healthcare benefits tied to the workplace
    (B) free market principle for businesses
    (C) low taxes
    (D) support for faith-based initiatives
    (E) crime fighting by curing social and economic reasons for crimes

20. Which of the following often results from divided government?

(A) The president and vice president do not support the same programs.
(B) Congress finds it difficult to pass legislation that the president will sign.
(C) The Majority and Minority Leaders in the Senate cannot compromise.
(D) The Supreme Court does not take cases for review.
(E) The president's executive orders cannot be issued.

(Questions 21 and 22 are based on the following table):

ELECTION RESULTS 2008		
	Barack Obama (Democrat)	**John McCain (Republican)**
Vote by Gender:		
Male	50%	50%
Female	57%	43%
Vote by Race:		
White	44%	56%
African-American	99%	1%
Hispanic	66%	32%
Vote by Age:		
Under 30 years	61%	38%
Under 50 years	53%	47%
50-64 years	54%	46%
65+ years	46%	54%
Vote by Income:		
Less than $50,000	60%	38%
$50,000 - $99,000	49%	49%
$100,000 +	49%	50%
Vote by Education:		
Grade School	67%	33%
H.S. Graduate	47%	53%
Some College	52%	48%
College Graduate	51%	49%
Postgrad Study	65%	35%
Vote by church-going:		
Weekly	45%	55%
Monthly	51%	49%
Seldom/Never	62%	38%

21. Which of the above categories appears to have the most effect on how people voted in 2008?

    (A) gender
    (B) race
    (C) age
    (D) income
    (E) education

22. The chart confirms all of the following voting patterns EXCEPT:

    (A) The more education an individual had, the more likely s/he was to vote for McCain.
    (B) Frequent church-goers were more likely to vote for McCain.
    (C) Women were more likely to vote for Obama than McCain.
    (D) Hispanics were more likely to vote for Obama than McCain.
    (E) People making less than $50,000 a year were more likely to vote for Obama than McCain.

23. In contrast to categorical grants, block grants allow the national Congress

    (A) more control over how states spend federal grant money
    (B) less control over how states spend federal grant money
    (C) to make larger overall grants to states
    (D) more discretion in terms of whether or not mandates receive federal funding
    (E) more control over how states fund education programs

24. The U.S. political culture today is characterized by all of the following values/principles EXCEPT:

    (A) individualism
    (B) democracy
    (C) civic duty
    (D) rule of law
    (E) economic equality

25. Dual federalism has become less characteristic of the U.S. political system since the mid-20th century because

    (A) the federal budget has not been able to fund state programs because of defense demands.
    (B) the federal government began devolving more and more responsibilities to the states
    (C) state courts have made it difficult to accept federal monies for state programs.
    (D) revenue sharing became so popular that the federal government significantly reduced regulations on the states.
    (E) state and federal governments have worked closely together in order to solve political and social problems.

26. The position of "party whip" exists as a leadership role in

    (A) the organizational structure of the Democratic Party, but not the Republican Party.
    (B) the organizational structure of the Republican Party, but not the Democratic Party.
    (C) the House of Representatives, but not the Senate
    (D) the Senate, but not the House of Representatives
    (E) both the Senate and the House of Representatives

27. The political term " bully pulpit" is a reference to

    (A) the ability of the president to use his popularity and visibility to gain public approval for policy.
    (B) the ability of the Supreme Court to order a public official to take action.
    (C) the public attention Congress gains during public hearings to promote a cause.
    (D) the opportunity for presidential candidates to articulate their views during the primaries.
    (E) the effect negative ads have on the public during campaigns.

28. Which of the following is the BEST definition of a parliamentary system of government?

    (A) A parliamentary system almost always has both a president and a prime minister.
    (B) A parliamentary system usually has a president, but does not have a prime minister.
    (C) A parliamentary system is governed by the legislature, and usually does not have a strong executive body.
    (D) A parliamentary system usually has a prime minister whose party has a majority in the legislature.
    (E) A parliamentary system usually has a one-house legislative branch.

29. An example of an entitlement program is

    (A) the Federal Elections Commission
    (B) No Child Left Behind
    (C) the National Aeronautics and Space Administration
    (D) the Central Intelligence Agency
    (E) Medicare

30. In *United States v. Nixon* (1974) President Nixon refused to turn over recordings of his office conversations based on his power of

    (A) executive privilege
    (B) impoundment
    (C) commander-in-chief
    (D) chief diplomat
    (E) chief negotiator

31. Which of the following is a power expressly granted to the president in Article II of the Constitution?

    (A) executive privilege
    (B) the line item veto
    (C) impoundment of funds
    (D) the right to initiate legislation
    (E) commander-in-chief of the armed forces

32. Which of the following people would a Republican president LEAST likely appoint as a federal judge?

    (A) a female judge from the South
    (B) a black judge from the Midwest
    (C) a judge affiliated with the Democratic Party
    (D) a judge whose experience has been exclusively on state courts
    (E) a judge that has never been politically active

(Questions 33 and 34 are based on the following hypothetical chart):

Percentage Change in Audience, 2007 to 2008, Across Media

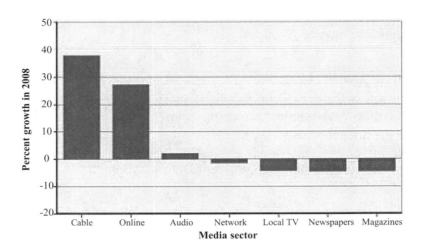

Pew Research Center

33. Which of the following statements is supported by the chart above?

   (A) Network TV maintained its viewership from 2007-2008.
   (B) Most Americans got their news from internet sources in 2007 and 2008.
   (C) Local TV, newspapers and magazines lost consumers at roughly the same rate during the period.
   (D) Radio (audio) and the Networks increased viewer in roughly the same route during the period.
   (E) Cable viewership surprisingly declined during the period.

34. Which of the following situations in the Senate would most likely lead to a filibuster?

   (A) A growing number of senators.
   (B) A relatively large number of elderly senators.
   (C) A small number of independent senators.
   (D) A narrow split between Democratic and Republican senators.
   (E) A significant number of new members elected to the Senate.

35. A frequent criticism of the media in covering candidates during a campaign is that

   (A) all media has a conservative bias when reporting on the candidates
   (B) candidate positions are reduced to soundbites rather than providing in-depth analysis
   (C) the media focuses too often on international news
   (D) internet sources of information are more credible than radio, TV and newspapers
   (E) too much focus is given to minor party candidates, which confuses the issues

36. Which of the following Supreme Court decisions was based on a case that used the Equal Protection Clause of the 14th Amendment?

    (A) *Mapp v Ohio*
    (B) *Gideon v. Wainwright*
    (C) *Brown v. Board of Education of Topeka*
    (D) *Roe v Wade*
    (E) *Schenck v United States*

37. Which of the following people would be MOST likely to vote for a Republican candidate for president?

    (A) a 40-year-old labor union member from Detroit, Michigan
    (B) a 19-year-old Hispanic female from California
    (C) a 52-year-old white farmer from Kansas
    (D) a suburban homemaker from New Jersey
    (E) an orthodox Jewish teacher from New York City

38. The filibuster is a powerful tool for senators primarily because it

    (A) is best used by the majority party to keep the minority party from gaining power
    (B) sends a message to the president that the Senate opposes his policies
    (C) forces the House of Representatives to comply with the Senate version of a proposed piece of legislation
    (D) brings the work of the Senate to a halt so that no legislation can pass
    (E) determines which senators are named as chairs of standing committees

39. Which of the following represents a major change in voting patterns that occurred during the election of 2008?

    (A) Battleground states in New England supported the Republican candidate for the first time in decades.
    (B) More southern states supported the Democratic candidate than in earlier elections.
    (C) More women voters supported the Republican ticket, probably because of a female vice-presidential candidate.
    (D) The percentage of young voters increased significantly as a percentage of all voters.
    (E) California supported the Republican candidate for the first time in decades.

40. Which of the following is the best description of a republic?

    (A) A government in which elected representatives make decisions for the people.
    (B) A government with a directly elected executive.
    (C) A government that has an independent judiciary.
    (D) A government with a bicameral legislature.
    (E) A government with clear separation of powers.

(Questions 41 and 42 are based on the following quote):

> "You have a right to remain silent and do not have to say anything at all.
>
> Anything you say can and will be used against you in Court.
>
> You have a right to talk to a lawyer of your own choice before we ask you any questions."

41. The quotation is required to be read to an individual who is

    (A) on trial for committing a crime
    (B) about to be sworn in as a police officer
    (C) being arrested by the police
    (D) about to testify in court against a defendant
    (E) being deported from the country

42. The quotation is based on a Supreme Court case called

    (A) *Roe v. Wade*
    (B) *Munn v. Illinois*
    (C) *Miranda v. Arizona*
    (D) *Barron v. Baltimore*
    (E) *Mapp v. Ohio*

43. Primary elections in which of the following states generally have the most impact in shaping who the political parties nominate for president?

    (A) California
    (B) Texas
    (C) New Hampshire
    (D) Pennsylvania
    (E) Florida

44. Which of the following individuals is most likely to vote in a national election?

    (A) an 18-year-old college student
    (B) a white male with a high school education
    (C) a church-going female with a college education
    (D) a 60 year old non-churchgoer with an 8th grade education
    (E) a 21-year-old factory worker in the Midwest

45. When the president refuses to spend all the funds appropriated by Congress for a program it is known as

    (A) malapportionment
    (B) gerrymandering
    (C) impoundment
    (D) frontloading
    (E) pigeonholing

46. Which of the following interest groups would be LEAST likely to support a Republican candidate for president?

    (A) American Medical Association
    (B) National Rifle Association
    (C) National Association for the Advancement of Colored People
    (D) Christian Coalition
    (E) National Association of Manufacturers

Borgman © 2007 The Cincinnati Enquirer. Reprinted by permission of Universal Press Syndicate. All rights reserved.

47. Which of the following is the view expressed in the cartoon above?

   (A) Military spending in the war on terrorism is hurting federal education programs.
   (B) The government must reform Social Security in order to reduce spending.
   (C) Funding for the No Child Left Behind Program must be cut.
   (D) The increased spending on children's health plans will dramatically increase the government's debt.
   (E) Increased overall government spending will create a problem that must be handled by future generations.

48. A person with a liberal political ideology would be most likely to support

   (A) increased military spending
   (B) affirmative action programs
   (C) active participation of religious groups in the political process
   (D) legislation to protect the use of the nation's flag
   (E) prayer in public schools

49. Voters in primary elections are much more likely than voters in general elections to be

   (A) more conservative
   (B) more liberal
   (C) men than women
   (D) black or Hispanic rather than white
   (E) more politically active

(Questions 50 and 51 are based on the following table):

Trends in Believability for TV News Outlets						
Believe **all or most** of what organization says	<u>1998</u>	<u>2000</u>	<u>2002</u>	<u>2004</u>	<u>2006</u>	<u>2008</u>
	%	%	%	%	%	%
CNN	42	39	37	32	28	30
60 Minutes	35	34	34	33	27	29
Local TV News	34	33	27	25	23	28
NPR	19	25	23	23	22	27
C-SPAN	32	33	30	27	25	26
NBC News	30	29	25	24	23	24
ABC News	30	30	24	24	22	24
MSNBC	--	28	28	22	21	24
FOX News Channel	--	26	24	25	25	23
News Hour	29	24	26	23	23	23
CBS News	28	29	26	24	22	22
BBC	--	--	--	--	--	21

Percentages based on those who could rate each organization.
Pew Research Center

50. Which of the following trend is reflected in the chart above?

   (A) Cable news outlets gradually became more believable to viewers from 2002 – 2008.
   (B) Network news generally gained then lost credibility with the public during the period.
   (C) The only news source that increased in consumer believability during the period was NPR.
   (D) Local TV news was more believable to viewers than network news during the period.
   (E) C-Span was the only news outlet to gain credibility during the period.

51. Which of the following is a likely outcome of the trends in believability for TV News?

    (A) The public will continue to gain most of its news from television.
    (B) Politicians will look for other ways to use television to gain the public confidence.
    (C) The public may turn to other sources of information that they feel are more believable.
    (D) Television will lose many of its viewers to radio as a source of information for the public.
    (E) Television networks will provide more news magazine shows such as 60 Minutes and Dateline.

52. The belief that the government must manage the economy by spending money during a recession is known as

    (A) socialist market economics
    (B) command economics
    (C) Keynesianism economics
    (D) activist economics
    (E) laissez-faire economics

53. Which of the following would a modern president be MOST likely to appoint as a senior member of the White House staff?

    (A) a well-known congressional leader
    (B) a popular governor from a well-populated state
    (C) a hard-working, loyal member of his campaign staff
    (D) the most prominent national leader of the opposition political party
    (E) a White House staff member from the previous president's administration

(Questions 54 and 55 are based on the following quote):

"No State shall…deny to any person within its jurisdiction the equal protection of the law."

54. The quote comes from

    (A) *Federalist #10*
    (B) the Civil Rights Act of 1964
    (C) the 1st Amendment of the Constitution
    (D) the majority opinion of *Marbury v. Madison*
    (E) the 14th Amendment

55. The quote has been applied by federal courts most frequently in cases that have defined

    (A) the relationship between state and national governments
    (B) the balance of power among the three branches of government
    (C) civil liberties
    (D) civil rights
    (E) rights of those accused of federal crimes

56. When the Supreme Court agrees to hear and review a case it issues a(n)

    (A) *ex post facto* document
    (B) writ of *habeas corpus*
    (C) bill of attainder
    (D) *amicus curiae* brief
    (E) writ of certiorari

Use the table below for questions #57 and #58.

FEDERAL CIVILIAN EMPLOYMENT BY AGENCY 2000-2007				
AGENCY	**2000**	**2005**	**2006**	**2007**
Federal Communications Commision	1,965	1,936	1,857	1,827
NASA	18,819	19,105	18,448	19,378
Peace Corps	1,065	1,064	1,075	1,077
Security & Exchange Commission (SEC)	2,955	3,933	3,760	3,534
Social Security Administration	64,474	65,861	64,885	62,769
Tennesee Valley Authority	13,145	12,721	12,624	12,293
Postal Service	860,726	767,972	760,039	753,254

Statistical Abstract of the United States

57. According to the table above, which of the following federal agencies employs the most civilians?

    (A) Social Security Administration
    (B) NASA
    (C) Security and Exchange Commission
    (D) Postal Service
    (E) Tennessee Valley Authority

58. Which of the following trends is demonstrated in the chart?

    (A) The Peace Corps demonstrated a significant increase in employees during the period.
    (B) The Social Security Administration experienced a decrease in employees by 2007.
    (C) The Federal Communications Commission consistently increased in the number of employees then had a sudden drop in 2007.
    (D) The Postal Service rate of employees remained stable during the time period.
    (E) The Security & Exchange Commission is the only agency that had an increase in the number of employees during the period.

59. The cabinet official most directly charged with enforcing federal law is the

    (A) secretary of defense
    (B) secretary of the treasury
    (C) secretary of state
    (D) attorney general
    (E) president's chief of staff

60. The term "divided government" defines a situation in which

    (A) the majority in the House of Representatives is from one party, and the majority in the Senate is from the other party
    (B) the president is from one party, and the vice president is from the other party
    (C) the legislature and executive are dominated by one party, and the judiciary tends to support the views of the other party
    (D) most of the state governments are dominated by one party, and the national government is dominated by the other party
    (E) both houses of the legislature are dominated by one party, and the president is a leader of the other party

FREE RESPONSE QUESTIONS

<u>Section II</u>
Time – 100 minutes

Directions: You have 100 minutes to answer all four of the following questions. Unless the directions indicate otherwise, respond to all parts of all four questions. It is suggested that you take a few minutes to plan and outline each answer. <u>Spend approximately one-fourth of your time (25 minutes) on each question</u>. In your response, use substantive examples where appropriate. Make certain to number each of your answers as the question is numbered below.

1. The United States president has the ability to use both formal and informal powers.

   a) Identify two formal powers of the president.
   b) Explain how each of the powers identified in (a) have led to increasing the power of the presidency.
   c) Identify two informal powers of the president.
   d) Explain how each of the powers identified in (c) have led to increasing the power of the president.

2. There are many different forms of citizen political participation in the United States political system.

   a) Describe one provision of the United States Constitution that protects the political participation of citizens.
   b) Describe two types of political participation that exist today but are not specifically mentioned in the Constitution.
   c) Explain one advantage and one disadvantage of the first type of participation you described in (b).
   d) Explain one advantage and one disadvantage of the second type of participation you described in (b).

By permission of Marshall Ramsey and Creators Syndicate, Inc.

3. a) Describe the message in the cartoon regarding how voters decide who to support in campaigns for public office.

   b) Explain two ways that the media shapes voters' attitudes toward candidates for public office.

   c) Describe one positive impact that the long campaign process has on voter attitudes toward candidates for public office.

   d) Describe one negative impact that the long campaign process has on voter attitudes toward candidates for public office.

4. The framers of the Constitution included a system of checks and balances in the United States governmental system in order to control power.

   a) Describe two Constitutional checks that Congress has over the Judiciary to control its power

   b) Describe two Constitutional checks that Congress has over the Executive to control its power.

   c) Describe one way that the Judiciary may check the power of Congress.

   d) Explain one reason that the founders created a system of checks and balances.

   e) Explain one problem that the American political system has experienced because of checks and balances.